Classical Subjects Creati

SONGSCHOOL LATIN
Book 2

Teacher's Edition

Amy Rehn
with Dr. Christopher A. Perrin

Song School Latin Book 2 Teacher's Edition

Version 1.1

Classical Academic Press
515 S. 32nd Street
Camp Hill, PA 17011

www.ClassicalAcademicPress.com

ISBN: 978-1-60051-081-6

Song School Latin Book 2 Music Credits:
Guitar: Grant Durrell, Christopher Perrin
Keyboard and Percussion: Matthew Monticchio
Vocals: Val McClymont, Amanda Struble, Christopher Perrin

3D illustrations by:
Rob Baddorf

Book design by:
Lenora Riley

Illustrations by:
David Gustafson and Lenora Riley

PGP.09.21

Table of Contents
for Teacher's Edition

Introduction to the Teacher's Edition 1

Song School Latin Book 2 **student book with answers** 7

CD Track Information 7
Pronunciation Guide 8
Introduction 9
Chapter 1: What Day Is It? 11
Chapter 2: Days of the Week 13
Chapter 3: Months of the Year 15
Chapter 4: More Months of the Year 17
Chapter 5: Numbers 21
Chapter 6: More Numbers 25
Chapter 7: Review 28
Chapter 8: Helping at Home 34
Chapter 9: Communicating with Others 37
Chapter 10: Ways to Travel 41
Chapter 11: Things to Learn in School 44
Chapter 12: Celebration 47
Chapter 13: Review 51
Chapter 14: Royalty 58
Chapter 15: Military Matters 60
Chapter 16: Everyday Actions 63
Chapter 17: Adverbs: How We Do Things 66
Chapter 18: More Adverbs 68
Chapter 19: Review 71
Chapter 20: When I Grow Up, Part I 76
Chapter 21: When I Grow Up, Part II 80
Chapter 22: Where Things Are, Part I 83
Chapter 23: Where Things Are, Part II 87
Chapter 24: Growing Virtues 90
Chapter 25: Review 94
Chapter 26: Time for Bed! 101
Chapter 27: A Time for Everything 105
Chapter 28: Colors 109
Chapter 29: Around the Palace 112
Chapter 30: Adjectives 116
Chapter 31: Review 121
Chapter 32: End-of-Book Review 129
Appendix A: Chapter-by-Chapter Glossary: New Vocabulary 133
Appendix B: Alphabetical Glossary: Review Vocabulary 135
Appendix C: Alphabetical Glossary 138
Appendix D: Summary of Grammar 142
Appendix E: Reference Charts 147
Appendix F: Classroom Commands 151

Song School Latin Book 2 **Activities** 152

Song School Latin Book 2 **Activity Answers** 200

Introduction
to the Teacher's Edition

Welcome to *Song School Latin Book 2*!

> In addition to this introduction, we also encourage you to read the introduction to the student edition of *Song School Latin Book 2*, which is also included in this book.

This teacher's edition (TE) has been designed to help you easily and effectively use *Song School Latin Book 2* (*SSL2*) to teach young students Latin. The TE contains the complete text of the student edition (SE) along with several other important elements, including:

- **Answer Key:** The answer key provides answers to all questions, exercises, puzzles, and activities on the same pages as the SE for easy and quick assessment.
- **Teaching Tips:** Suggestions, guidance, and ideas for how to use the text with students are provided throughout the text.
- **Additional Activities and Practice:** This TE contains over forty pages of additional activities and exercises corresponding to each chapter in the SE. These extra activities can be assigned as supplemental work for older or advanced students, or for enthusiastic learners who simply want more Latin study. See pages 153–199 to review the activities and page 200 and following for the key to the activities. The activities may also be photocopied for use in a class or family.

Target Grade Range of *Song School Latin Book 2*

Song School Latin Book 2 has been designed for use by students in grades 2–4 and assumes students have completed *Song School Latin Book 1* (*SSL1*) or another introductory Latin book. This book has also been designed to lead naturally and seamlessly into *Latin for Children Primer A* (*LFCA*). In fact, students who have completed *SSL2* will have already learned sixty Latin words from *LFCA* and the first unit's worth of grammar.

The Teaching Method of Song School Latin

Classical Academic Press has designed our Song School line of curricula to take advantage of the natural capacity of young children to learn and master language by song as well as by reading, writing, listening, and speaking. The audio CD of songs and chants included with the SE, therefore, is a key means to teaching the course. The songs and chants should be played and sung frequently. *Song School Latin Book 2* contains at least one song/chant per chapter that teaches Latin vocabulary and some basic grammar in a way that children will enjoy and mimic. For a language to be learned well, it is best to study it regularly in shorter segments of time rather than occasionally in longer segments. We encourage you, therefore, to have students review Latin vocabulary and phrases frequently and to have them play the audio CD around the house and while traveling in the car. Students will soon be singing these catchy songs throughout the day—even when you might want them to stop!

Additional Resources

Classical Academic Press has made available several resources that supplement the *SSL2* SE and TE. Please review and consider using the following:

- **My Library:** The CAP My Library platform collects your streaming video, audio, and digital purchases into a single location, and also provides you with extra practice activities and games for *SSL2*! If you purchase the *SSL2* streaming video from CAP, you will receive the free My Library bonus content for *SSL2*, including our FlashDash vocabulary game, to take students' learning further while they're having fun!
- **Latin Monkey Match Vocabulary Cards:** These cards, which contain all of the vocabulary from *SSL2*, play like the Memory Game, in which students seek to match one Latin card with its English twin. The cards can also be used as typical vocabulary flash cards. You may see a sample of these cards on the product page for *Song School Latin Book 2* at ClassicalAcademicPress.com.
- **Latin Pronunciation Files:** While the *SSL2* audio CD teaches Latin pronunciation well, it is also helpful for students (and teachers) to hear each word pronounced. To download mp3 files of all of the vocabulary being pronounced, visit the *Song School Latin Book 2* product page at ClassicalAcademicPress.com and click the Support tab beneath the product photo. You may download a file that features either the classical or ecclesiastical pronunciation.
- **Ask the Magister:** Parents and teachers may ask questions about this text and seek guidance from other Latin teachers by clicking on the "Ask the Magister" link under the Resources tab at ClassicalAcademicPress.com.

Other Song School Products from Classical Academic Press

If your students enjoy *Song School Latin Book 2*, we encourage you also to review our other Song School curricula, including *Song School Latin Book 1*, *Song School Greek*, and *Song School Spanish Book 1*.

A Suggested Schedule for Teaching *Song School Latin Book 2*

Song School Latin Book 2 was designed to be flexible and easy to teach in various settings. It can be taught once a week in a gathered class (for about forty-five to sixty minutes) with students doing some workbook activities at home (with parental guidance) and listening to the audio CD songs/chants until the next class period. However, our suggested method consists of more frequent study in shorter time segments. Therefore, we generally recommend a three- to four-day rhythm with the student doing some of the workbook exercises and singing/chanting along with the audio CD during each session. Each of these sessions should take only ten to twenty minutes. We also recommend that students play the audio CD around the home, in the classroom, and in the car, which will aid them in learning much even without the workbook.

What follows is a generic, three-day (or three-session) schedule that teachers and parents should be able to easily adapt to other rhythms and patterns.

Day One: Have students study the first page and read out loud all the new Latin words/phrases for the week. For proper pronunciation, students should listen to the audio file of the Latin words/phrases being spoken, in either the classical or ecclesiastical pronunciation. These files can be downloaded from the Support tab on the *Song School Latin Book 2* product page of ClassicalAcademicPress.com. Then students should listen to the chapter song(s)/chant(s) on the audio CD. The songs/chants will help them to remember the words and pronounce them correctly.

Day Two: Have students review the chapter's Latin words/phrases once more and practice speaking them, both by reading them out loud and by speaking them from memory. Have students practice speaking the words to another student or to you or a parent. Next, students should sing/chant along with the CD and also see if they can sing/chant from memory. Students should then read the chapter lesson in the book and do any exercises that follow it, being sure to stop when they reach the Show What You Know section—they'll do that section during the third lesson. End the lesson by having students recite from memory all the Latin words/phrases in the chapter and having them sing/chant the song(s)/chant(s) from memory, too.

Day Three: Have the students, from memory, say out loud all of the chapter's Latin words/phrases. Next they should sing/chant the song(s)/chant(s) from memory and then sing/chant along with the audio CD a couple of times. It is also a good idea to have them review the songs/chants from past chapters, an activity students should find enjoyable. Finally, have students do the Show What You Know section and finish the chapter.

More About *Song School Latin Book 2*

Scores of customers using *Song School Latin Book 1* have asked us to produce this book for two main reasons: 1) many students who completed the first book were younger students not yet ready for a Latin grammar (such as our *Latin for Children Primer A*); 2) students, parents, and teachers simply loved *SSL1* and wanted more.

We have created *SSL2*, therefore, to continue the Song School Latin adventure and to fully prepare students for the study of reading and translating Latin. For students up to the third or fourth grade level it is an ideal preparation for the Latin for Children series.

In addition to preparing students for reading and translating Latin, *SSL2* has the following central goals:

- to impart a love and taste for the Latin language that will inspire students to future study
- to impart a mastery of over 150 high-frequency Latin words
- to gently introduce basic grammatical concepts

Using the Audio CD with the Book

As you know by now, the Song School books are more than just books—they are a uniquely integrated approach to learning that combines text with music to create an engaging learning experience for young students. The songs help impart mastery of vocabulary and some grammar, as well as making the learning process delightful to students who naturally love to sing and sing again. The audio CD should be used generously, even outside of class. Each content chapter features at least one song/chant that will help students master their Latin vocabulary. To facilitate the students' learning and memorization of the songs/chants, the audio CD should be played in conjunction with the chapter-by-chapter study through the book. The songs can be played before or after (or both) study to engage the chapter lesson. The audio CD can also be used to further impart vocabulary mastery outside of the class by playing it in the car, around the house, or on an mp3 player.

The Scope of Learning in *Song School Latin Book 2*

Song School Latin Book 2 picks up where *SSL1* left off. Much of the *SSL1* vocabulary is reviewed in *SSL2*, but then 175 new vocabulary words are introduced and students also learn a few new forms and a bit of grammar.

The grammar covered in *SSL2* includes:

- **Three Verb Tenses:** Students learn about the present, imperfect (past), and future tenses. The tense endings are taught and simple Latin sentences using verbs are studied.
- **Two Noun Declensions:** Students are introduced to the first and second declension noun endings.
- **Introduction to the Idea of Cases and Noun Jobs:** We present all five case endings for memorization, but only gently introduce the function or job performed by the nominative and accusative cases.
- **Subject-Verb Agreement:** We show students by means of chapter lessons and sample sentences how singular subject nouns require singular forms of the verb and how plural subject nouns require plural forms of the verb.
- **Adjective-Noun Agreement:** We introduce the concept that adjectives must "match" the nouns they describe in number and case. We also let students know that nouns and adjectives have gender, but leave the study of this for later learning.
- **Use of Linking Verbs:** By means of chapter lessons and sample sentences we teach students the forms of the being/linking verb **sum** in the imperfect, present, and future tenses and show students how linking verbs function in simple Latin sentences.

Conventions/Methods

Song School Latin Book 2 makes use of an engaging pedagogy blending singing, chanting, regular review and repetition, weekly exercises and assessment, and a grammatical approach that seeks to show, study, and replicate. Note the following key pedagogical tools:

- **Songs, Chants, and Memorization:** Committing forms and vocabulary to deep memory is accomplished by means of singing, chanting, and regular review.
- **General Use of the Nominative Case:** In this book, the sample sentences and diglot weaves (stories in Latin and English) will almost always feature the nominative forms of nouns. Exceptions to this will be a few sample sentences in which we list a noun functioning as a direct object in the accusative case. In these instances we note the new noun ending and alert students that these endings will be explained later in their Latin study. This means that in the diglot stories you will sometimes see some Latin nouns recorded in the nominative case, even when you would expect them in the accusative case. We have done this to avoid confusing students with different case endings before they have learned how they function, and because the main purpose of the Latin in the stories is to teach vocabulary, not case function.
- **Diglot Weaves:** We present a few diglot weaves in the book to reinforce Latin vocabulary learning and to create some delightful learning activities. As noted above, the nominative case for nouns will be featured in these stories.
- **Sample Sentences:** Throughout the book we present sample sentences in Latin with their English translations. We think it is important to begin to show students how Latin works without at first also requiring them to translate the Latin. By showing students a variety of Latin sentences in translation, Latin sentence patterns will become familiar and then translation skills will follow more easily.
- **Light Translation:** After studying sample sentences, students will gradually be asked to do some of their own translation, modeled after the sentences they have studied. These translation exercises will be gentle and light, appropriate for new Latin learners. Translation exercises increase slowly throughout the book, but translation as a skill will pick up significantly in a more advanced book such as *Latin for Children Primer A.*
- **Using Vocabulary from *Song School Latin Book 1*:** As noted previously, much of the vocabulary from *SSL1* will be reviewed and used in this book. This will help students retain and master vocabulary from previous study and prepare them well for future study in the Latin for Children curriculum. All of the vocabulary for both books is included in the alphabetical glossary at the end of the book.
- **Various Exercises:** Each chapter will feature various exercises that reinforce the learning of vocabulary, forms, and basic grammar in the book. These exercises are varied to maintain student interest and engagement.

Table of Contents

CD Track Information iv
Pronunciation Guide 1
Introduction 3
Chapter 1: What Day Is It? 7
Chapter 2: Days of the Week 11
Chapter 3: Months of the Year 15
Chapter 4: More Months of the Year. 20
Chapter 5: Numbers. 28
Chapter 6: More Numbers 36
Chapter 7: Review 41
Chapter 8: Helping at Home 54
Chapter 9: Communicating with Others 60
Chapter 10: Ways to Travel. 67
Chapter 11: Things to Learn in School. 74
Chapter 12: Celebration. 80
Chapter 13: Review. 87
Chapter 14: Royalty. 101
Chapter 15: Military Matters 106
Chapter 16: Everyday Actions 111
Chapter 17: Adverbs: How We Do Things . . .117
Chapter 18: More Adverbs 122
Chapter 19: Review. 128
Chapter 20: When I Grow Up, Part I. 138
Chapter 21: When I Grow Up, Part II. 145
Chapter 22: Where Things Are, Part I 152
Chapter 23: Where Things Are, Part II 159
Chapter 24: Growing Virtues 165
Chapter 25: Review 173
Chapter 26: Time for Bed! 188
Chapter 27: A Time for Everything 195
Chapter 28: Colors 203
Chapter 29: Around the Palace 210
Chapter 30: Adjectives. 217
Chapter 31: Review. 227
Chapter 32: End-of-Book Review 243
Appendix A: Chapter-by-Chapter Glossary: New Vocabulary 251
Appendix B: Chapter-by-Chapter Glossary: Review Vocabulary 256
Appendix C: Alphabetical Glossary 261
Appendix D: Summary of Grammar. 269
Appendix E: Reference Charts. 279
Appendix F: Classroom Commands 288

CD Track Information

Classical

Track Number & Name		Chapter	Page	Time
1	When You Wake Up in the Mornin'	1	7	1:28
2	Days of the Week Song	2	11	1:26
3	Months of the Year, Part I	3	15	1:06
4	Months of the Year, Parts I & II	4	21	1:34
5	**O-S-T** Song, Parts I & II	3, 4	16, 22	1:16
6	Numbers Chant, Part I	5	28	2:02
7	Numbers Chant, Parts I & II	6	36	2:09
8	**Decem** Little Romans	6	37	0:51
9	The Working Song	8	54	1:51
10	Speaking and Writing Song	9	61	1:14
11	Walk and Ride Song	10	68	2:00
12	The Subjects Song	11	74	2:09
13	**Celebratio** Song	12	81	1:42
14	**Rex** and **Regina** Song	14	101	1:00
15	The Mighty **Miles** Song	15	106	0:54
16	**Porto-Amo** Song	16	111	1:25
17	Bonus Chant: Being Chant	16	112	0:49
18	**Cito-Lente** Song	17	117	1:08
19	**Forte** Song	18	122	1:08
20	The **Negotium** Song, Part I	20	138	0:59
21	The **Negotium** Song, Part II	21	146	0:59
22	The Shoe Song	22	152	1:14
23	Visiting Song	23	159	1:14
24	Grow My **Virtus**	24	166	1:15
25	Bonus Chant: First Declension Endings Chant	24	167	0:49
26	Bedtime Song	26	189	2:08
27	Grand Old Father Time	27	196	1:49
28	The **Colores** Song	28	204	2:05
29	Mr. King **Folium**	29	210	1:41
30	Adjectives Chant	30	218	0:54

Ecclesiastical

Track Number & Name		Chapter	Page	Time
31	When You Wake Up in the Mornin'	1	7	1:28
32	Days of the Week Song	2	11	1:26
33	Months of the Year, Part I	3	15	1:06
34	Months of the Year, Parts I & II	4	21	1:34
35	**O-S-T** Song, Parts I & II	3, 4	16, 22	1:16
36	Numbers Chant, Part I	5	28	2:02
37	Numbers Chant, Parts I & II	6	36	2:09
38	**Decem** Little Romans	6	37	0:51
39	The Working Song	8	54	1:51
40	Speaking and Writing Song	9	61	1:14
41	Walk and Ride Song	10	68	2:00
42	The Subjects Song	11	74	2:09
43	**Celebratio** Song	12	81	1:42
44	**Rex** and **Regina** Song	14	101	1:00
45	The Mighty **Miles** Song	15	106	0:54
46	**Porto-Amo** Song	16	111	1:25
47	Bonus Chant: Being Chant	16	112	0:49
48	**Cito-Lente** Song	17	117	1:08
49	**Forte** Song	18	122	1:08
50	The **Negotium** Song, Part I	20	138	0:59
51	The **Negotium** Song, Part II	21	146	0:59
52	The Shoe Song	22	152	1:14
53	Visiting Song	23	159	1:14
54	Grow My **Virtus**	24	166	1:15
55	Bonus Chant: First Declension Endings Chant	24	167	0:49
56	Bedtime Song	26	189	2:08
57	Grand Old Father Time	27	196	1:49
58	The **Colores** Song	28	204	2:05
59	Mr. King **Folium**	29	210	1:41
60	Adjectives Chant	30	218	0:54

Pronunciation Guide

There are twenty-four letters in the Latin alphabet—there is no *j* or *w*. Although the letters *k*, *y*, and *z* are included in the Latin alphabet, they are used very rarely. Latin vowels are the same as English vowels: *a*, *e*, *i*, *o*, and *u*. Letters in Latin are never silent.

Classical or Ecclesiastical Pronunciation?

There are two systems of pronunciation in Latin—classical and ecclesiastical. Both pronunciations are really quite similar, so ultimately the decision is not a significant one. The classical attempts to follow the way the Romans spoke Latin (an older pronunciation) while the ecclesiastical follows the way Latin pronunciation evolved within the Christian Church during the Middle Ages, particularly within the Roman Catholic Church.

The main difference between the two pronunciations is the way **c/ch** and **v** are pronounced. The classical pronounces **c/ch** as an English *k*, whereas the ecclesiastical pronounces it (Italian style) as an English *ch* (as in *ch*eck). The ecclesiastical pronounces **v** as the English *v* (as in *v*ictory) whereas the classical pronounces it as an English *w*. In the ecclesiastical, a **j** occasionally appears in place of an **i** and the **t** has a special pronunciation (when followed by an *i* and another vowel), like **ts** as in ca*ts*.

So, take your pick and stick with it! Either choice is a good one. Our audio and video files contain both pronunciations.

Classical Pronunciation

Latin Consonants: In the classical pronunciation, consonants are pronounced the same as they are in English with the following exceptions.

Letter	Pronunciation	Example	Sound
b	before **s** or **t** like English *p*	**urbs:** city	*urps*
c/ch	always hard like English *k*	**cantō:** I sing	*kahn-toh*
g	always hard like English *g*oat	**gaudium:** joy	*gow-diyum*
gn	in the middle of the word like English *ngn* in ha*ngn*ail	**magnus:** big	*mang-nus*
i	before a vowel it is a consonant like the English *y*	**iaceō:** I lie down	*yah-keh-oh*
r	should be rolled as in Spanish or Italian	**rēgīna:** queen	*ray-geen-ah*
s	always like the *s* in the English *s*ing	**servus:** servant	*ser-wus*
v	always as an English *w*	**vallum:** wall	*wa-luhm*

Diphthongs: Diphthongs are two vowels with a single sound.

ae	au	ei	oe	ui
as in *eye*	as in *ou*t	as in str*ay*	as in c*oi*l	not a diphthong; pronounced *oo-ee*

Latin Short and Long Vowels: Vowels can be short or long in Latin. When they are long, they have a little dash called a macron placed over them. Long vowels take about twice as long to say as short ones. In this book we don't display macrons, but they are often displayed in Latin grammar textbooks.

Short Vowels			Long Vowels		
Letter	Example	Sound	Letter	Example	Sound
a in Dinah	**casa:** house	*ka-sa*	ā in father	**stāre:** to stand	*stah-reh*
e in pet	**ventus:** wind	*wen-tus*	ē in they	**vidēre:** to see	*wi-dey-reh*
i in pit	**silva:** forest	*sil-wah*	ī in machine	**īre:** to go	*ee-reh*
o in pot	**bonus:** good	*bah-nus*	ō in hose	**errō:** I wander	*er-roh*
u in put	**cum:** with	*kum*	ū in rude	**lūdus:** school	*loo-duhs*

Ecclesiastical Pronunciation

There is no *w* in the ecclesiastical pronunciation of Latin. The letters *k*, *y*, and *z* were used very rarely. Letters in Latin are never silent.

Latin Consonants: In the ecclesiastical pronunciation, consonants are pronounced the same as they are in English with the following exceptions. The pronunciations specific to the ecclesiastical pronunciation have been shaded.

Letter	Pronunciation	Example	Sound
b	before **s** or **t** like English *p*	**urbs:** city	*urps*
c	before **e, i, ae, oe,** and **y** always like English *ch*	**cēna:** food	*chey-nah*
c	before other letters, hard *c* like English *c*ap	**cantō:** I sing	*kahn-toh*
g	soft before **e, i, ae,** and **oe** like English *g*erm	**magistra:** teacher	*mah-jee-stra*
g	before other letters, hard like English *g*oat	**gaudium:** joy	*gow-diyum*
gn	in the middle of the word like English *ngn* in ha*ngn*ail	**magnus:** big	*mang-nus*
j	like the English *y* in *y*es	**jaceō:** I lie down	*yah-keh-oh*
r	should be rolled as in Spanish or Italian	**rēgīna:** queen	*ray-geen-ah*
s	always like the *s* in the English *s*ing	**servus:** servant	*ser-vus*
t	when followed by **i** and a vowel, like *tsee*	**silentium:** silence	*see-len-tsee-um*
v	always as an English *v*	**vallum:** wall	*va-luhm*

Diphthongs: With the exception of *ae*, which is pronounced "ay" in the ecclesiastical pronunciation, diphthongs are pronounced the same in both classical and ecclesiastical pronunciations. See the chart on the previous page for the other pronunciations.

Latin Short and Long Vowels: The ecclesiastical short and long vowels are pronounced the same way as in the classical pronunciation. See the table on the preceding page for the pronunciations.

Introduction

Welcome to "Song School," a place for you and your students to enjoy acquiring Latin vocabulary and start learning the basics of Latin grammar. This book is designed to lay the foundation of a strong vocabulary in Latin, taking advantage of young children's incredible capacity for memorization and the fun they can have singing and chanting. Through songs and chants, games, and simple workbook activities, students will learn 175 new vocabulary words as well as some basic Latin grammar.

Song School Latin Book 2 (*SSL2*) has been designed for use by students in grades 2–4 and assumes students have completed *Song School Latin Book 1* (*SSL1*) or another introductory Latin book. This book has also been designed to lead naturally and seamlessly into *Latin for Children Primer A* (*LFCA*). In fact, students who have completed *SSL2* will have already learned seventy-five Latin words from *LFCA* and the first unit's worth of grammar.

Schedule and Pacing

Song School Latin Book 2 is designed for your class to cover one chapter a week, completing thirty-two chapters during a September-to-May school year. Most chapters contain a small review of words from *SSL1*. Review chapters are built in every few weeks to help students master the content before moving on. Memorizing the songs/chants works well as part of a daily classroom routine, and students should be encouraged to listen to the CD in the car and at home. The workbook pages can be completed in one class period (for Latin teachers who see their classes once a week for a full school period) or with ten to fifteen minutes per day, spread over the school week.

Chapter Lessons and Grammar

A secondary goal of this text is to open children's eyes gently to the process of language learning. The chapter lessons address some of the frustrations students have when they first begin studying a language—for example, dismay at encountering a phrase in Latin that has fewer words than its English translation. Many students are surprised to find that foreign languages have different rules than English does—some are even surprised to find that language has rules at all. Our hope is that your students will find these new rules exotic and intriguing, rather than an obstacle to surmount.

To create this level of comfort and interest in studying grammar, the few "rules" that we teach are presented gently and with examples and frequent review. We've chosen to focus on three verb tenses, noun-verb agreement, and noun-adjective agreement. We introduce and teach the nominative case (singular and plural), and briefly touch on the accusative case and noun genders. Students will also learn how being (linking) verbs function in Latin. Students will memorize case and verb endings, some of which will be used later in their next year of Latin study.

A Note About Code Switching

Code switching is the linguistic term for changing languages mid-speech. In recent years, code switching has been discouraged in the language classroom, where teachers aim for a "full immersion" situation, and ask their students not to speak their native language. At Classical Academic Press, we believe in using a child's native language as a scaffold to facilitate a more rapid acquisition of grammar concepts and vocabulary.

There is a significant amount of research on the phenomenon of code switching, establishing it as a common, and "natural," occurrence in bilingual communities. In the songs/chants and exercises in this book, we have attempted to respect the patterns of native Latin in the code switching as much as possible.

We hope you and your students have a great experience with *Song School Latin Book 2*. Feel free to contact us at info@ClassicalSubjects.com with any questions about the text or the audio CD.

Additional Resources

Classical Academic Press has designed several resources that supplement the student edition (SE) of this book. The teacher's edition (TE) provides all the answers to exercises as well as teaching tips and more than forty pages of additional activities and exercises corresponding to each chapter in the SE. These activities are ideal for advanced students or enthusiastic learners who simply want more Latin study. In addition, the following is available:

- **My Library:** The CAP My Library platform collects your streaming video, audio, and digital purchases into a single location, and also provides you with extra practice activities and games for *SSL2*! If you purchase the *SSL2* streaming video from CAP, you will receive the free My Library bonus content for *SSL2*, including our FlashDash vocabulary game, to take students' learning further while they're having fun!
- **Latin Monkey Match Vocabulary Cards:** These cards, which contain all of the vocabulary from *SSL2*, play like the Memory Game, in which students seek to match one Latin card with its English twin. The cards can also be used as typical vocabulary flash cards. You may see a sample of these cards on the product page for *Song School Latin Book 2* at ClassicalAcademicPress.com.
- **Latin Pronunciation Files:** While the *SSL2* audio CD teaches Latin pronunciation well, it is also helpful for students (and teachers) to hear each word pronounced. To download mp3 files of all of the vocabulary being pronounced (in either the classical or ecclesiastical pronunciation), visit the *Song School Latin Book 2* product page at ClassicalAcademicPress.com and click the Support tab.

• **Ask the Magister:** Parents and teachers may ask questions about this text and seek guidance from other Latin teachers by clicking on the "Ask the Magister" link under the Resources tab at ClassicalAcademicPress.com.

Other Song School Products from Classical Academic Press

If your students enjoy *Song School Latin Book 2*, we encourage you also to review our other Song School curricula, including *Song School Latin Book 1*; *Song School Greek*; and *Song School Spanish*.

A Suggested Schedule for Teaching *Song School Latin Book 2*

Song School Latin Book 2 was designed to be flexible and easy to teach in various settings. It can be taught once a week in a gathered class (for about forty-five to sixty minutes) with students doing some workbook activities at home (with parental guidance) and listening to the audio CD songs/chants until the next class period. However, our suggested method consists of more frequent study in shorter time segments. Therefore, we generally recommend a three- to four-day rhythm with the student doing some of the workbook exercises and singing/chanting along with the audio CD during each session. Each of these sessions should take only ten to twenty minutes. We also recommend that students play the audio CD around the home, in the classroom, and in the car, which will aid them in learning much even without the workbook.

What follows is a generic, three-day (or three-session) schedule that teachers and parents should be able to easily adapt to other rhythms and patterns.

Day One: Have students study the first page and read out loud all the new Latin words/phrases for the week. For proper pronunciation, students should listen to the audio file of the Latin words/phrases being spoken (in either the classical or ecclesiastical pronunciation). These files can be downloaded from the Support tab on the *Song School Latin Book 2* product page of ClassicalAcademicPress.com. Then students should listen to the chapter song(s)/chant(s) on the audio CD. The songs/chants will help them to remember the words and pronounce them correctly.

Day Two: Have students review the chapter's Latin words/phrases once more and practice speaking them, both by reading them out loud and by speaking them from memory. Have students practice speaking the words to another student or to you or a parent. Next, students should sing/chant along with the CD and also see if they can sing/chant from memory. Students should then read the chapter lesson in the book and do any exercises that follow it, being sure to stop when they reach the Show What You Know section—they'll do that section during the third lesson. End the lesson by having students recite from memory all the Latin words/phrases in the chapter and having them sing/chant the song(s)/chant(s) from memory, too.

Day Three: Have the students, from memory, say out loud all of the chapter's Latin words/phrases. Next they should sing/chant the song(s)/chant(s) from memory and then sing/chant along with the audio CD a couple of times. It is also a good idea to have them review the songs/chants from past chapters, an activity students should find enjoyable. Finally, have students do the Show What You Know section and finish the chapter.

Chapter 1

What Day Is It?

Phrases to Learn

1. **Qui dies est?** What day is it?
2. **Hodie est ______.** Today is ______.

Review Words

1. **salve** hello
2. **vale** good-bye
3. **discipuli** students
4. **magister** male teacher
   magistra female teacher

Chapter Song

When You Wake Up in the Mornin' [Track 1(C)/31(E)]

When you wake up in the mornin'
and you don't know the day,
Qui dies est? is the way to say:
What's the day?
What's the day?

When you wake up in the mornin'
and you're in the know,
Hodie est is the way to show:
It's today,
It's today,
It's today!

Famous Saying

Acta non verba = Actions, not words!

Sometimes we need to stop talking and just do our work! Words are important too, though, and in this chapter we are looking at words *and* actions.

Chapter Lesson

Jumping, eating, talking, running, splashing, yelling, washing, breathing . . . how are all these words alike? These are all things you can *do*; they are action words. Do you remember the name for words that show action? They are called *verbs*. There is a verb to name any action that you can do. What verbs can you think of? Don't get confused by other types of words, such as nouns. (Remember, a noun usually names a person, place, or thing.) If you want to know if a word is an action verb, try to picture someone "doing" that word. Can you picture a person toe-ing? No! Can you picture a person singing? Yes. Think of as many action words as you can and test them out by trying to picture a person doing them.

Grow Your English

The Latin word **dies** gives us many English words relating to days. What do you call a little book in which you might write down what happens each *day*? A *diary*! Something that happens every day is a *diurnal* event. You would also say that an animal that sleeps at night and is active in the daytime is diurnal. This is the opposite of nocturnal, which means happening, or being active, at night. Are you a diurnal or nocturnal creature?

Practice Your Latin

I. Practice writing your new Latin phrases by tracing the dots.

Qui dies est?

Hodie est

II. **Time to Talk!** Practice asking people what day it is in Latin and giving the answer starting with the correct Latin phrase. Be sure to use the greetings in the Review Words section of this chapter as well as your new Latin phrases. Soon you will learn the days of the week in Latin, too, so you will be able to give the answer completely in Latin.

III. Simeon is confused. Help him figure out the best way to get from **Qui dies est?** to **Hodie est**. When he gets out of the maze, write a message telling him what day of the week it is, starting with the correct Latin phrase and ending with the day of the week in English.

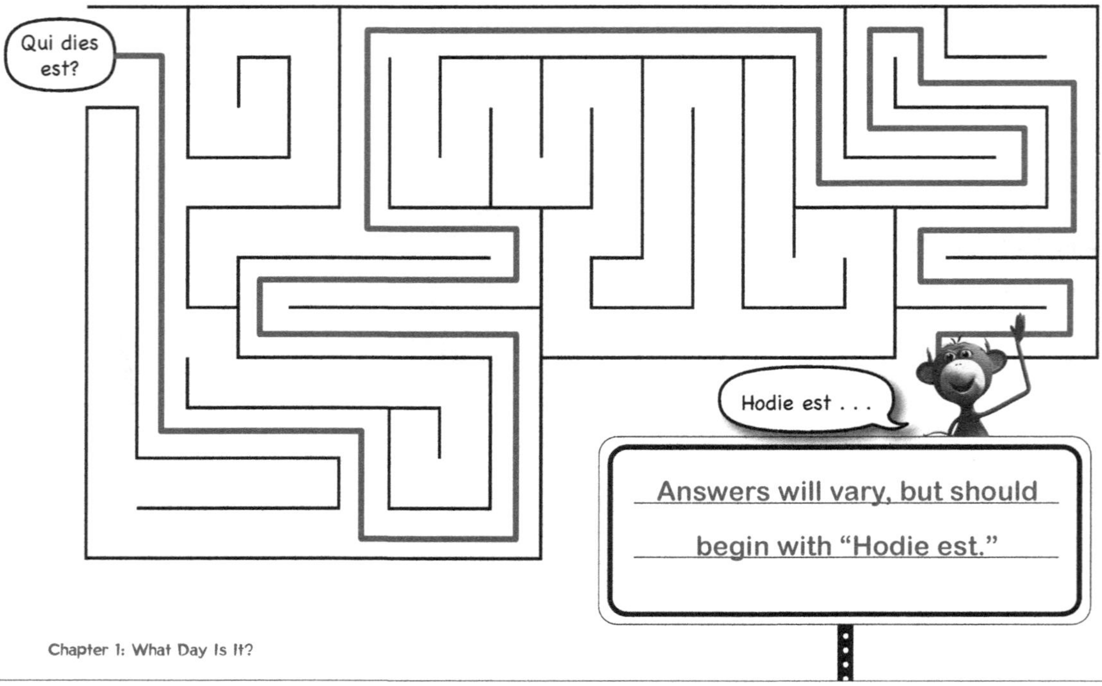

Answers will vary, but should begin with "Hodie est."

IV. Circle the best answer.

1. Which phrase means "What day is it?"

a. **Qui hodie?** b. **Hodie est?** (c. **Qui dies est?**) d. **Carpe diem?**

2. Which phrase means "today is"?

a. **qui est dies** (b. **hodie est**) c. **hodie qui** d. **hodie dies**

Show What You Know

I. Write "What day is it?" in Latin. Qui dies est?

II. Write "today is" in Latin. hodie est

III. What is the name for an action word? verb

IV. Circle the action words in this list (remember to try to picture someone doing each word).

1. book◊
2. (sit)
3. car
4. bird
5. (hold)
6. (sing)
7. computer
8. (write)
9. (sleep)
10. (shoot)
11. table
12. (whistle)◊◊
13. marshmallow
14. sandal
15. peanut butter
16. (tickle)
17. (drive)
18. teddy bear
19. cake◊
20. (jump)◊◊

◊ Students will likely gravitate toward the noun meanings of the words marked with ◊, but in case there's confusion, you may need to point out that the indicated words can be both nouns and verbs.

◊◊ These words can also be nouns as well as verbs.

Chapter 2

Days of the Week

Words/Phrases to Learn

1. **Dies Solis** Sunday
2. **Dies Lunae** Monday
3. **Dies Martis** Tuesday
4. **Dies Mercurii** Wednesday
5. **Dies Iovis** Thursday
6. **Dies Veneris** Friday
7. **Dies Saturni** Saturday

Review Phrases

1. **Quid est tuum praenomen?** What is your name?
2. **Meum praenomen est . . .** My name is . . .

Chapter Song

Days of the Week Song [Track 2(C)/32(E)]

Sunday **Solis**
Monday **Lunae**
Tuesday **Martis**
Wednesday **Mercurii**
Thursday **Iovis**
Friday **Veneris**
Saturday **Saturni**

Famous Saying

Carpe diem = Seize the day!

◊ You may enjoy incorporating **carpe diem** as a common phrase in your classroom to remind students that they should be working hard and making the most of their time, whether it is by listening, studying, doing extracurricular activities, or interacting with their peers. You may open a discussion by asking students to think about the opportunities that come across their paths daily to learn, do good things for others, and enjoy life. Build on their responses if you would like to take the discussion further or remind them at later times to **carpe diem** in their own unique worlds.

This is a very famous quote by Horace, a Roman poet. We think that he was saying to take the opportunities that come and make the most of each day. You might often hear this saying changed, with another word after **carpe**, telling people to seize something else. For example, **Carpe noctem!** which means "Seize the night!" Here are some other fun variations: **Carpe crustulum!** (Seize the cookie!) or **Carpe canem!** (Seize the dog!) How can you **Carpe diem!** today?◊

Chapter Lesson

Do you remember the name for action words? Yes, action words are called verbs! Latin verbs have all kinds of special endings that are kind of like codes. The endings give us more information about the action, such as who is doing it and when it is being done. In this chapter, you will start learning some of these verb endings, and in the next chapter you will learn what they mean. These endings are fun to chant. Here they are: ◊◊

◊◊ The o-s-t chant is fun to chant with two quick claps between the singular (**-o, -s, -t**) and plural (**-mus, -tis, -nt**) endings. (Think "Mexican Hat Dance.")

O-S-T Chant	
-o	**-mus**
-s	**-tis**
-t	**-nt**

Grow Your English

If you listen carefully, you can hear one of the English weekday names in one of the Latin weekday names. Can you figure out which one? Saturday sounds almost like "saturnday" or **dies saturni**. Do you remember what **sol** and **luna** mean? Sun and moon! So, the week starts with the Day of the Sun (**dies solis**) and is followed by the Day of the Moon (**dies lunae**)—Sunday and Moonday (Monday).

Practice Your Latin

I. Practice writing the days of the week by tracing the dots.

Dies Solis Dies Lunae

Dies Martis Dies Mercurii

Dies Iovis Dies Veneris

Dies Saturni

II. Circle the best answer.

1. Which day is right in the middle of the week?

   a. **Dies Saturni** b. **Dies Lunae** c. **Dies Mercurii**

2. What day starts your school week?

   a. **Dies Lunae** b. **Dies Iovis** c. **Dies Veneris**

3. On which of these days do you not go to school?

   a. **Dies Mercurii** b. **Dies Saturni** c. **Dies Martis**

4. What is the very first day of the week?

   a. **Dies Solis** b. **Dies Iovis** c. **Dies Veneris**

5. Which day comes next after **Dies Iovis**?

   a. **Dies Saturni** b. **Dies Solis** c. **Dies Veneris**

III. What is your favorite day of the week? **Dies** Answers will vary.

IV. In the box provided, draw a picture showing what you like best about your favorite day of the week!

Show What You Know

Draw lines connecting the days of the week in Latin to the English days of the week.

1. Sunday	**Dies Mercurii**
2. Monday	**Dies Saturni**
3. Tuesday	**Dies Martis**
4. Wednesday	**Dies Veneris**
5. Thursday	**Dies Solis**
6. Friday	**Dies Lunae**
7. Saturday	**Dies Iovis**

Chapter 3

Months of the Year

Words/Phrases to Learn

1. **Qui mensis est?** — What month is it?
2. **Hic mensis est . . .** — This month is . . .
3. **Ianuarius** — January
4. **Februarius** — February
5. **Martius** — March
6. **Aprilis** — April

Review Words

1. **hiems** — winter
2. **ver** — spring
3. **autumnus** — fall
4. **aestas** — summer

Chapter Song

<u>Months of the Year, Part I</u> [Track 3(C)/33(E)]

Ianuarius comes first in the year,
Februarius brings us coats to wear.
Martius marches into town,
Aprilis brings the showers down. *(x2)**
The first four months of the year!

*That number at the end of the verse is there to tell you how many times you should sing the verse.

Famous Saying

Per mensem = monthly, every month, or by the month

◊ **Per diem means "per day." Sometimes it refers to a set expense allowance per day or to the way a contract is set up, but essentially it means "per day."**

Someday, when you have a job, you may be paid **per mensem**, but more likely you will be paid by the week or every two weeks. You might get a **per mensem** allowance right now, and you might turn your calendar page **per mensem**. If **per mensem** means "monthly," what do you think **per diem** means?◊

Chapter Lesson

It's time to learn the meanings of the verb endings you learned last week! In this chapter, you will learn the meanings of the first three of the endings. These are the singular endings. You'll learn the plural endings in the next chapter. (Do you remember what singular and plural mean? Singular means "only one." Plural means "more than one.") These verb endings tell you *who* is doing the action. To the right is the first half of the **o-s-t** chant with the meanings:

O-S-T Chant: Singular		
First Person ◊◊	**-o**	I
Second Person	**-s**	you
Third Person	**-t**	he/she/it

◊◊ **Students will learn about person later in this book, but it's a good idea to get them used to the terminology as they're learning the chant.**

To help you remember these meanings, you can chant them like this:

-o means *I*
-s means *you*
-t means *he/she/it*

Or you can *sing* them, like this!

<u>**O-S-T Song, Part I**</u> [Track 5(C)/35(E)]

-O, **-o**, **-o** means *I*
-S means only *you*
-T means *he*, *she*, or *it*
Three more and then we're through.

Grow Your English

In many schools and most colleges, the year is divided up into two *semesters*. Can you see the Latin word for "month" in that word? The word "semester" actually comes from two Latin words: the word for *month* (**mensis**) and the word for the number *six* (**sex**). Most semesters aren't actually six months long any more, but that is the original meaning of the word ("six months").

Practice Your Latin

I. Trace the dots to practice writing the months of the year and the questions that go with them.

Qui mensis est?

Hic mensis est . . .

Ianuarius Februarius

Martius Aprilis

II. Circle the best answer.

1. What is the third month of the year?

   a. **Februarius** b. **Aprilis** c. **Martius** d. **Ianuarius**

2. In what month is Valentine's Day?

   a. **Martius** b. **Februarius** c. **Ianuarius** d. **Aprilis**

3. What is the first month of the year?

   a. **Aprilis** b. **Ianuarius** c. **Martius** d. **Februarius**

4. Which of these months do you think would be the warmest?◊◊◊

   a. **Ianuarius** b. **Martius** c. **Februarius** d. **Aprilis**

◊◊◊ Answers to the indicated exercises may vary depending on your local climate. Give guidance, feedback, and/or instructions appropriate to your local climate.

III. Circle the best picture for each month and then color it.◊◊◊◊

◊◊◊◊ Answers to the indicated exercises may vary depending on your local climate. Give guidance, feedback, and/or instructions appropriate to your local climate.

1. **Ianuarius**

2. **Februarius**

3. **Martius**

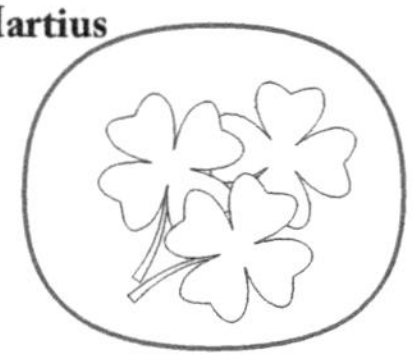

4. **Aprilis**

IV. **Time to talk!** Take turns with your classmates asking and answering the month questions. In the next chapter, you'll learn the remaining month names, but until then, you may have to pretend it's January, February, March, or April. After the next chapter you will be able to answer correctly anytime!

Show What You Know

I. Draw lines to match the Latin month name to the correct English month name.

1. January	**Aprilis**
2. February	**Martius**
3. March	**Ianuarius**
4. April	**Februarius**

II. Circle the best answer.

1. Which Latin phrase means "What month is it?"

a. **Qui mensis est?** b. **Hic mensis est?** c. **Hic mensis qui?**

2. Which Latin phrase means "This month is"?

a. **Qui mensis est** b. **Hic mensis est** c. **Hic mensis qui**

3. Draw lines to match the endings in the **o-s-t** chant to their meanings.

a. **-o**	you
b. **-s**	he/she/it
c. **-t**	I

Chapter 4

More Months of the Year

Words to Learn

1. **Maius**	May
2. **Iunius**	June
3. **Iulius**	July
4. **Augustus**	August
5. **September**	September
6. **October**	October
7. **November**	November
8. **December**	December

Review Words/Phrases

1. **Quid agis?**	How are you?
2. **bene**	well, fine
3. **optime**	best
4. **pessime**	badly, terrible
5. **pater**	father
6. **mater**	mother

Chapter Song

Months of the Year, Parts I & II [Track 4(C)/34(E)]

Ianuarius comes first in the year,
Februarius brings us coats to wear.
Martius marches into town,
Aprilis brings the showers down.
The first four months of the year!

Maius blooms in flowers and berries,
Iunius loves the bright red cherries,
Iulius starts with a bang and a flash,
Augustus—off to the beach we dash.
The next four months of the year.

September—lots of cookies to bake,
October scatters leaves to rake,
November—off to Grandma's we go,
December shovels white, white snow.
The last four months of the year.

Famous Saying

Ad idem = of the same mind

What do you think it means to be "of the same mind"? Being "of the same mind" generally means thinking the same thing as someone else. You may agree on a specific topic, such as your feelings about chocolate ice cream. If you're of the same mind with someone who dislikes chocolate ice cream, that means that you also dislike it. In other words, being "of the same mind" means that you agree with one another. Sometimes when someone says they are "of the same mind" with someone else, they mean it in a bigger, broader way than just one specific topic. They are saying that they have similar views on many or most things. So, can you think of someone with whom you are "of the same mind"?

Chapter Lesson

It's time to learn the rest of the meanings of the **o-s-t** chant! Last week you learned the singular endings and their meanings and now you will learn the plural endings and their meanings.

O-S-T Chant				
Person	Singular		Plural	
First Person	**-o**	I	**-mus**	we
Second Person	**-s**	you	**-tis**	you all◊
Third Person	**-t**	he/she/it	**-nt**	they

◊ "You (plural)" is often given for this ending as well. "You all" is used throughout this book because it is simpler for younger students to understand and remember.

Chant the endings like this . . .

-o means *I*
-s means *you*
-t means *he/she/it*
-mus means *we*
-tis means *you*
and **-nt** means *they* all day.

. . . and sing them like this!

O-S-T Song, Parts I & II [Track 5(C)/35(E)]

-O, **-o**, **-o** means *I*
-S means only *you*
-T means *he*, *she*, or *it*
Three more and then we're through.

-Mus, **-mus**, **-mus** means *we*
-Tis means *you* and *you*
-Nt means *they*, **-nt** means *they*
Six endings, now we're through.

Example

Do you remember the word **laudo** from *SSL1*? **Laudo** means "I praise." If we add all the present tense endings (**-o, -s, -t, -mus, -tis, -nt**) to **laudo**, here is what we get:

Laudo with Endings	
laud*o*	***I*** praise
lauda*s*	***you*** praise
lauda*t*	***he/she/it*** praises
lauda*mus*	***we*** praise
lauda*tis*	***you all*** praise
lauda*nt*	***they*** praise

You might notice that, except for the first-person singular, we add an **a** to **laud** before we put on the endings. We call that **a** our *connecting vowel*. Next week, we will study this chart some more.

Grow Your English

If you ever wondered how we got our English month names, just look at the Latin month names! You can see that the English and Latin are very much alike. In fact, some are spelled identically! Do you see which ones are spelled the same? Of course, the names would have sounded different when a Roman said them because of pronunciation and accent differences. However, the month names remind us how much of the English language came from Latin!

Practice Your Latin

I. Practice your new and review vocabulary by tracing the dots.

Qui mensis est? Quid agis?

Maius Iunius Iulius

Augustus September

October November

December

II. Draw lines from the month name to the picture that best matches it.◊◊

◊◊ If necessary, help students find pictures appropriate for each month according to your local climate.

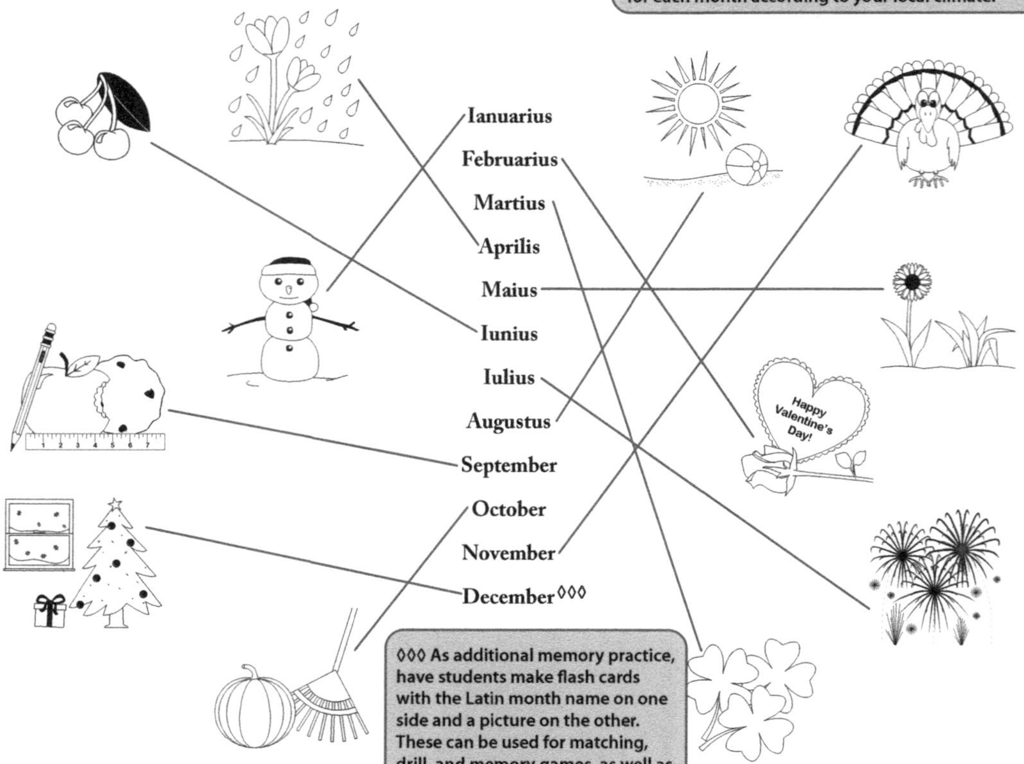

Ianuarius

Februarius

Martius

Aprilis

Maius

Iunius

Iulius

Augustus

September

October

November

December◊◊◊

◊◊◊ As additional memory practice, have students make flash cards with the Latin month name on one side and a picture on the other. These can be used for matching, drill, and memory games, as well as personal review.

III. On the lines provided, write the best answer in Latin.

1. What month is it right now? **Answers will vary.**
2. In which month is your birthday? **Answers will vary.**
3. In which month is your teacher's birthday? **Answers will vary.**
4. What is the hottest month of the year where you live? **Answers will vary.**
5. In which month is your dad's birthday? **Answers will vary.**
6. In which month is Thanksgiving? **November**
7. In which month does spring start? **Martius**
8. In which month is Valentine's Day? **Februarius**

IV. Pick your favorite month and draw a picture of Simeon doing something in that month.

V. With your classmates, take turns asking what month it is and giving the answer to the question.

Show What You Know

I. Draw lines to match the Latin month name to the English month name.

1. **Ianuarius**	October
2. **Februarius**	May
3. **Martius**	January
4. **Aprilis**	December
5. **Maius**	March
6. **Iunius**	November
7. **Iulius**	September
8. **Augustus**	February
9. **September**	April
10. **October**	June
11. **November**	July
12. **December**	August

II. Draw lines to match the endings to their meanings.

1. **-o**	they
2. **-s**	he/she/it
3. **-t**	we
4. **-mus**	you all
5. **-tis**	I
6. **-nt**	you

Chapter 5 Numbers

Words to Learn

1. **unus** one
2. **duo** two
3. **tres** three
4. **quattuor** four
5. **quinque** five

Review Words

1. **soror** sister
2. **frater** brother
3. **puella** girl
4. **puer** boy
5. **vir** man
6. **femina** woman

Chapter Song

<u>Numbers Chant, Part I</u> [Track 6(C)/36(E)]

One, two, three, four!
Unus, duo, tres, quattuor! *(x2)*

Give me one and give me two
Unus! Duo! One and two! *(x2)*

Three and four I adore
Tres and then comes **quattuor**! *(x2)*

And now **quinque** does arrive
That very special number five. *(x2)*

Unus–quinque, one to five
Chant again and look alive! *(x2)*

Famous Saying

Auxilio ab alto = by help from on high

Discuss as a class what you think "help from on high" means. Think about trying to accomplish your hardest challenges "by help from on high"! ◊

◊ **Guide this discussion in a manner suited for your setting and your students.**

Chapter Lesson

Practice! Review the **o-s-t** chant and the meanings.

O-S-T Chant				
PERSON	SINGULAR		PLURAL	
First Person	**-o**	I	**-mus**	we
Second Person	**-s**	you	**-tis**	you all
Third Person	**-t**	he/she/it	**-nt**	they

Sing the **o-s-t** song.

<u>O-S-T Song</u> [Track 5(C)/35(E)]

-O, **-o**, **-o** means *I*
-S means only *you*
-T means *he*, *she*, or *it*
Three more and then we're through.

-Mus, **-mus**, **-mus** means *we*
-Tis means *you* and *you*
-Nt means *they*, **-nt** means *they*
Six endings, now we're through.

<u>A Conjugation Chart</u>

Do you remember this chart from last week? It shows the verb **laudo** with all the endings you have learned (**-o, -s, -t, -mus, -tis, -nt**). This chart is called a *conjugation chart*. The word "conjugation" comes from the Latin word **conjugo**, which means "I join together." In a conjugation chart, we join together the verb and all its endings so that you can see how Latin verbs are made. Learning conjugation charts will come in handy in your later study of Latin.

Laudo with Endings	
laud*o*	***I*** praise
laud*as*	***you*** praise
laud*at*	***he/she/it*** praises
laud*amus*	***we*** praise
laud*atis*	***you all*** praise
laud*ant*	***they*** praise

Now let's make a conjugation chart using another verb—the verb **do**. In *SSL1* you learned that the Latin verb **do** means "I give."

Do with Endings	
d*o*	***I*** give
d*as*	***you*** give
d*at*	***he/she/it*** gives
d*amus*	***we*** give
d*atis*	***you all*** give
d*ant*	***they*** give

Notice that the connecting vowel **a** is used for **do** just as it is for **laudo**.

Grow Your English

The Latin number **unus** is the root of many of our English words. To *unify* means to join together as *one*. A *uniform* is *one* outfit for everyone. How many wheels does a *unicycle* have? Say the number in Latin! There is only one *universe*. What other words can you think of that contain part of the word **unus**? ◊◊

The Latin word **duo** gives us words such as duel, dual, and duplicate. Do you know what these words mean? ◊◊◊

What does the word **quattuor** remind you of? If you thought of *quarter*, you are thinking like a word scholar! What English derivative of **quattuor** refers to four people singing together?

A quartet is four people singing together.

Practice Your Latin

I. Trace the dots to practice writing the Latin numbers one to five. Then, write their English meanings on the blanks next to them.

unus — one

duo — two

tres — three

quattuor — four

quinque — five

> ◊◊ Other derivatives of **unus** include unity, unite, reunite, onion (all parts form one), unit, unicorn, unanimous, unique, union, and unison.

> ◊◊◊ The following is a quick reference for informal definitions of the words mentioned here: A duel is a fight between two people, sometimes to the death—it can be a real physical fight, a duel with words, or a duel of checkers, for example. Dual means "double, two of them"—dual wheels, dual engines on planes, dual rings on pipes, etc.—anything that comes in pairs can be called "dual." To duplicate something is to make an exact second copy so now there are *two* of the thing that was copied.

II. How many are there? Count the number of the items in the pictures and write the answer in Latin.

quinque

unus

quattuor

duo

quinque

tres

III. Help each fisherman catch his fish by drawing a line from his fishing rod to the fish that matches his number.

IV. Color all the **unus** shapes blue, the **duo** shapes green, the **tres** shapes red, the **quattuor** shapes yellow, and the **quinque** shapes orange.

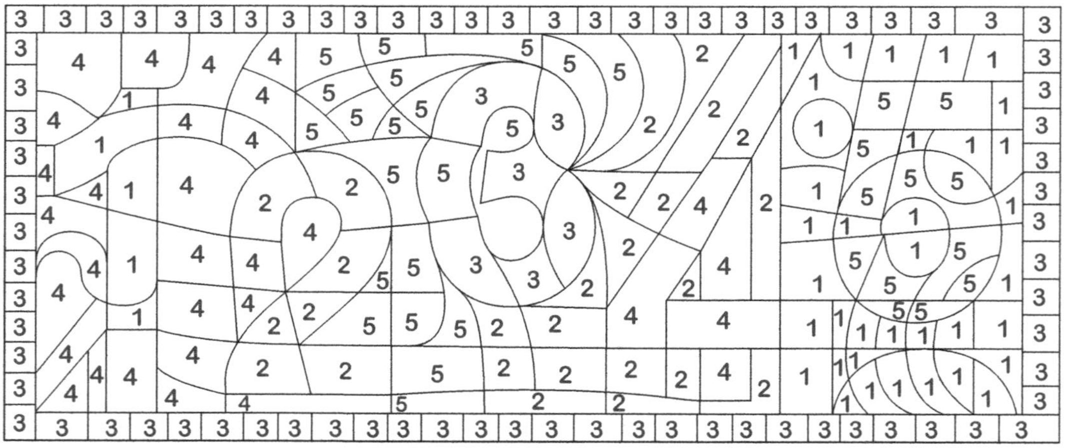

Show What You Know

I. Draw lines to match the Latin numbers to the English numbers.

1. one — **quattuor**
2. two — **unus**
3. three — **quinque**
4. four — **duo**
5. five — **tres**

II. Fill in just the endings of the **o-s-t** chant (don't include the meanings of the endings).

O-S-T Chant		
Person	Singular	Plural
First Person	-o	-mus
Second Person	-s	-tis
Third Person	-t	-nt

III. Write the answers in Latin.

1. How many fingers do you have on each hand? quinque
2. How many arms do you have? duo
3. How many noses do you have? unus
4. How many wheels does a tricycle have? tres
5. How many seasons are in a year? quattuor

Chapter 6

More Numbers

Words to Learn

1. **sex** six
2. **septem** seven
3. **octo** eight
4. **novem** nine
5. **decem** ten

Review Words

1. **mensa** table
2. **sella** chair
3. **stylus** pencil
4. **liber** book

Chapter Songs

<u>Numbers Chant, Parts I & II</u> [Track 7(C)/37(E)]

One, two, three, four!
Unus, duo, tres, quattuor! *(x2)*
Give me one and give me two
Unus! Duo! One and two! *(x2)*
Three and four I adore
Tres and then comes **quattuor**! *(x2)*
And now **quinque** does arrive,
That very special number five. *(x2)*
Six, seven! Eight, nine, ten!
Five more numbers up to ten. *(x4)*

Sex, septem! Six and seven,
Two more numbers we've been given. *(x2)*
Octo, novem, eight and nine,
Right up to the borderline. *(x2)*
Now there's **decem**, number ten,
The first ten numbers in Latin. *(x2)*
Unus–decem, one to ten,
Take a breath and count again! *(x2)*

Decem Little Romans [Track 8(C)/38(E)]

Unus, duo, tres little Romans
Quattuor, quinque, sex little Romans
Septem, octo, novem Romans
Decem Roman boys!

Decem, novem, octo Romans
Septem, sex, and **quinque** Romans
Quattuor, tres, and **duo** Romans
Unus Roman boy! *(x2)*

Famous Saying

Pater familias = father of the family

This is a saying or term that gives a little more importance to the title of "father." It even carries the idea of not just your own father, but of the oldest male in your extended family—your great grandfather, for example, is the **pater familias** of you all. However, you may also call your very own father **pater familias** to remind everyone of his very important role.

Chapter Lesson

Do you remember what kind of word uses the **o-s-t** endings? An action verb! Do you remember how to tell what an action verb is? Take time to think of examples of action verbs right now. The purpose of the **o-s-t** endings on action verbs is to show *who* is doing the action. In *SSL1*, you learned the word **laudo**, which means "I praise." What part of the word means "I"? That's right, the *o*! The chart below shows **laudo** with all of the **o-s-t** endings added:

Laudo with Endings				
	Singular◊		Plural	
Person	Ending	Meaning	Ending	Meaning
First Person	**laud*o***	I praise	**laud*amus***	we praise
Second Person	**laud*as***	you praise	**laud*atis***	you all praise
Third Person	**laud*at***	he/she/it praises	**laud*ant***	they praise

Practice chanting **laudo** with the endings!

◊ You may want to review what singular and plural mean. You can use the following text to help you do so: Do you see that we labeled one side of the box "singular" and the other "plural"? That is because on the singular side just one *single* person is doing the action of praising ("I" means just one person, "you" means just one person, and "he," "she," or "it" means just one person or thing). The other side is plural because *more than one* person is doing the action of praising ("we," "you all," and "they" all refer to more than one person).

Sample Sentences

The following three sentences each use a different form of the verb **laudo**:

Laud*o* stellam.* *I* praise the star.

Laud*amus* stellam. *We* praise the star.

Laud*ant* stellam. *They* praise the star.

Grow Your English

Latin numbers give us many English derivatives. Can you remember some of the derivatives from the last lesson? **Octo** is another Latin number from which we take several English words. An octagon is a figure with *eight* sides. An octave is a series of *eight* notes. Can you think of a sea creature that has *eight* legs? **An octopus has eight legs.**

What Latin number do you think the word *decimal* came from? How many sides do you think a *decagon* has? How many years are in a *decade*?

All of these words are derived from the Latin word decem, which means "ten."

Practice Your Latin

I. Practice writing the Latin numbers **unus** through **decem** by tracing the dots.

unus duo tres quattuor

quinque sex septem

octo novem decem

*The word **stella** means star. We add an **m** to the end of many nouns when they are receiving the action of a verb. You will learn more about this in your later study of Latin.

II. Simeon's bananas are out of order! Read the Latin numbers and line them up in numerical order by drawing lines from the bananas to the correct numbered tab.

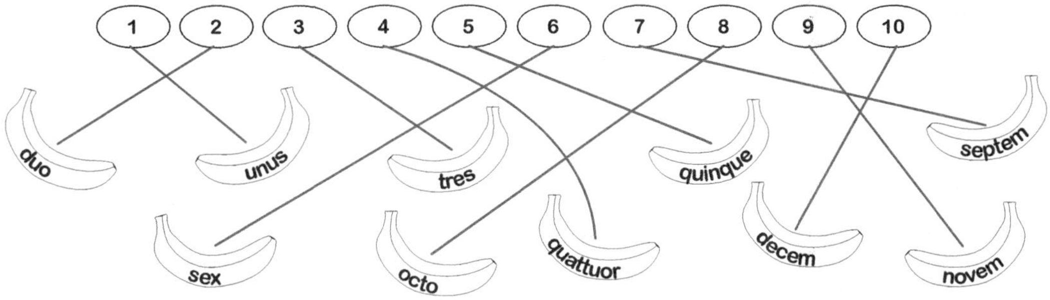

III. Draw the picture by connecting the dots in the order of their Latin number labels. **Hint:** You'll need to connect the dots of the first and last number to complete the picture. Color the picture when you finish!

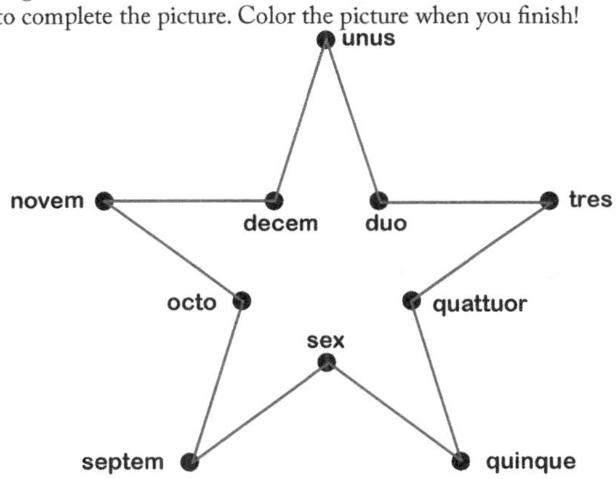

IV. **Number Games!**

1. **Number Sound-Off:** Line up with your classmates and then, starting at the beginning of the line, number off in Latin.◊◊
2. **Number Matching:** Your teacher will hand you a card with either a Latin or an English number on it, and you have to find your partner who has the same number in the other language.◊◊◊

◊◊ If you have more than ten students, have them just start over with **unus** after they get to **decem** and continue that way until all students have numbered off or until they make the desired number of rounds. If you have fewer than ten students, just have them arranged in a line or a circle so that the number comes back around to the first student and then have them continue until they reach **decem**.

Show What You Know

I. Write the numbers one to ten in Latin.

1. unus
2. duo
3. tres
4. quattuor
5. quinque
6. sex
7. septem
8. octo
9. novem
10. decem

◊◊◊ You will need two sets of cards for this exercise. One set should be numbered from 1 to 10 in English. The other set of cards should be numbered from **unus** to **decem** in Latin. Hand out, right-side down, an equal number of cards in Latin and English, ensuring that each card has a match. Also make sure that you mix the cards up so that students with matching numbers aren't standing right next to each other. Then have students turn their cards over and find their matches. You will need to adjust this exercise to match the configuration of your classroom. If you have an odd number of students, you can either hold a card and participate in the exercise yourself, or you can pull one student out and designate that student as the "last chance helper" for students who forget the translated counterpart of their number. If you have more than ten students, include multiple sets of as many numbers as needed. In this instance, there would be multiple possibilities for the pairing, which is fine. If you have fewer than ten students, rotate out the appropriate number of cards, doing several rounds so that all numbers get used. Make it as competitive as is appropriate for your classroom. You could give special recognition to the first one or two teams to be matched or you could go with an elimination approach, with the last team paired up being eliminated. The second round starts with cards redistributed, minus the last pair, and so on until you get down to a final four.

II. Fill in the **o-s-t** chant, including the meanings.

O-S-T Chant				
	Singular		Plural	
Person	Ending	Meaning	Ending	Meaning
First Person	-o	I	-mus	we
Second Person	-s	you	-tis	you all
Third Person	-t	he/she/it	-nt	they

Master Your Words

Well, **discipuli**, you have learned a bunch of new words. Now it's time to make sure you've mastered them. On the lines provided, write the correct English words for the Latin words.

Chapter 1 New Words/Phrases

1. **Qui dies est?** ______ What day is it? ______
2. **Hodie est ______.** ______ Today is ______. ______

Chapter 1 Review Words

1. **salve** ______ hello ______
2. **vale** ______ good-bye ______
3. **discipuli** ______ students ______
4. **magister** ______ male teacher ______
   magistra ______ female teacher ______

Chapter 2 New Words/Phrases

1. **Dies Solis** ______ Sunday ______
2. **Dies Lunae** ______ Monday ______
3. **Dies Martis** ______ Tuesday ______

4. **Dies Mercurii** ______ Wednesday ______
5. **Dies Iovis** ______ Thursday ______
6. **Dies Veneris** ______ Friday ______
7. **Dies Saturni** ______ Saturday ______

Chapter 2 Review Phrases

1. **Quid est tuum praenomen?** ______ What is your name? ______
2. **Meum praenomen est . . .** ______ My name is . . . ______

Chapter 3 New Words/Phrases

1. **Qui mensis est?** ______ What month is it? ______
2. **Hic mensis est . . .** ______ This month is . . . ______
3. **Ianuarius** ______ January ______
4. **Februarius** ______ February ______
5. **Martius** ______ March ______
6. **Aprilis** ______ April ______

Chapter 3 Review Words

1. **hiems** ______ winter ______
2. **ver** ______ spring ______

3. autumnus — fall

4. aestas — summer

Chapter 4 Words

1. Maius — May
2. Iunius — June
3. Iulius — July
4. Augustus — August
5. September — September
6. October — October
7. November — November
8. December — December

Chapter 4 Review Words/Phrases

1. Quid agis? — How are you?
2. bene — well, fine
3. optime — best
4. pessime — badly, terrible
5. pater — father
6. mater — mother

Chapter 5 Words

1. unus — one
2. duo — two
3. tres — three
4. quattuor — four
5. quinque — five

Chapter 5 Review Words

1. soror — sister
2. frater — brother
3. puella — girl
4. puer — boy
5. vir — man
6. femina — woman

Chapter 6 Words

1. sex — six
2. septem — seven
3. octo — eight

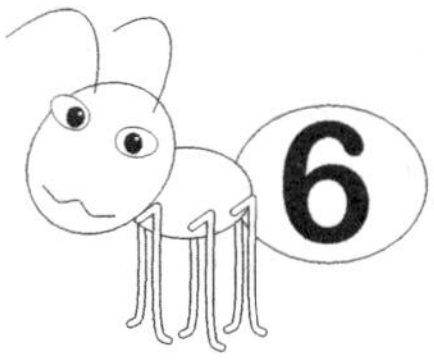

4. **novem** nine

5. **decem** ten

Chapter 6 Review Words

1. **mensa** table
2. **sella** chair
3. **stylus** pencil
4. **liber** book

Master Your Songs

<u>When You Wake Up in the Mornin'</u> [Track 1(C)/31(E)]

When you wake up in the mornin'
and you don't know the day,
Qui dies est? is the way to say:
What's the day?
What's the day?

When you wake up in the mornin'
and you're in the know,
Hodie est is the way to show:
It's today,
It's today,
It's today!

<u>Days of the Week Song</u> [Track 2(C)/32(E)]

Sunday **Solis**
Monday **Lunae**
Tuesday **Martis**
Wednesday **Mercurii**
Thursday **Iovis**
Friday **Veneris**
Saturday **Saturni**

<u>Months of the Year, Part I</u> [Track 3(C)/33(E)]

Ianuarius comes first in the year,
Februarius brings us coats to wear.
Martius marches into town,
Aprilis brings the showers down. *(x2)*
The first four months of the year!

<u>O-S-T Song, Part I</u> [Track 5(C)/35(E)]

-O, **-o**, **-o** means *I*
-S means only *you*
-T means *he*, *she*, or *it*
Three more and then we're through.

<u>Months of the Year, Parts I & II</u> [Track 4(C)/34(E)]

Ianuarius comes first in the year,
Februarius brings us coats to wear.
Martius marches into town,
Aprilis brings the showers down.
The first four months of the year!

Maius blooms in flowers and berries,
Iunius loves the bright red cherries,
Iulius starts with a bang and a flash,
Augustus—off to the beach we dash.
The next four months of the year.

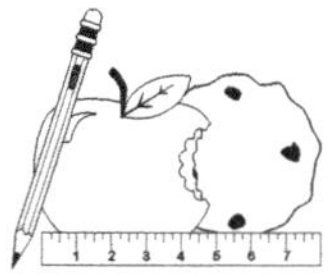

September—lots of cookies to bake,
October scatters leaves to rake,
November—off to Grandma's we go,
December shovels white, white snow.
The last four months of the year.

<u>O-S-T Song, Parts I & II</u> [Track 5(C)/35(E)]

-O, **-o**, **-o** means *I*
-S means only *you*
-T means *he*, *she*, or *it*
Three more and then we're through.

-Mus, **-mus**, **-mus** means *we*
-Tis means *you* and *you*
-Nt means *they*, **-nt** means *they*
Six endings, now we're through.

Numbers Chant, Part I [Track 6(C)/36(E)]

One, two, three, four!
Unus, duo, tres, quattuor! *(x2)*

Give me one and give me two
Unus! Duo! One and two! *(x2)*

Three and four I adore
Tres and then comes **quattuor**! *(x2)*

And now **quinque** does arrive
That very special number five. *(x2)*

Unus–quinque, one to five
Chant again and look alive! *(x2)*

Decem Little Romans [Track 8(C)/38(E)]

Unus, duo, tres little Romans
Quattuor, quinque, sex little Romans
Septem, octo, novem Romans
Decem Roman boys!

Decem, novem, octo Romans
Septem, sex, and **quinque** Romans
Quattuor, tres, and **duo** Romans
Unus Roman boy! *(x2)*

Numbers Chant, Parts I & II [Track 7(C)/37(E)]

One, two, three, four!
Unus, duo, tres, quattuor! *(x2)*

Give me one and give me two
Unus! Duo! One and two! *(x2)*

Three and four I adore
Tres and then comes **quattuor**! *(x2)*

And now **quinque** does arrive,
That very special number five. *(x2)*

Six, seven! Eight, nine, ten!
Five more numbers up to ten. *(x4)*

Sex, septem! Six and seven,
Two more numbers we've been given. *(x2)*

Octo, novem, eight and nine,
Right up to the borderline. *(x2)*

Now there's **decem**, number ten,
The first ten numbers in Latin. *(x2)*

Unus–decem, one to ten,
Take a breath and count again! *(x2)*

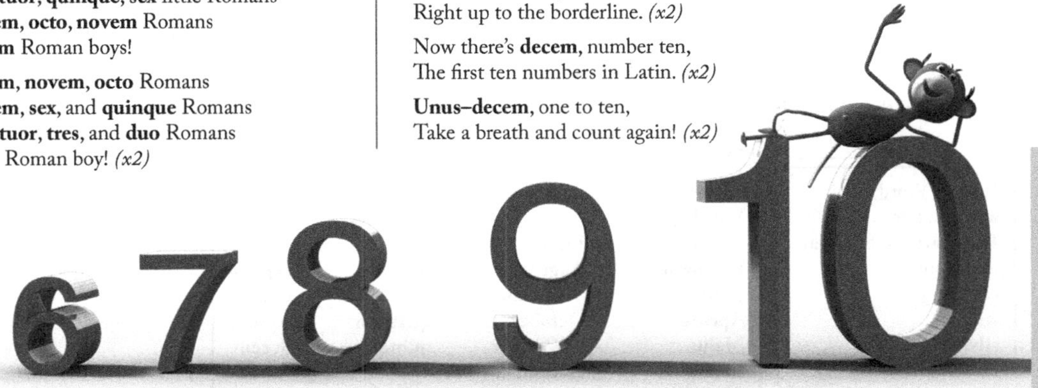

Word Review Activities

I. **Word Search:** Find and circle the Latin words that match the meanings of the words in the box.

C	J	Q	O	N	O	V	E	M	B	E	R	S	M	H	K	A	M	B	O
Q	E	N	C	J	E	Q	H	D	I	E	S	M	A	R	T	I	S	T	E
U	S	D	T	F	K	D	T	D	I	E	S	M	E	R	C	U	R	I	I
I	O	I	O	D	S	I	M	A	R	T	I	U	S	W	R	S	J	E	U
N	A	E	B	E	U	E	K	S	E	X	V	H	O	D	I	E	E	S	T
Q	U	S	E	C	B	S	P	D	L	P	C	I	D	R	T	L	A	L	I
U	G	I	R	E	C	S	A	T	Y	F	G	R	E	J	D	E	P	R	A
E	U	O	W	M	I	A	I	D	E	S	O	N	C	Q	I	B	R	F	O
D	S	V	G	B	A	T	B	H	U	M	E	D	E	D	E	D	I	M	H
X	T	I	A	E	N	U	I	N	X	V	B	I	M	U	S	O	L	I	S
I	U	S	S	R	U	R	U	Z	S	M	T	E	Z	O	S	C	I	U	E
V	S	N	F	P	A	N	N	E	N	G	P	S	R	I	O	T	S	L	P
T	Q	O	P	L	R	I	I	R	K	H	T	L	F	C	L	O	I	I	T
B	L	I	K	C	I	D	U	F	E	B	R	U	A	R	I	U	S	U	E
Y	W	A	N	T	U	V	S	E	O	Q	E	N	P	M	S	A	O	S	M
O	R	C	J	G	S	M	F	P	K	H	S	A	D	N	O	V	E	M	E
H	Q	U	A	T	T	U	O	R	I	B	L	E	R	Q	K	E	G	U	S

DIES SOLIS	APRILIS
HODIE EST	UNUS
DIES LUNAE	IULIUS
IANUARIUS	IUNIUS
DIES MARTIS	DUO
FEBRUARIUS	TRES
DIES MERCURII	SEX
DIES IOVIS	OCTO
DIES VENERIS	NOVEM
DIES SATURNI	SEPTEM
AUGUSTUS	DECEM
SEPTEMBER	MARTIUS
OCTOBER	
QUATTUOR	
NOVEMBER	
QUINQUE	
DECEMBER	

II. From the word bank, choose a Latin number or month to fill in each of the blanks in the following paragraphs. Then, draw a picture in the box to illustrate the paragraph. You'll see that we've included some Latin words that you've already learned, but just in case you can't remember them, we've provided a list of them along with their English translations.

Answers will vary.

1. It is ____________________, and the weather is starting to get cold! Simeon and Justus need to bring home ______________ cartloads of wood to stay warm for the winter. To do this, they need to cut down ______________ **arbores**!

2. Since it is **Dies Saturni**, Simeon and Justus start off early in the morning. They bring lunch, **unus** cart, ______________ axe(s), and ______________ **canis** with them.

Review Words:
arbores: trees
Dies Saturni: Saturday
unus: one
canis: dog
sol: sun
silva: forest
casa: house

Word Bank:

Ianuarius	**Iulius**	**unus**	**sex**
Februarius	**Augustus**	**duo**	**septem**
Martius	**September**	**tres**	**octo**
Aprilis	**October**	**quattuor**	**novem**
Maius	**November**	**quinque**	**decem**
Iunius	**December**		

Answers will vary.

3. The **sol** is shining brightly in the **silva**. As Simeon, Justus, and the ______________ **canis** came around a bend, there were ______________ deer in the path. The biggest one had ______________ points on his antlers. The smallest one had ______________ spots on his coat.

4. Simeon and Justus worked for ______________ hours and made ______________ trips back with wood. Now they have a fine stack of wood next to the **casa** for the cold months of ______________, ______________, ______________ and ______________. Their ______________ **canis** likes to climb on top of the stack!

Review Words:
arbores: trees
Dies Saturni: Saturday
unus: one
canis: dog
sol: sun
silva: forest
casa: house

Word Bank:

Ianuarius	**Iulius**	**unus**	**sex**
Februarius	**Augustus**	**duo**	**septem**
Martius	**September**	**tres**	**octo**
Aprilis	**October**	**quattuor**	**novem**
Maius	**November**	**quinque**	**decem**
Iunius	**December**		

III. **Pick up Toys!** Draw a line to match each numbered toy with the cubby that is labeled with the month that matches its order. (Hint: Which is the first month of the year? Match that month with the first Latin number.)

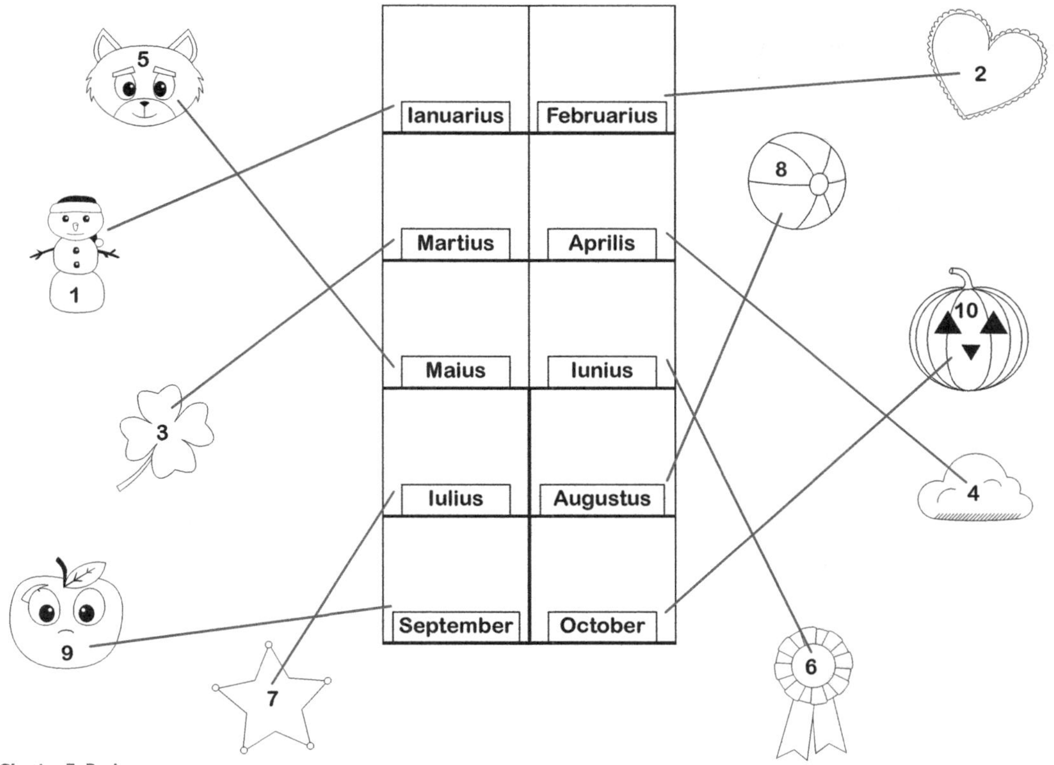

Master Your Famous Sayings

Acta non verba — Actions, not words!

Carpe diem — Seize the day!

Per mensem — monthly, every month, or by the month

Ad idem — of the same mind

Auxilio ab alto — by help from on high

Pater familias — father of the family

Master Your Derivatives

Circle the Latin word from which each English word is derived.

1. diary
   a. **unus** b. **Iulius** c. **dies** (circled)
2. Saturday
   a. **Dies Saturni** (circled) b. **October** c. **quinque**
3. July
   a. **Iunius** b. **Iulius** (circled) c. **Aprilis**
4. universe
   a. **Iunius** b. **unus** (circled) c. **tres**
5. quartet
   a. **quattuor** (circled) b. **septem** c. **quinque**

6. octagon

a. **octo** (circled) b. **augustus** c. **decem**

Master Your Verb Ending and Conjugation Charts

I. Fill in the **o-s-t** chant, including the meanings.

O-S-T Chant				
	Singular		Plural	
Person	Ending	Meaning	Ending	Meaning
First Person	-o	I	-mus	we
Second Person	-s	you	-tis	you all
Third Person	-t	he/she/it	-nt	they

II. Fill in the blanks to complete the **laudo** conjugation chart.

Laudo with Endings				
	Singular		Plural	
Person	Ending	Meaning	Ending	Meaning
First Person	**laud*o***	I praise	laudamus	we praise
Second Person	laudas	you praise	**laud*atis***	you all praise
Third Person	**laud*at***	he/she/it praises	laudant	they praise

Chapter 8

Helping at Home

Words to Learn

1. **laboro** I work
2. **lavo** I wash
3. **coquo** I cook
4. **pasco** I feed
5. **purgo** I clean

Review Words/Phrases

1. **casa** house
2. **porta** door, gate
3. **murus** wall
4. **fenestra** window
5. **Qui dies est?** What day is it?
6. **Hodie est ______.** Today is ______.

Chapter Song

<u>The Working Song</u> [Track 9(C)/39(E)]

Laboro, laboro, I work with my family,
Work with my family, work with my family.
Purgo, purgo, I clean up the dirty things,
Clean them happily.

I work with my family,
Work with my family,

Laboro, laboro, I work with my family,
Work with them happily.

Coquo, coquo, I help cook the food we eat,
Help cook the food we eat, help cook the food we eat.
Pasco, pasco, I feed the cat and parakeet,
Feed them happily.

I work with my family,
Work with my family,
Laboro, laboro, I work with my family,
Work with them happily.

Lavo, lavo, I wash dishes while I sing,
Wash dishes while I sing, wash dishes while I sing.
Purgo, purgo, I clean up everything,
Clean up happily.

I work with my family,
Work with my family,
Laboro, laboro, I work with my family,
Work with them happily.

Famous Saying

Ora et labora = Pray and work!

This famous saying comes from a monk named Benedict, who lived in Italy from about AD 480–547.

Chapter Lesson

Look at all the words you're learning in this chapter. What kind of words are they? Are they words you can *do*? If so, what are they called? That's right, they're called *verbs*! The chants you have been learning are for verbs. In chapter 4, you started learning the **laudo** chant. Remember, the chant is just the action word **laudo** with the **o-s-t** endings added to it. Review the **laudo** chant, shown below, by chanting it aloud several times.

Laudo Chant			
SINGULAR		PLURAL	
laud*o*	I praise	**laud*amus***	we praise
laud*as*	you praise	**laud*atis***	you all praise
laud*at*	he/she/it praises	**laud*ant***	they praise

If you would like, you can chant this chart without the English translations, as follows:

Laudo Chant	
SINGULAR	PLURAL
laudo	**laudamus**
laudas	**laudatis**
laudat	**laudant**

Now let's try creating a conjugation chart for a new verb. Here is one for **lavo**, which means "I wash."

Lavo Chant			
SINGULAR		PLURAL	
lav*o*	I wash	**lav*amus***	we wash
lav*as*	you wash	**lav*atis***	you all wash
lav*at*	he/she/it washes	**lav*ant***	they wash

Sample Sentences

Now let's create some sample sentences to study using the endings you have learned:

Lavo elephantum.*	I wash the elephant.
Lavas elephantum.	You wash the elephant.
Lavat elephantum.**	He, she, or it washes the elephant.
Lavamus ursam.*	We wash the bear. (That could be scary!)
Lavatis ursam.	You all wash the bear.
Lavant ursam.	They wash the bear.

Grow Your English

Can you think of any English words that may have come from the Latin word **laboro**? What do you call the place where scientists *work* and do experiments? A task that makes you work very hard can be called *laborious*. As you go through this book, you must *labor* hard in learning Latin!◊

◊ Laboro is such a useful word in English! In addition to labor, laborious, and laboratory, here are a few more derivatives of laboro: belabor, elaborate, and collaborate.

Practice Your Latin

I. Practice writing your new Latin words by tracing the dots.

laboro lavo coquo

pasco purgo

II. On the lines provided, answer the questions with words from this chapter.

1. When your pet is hungry, what should you do for it? pasco

2. What should you do with raw meat before eating it? coquo

*Note that we often add an **m** to nouns that are receiving the action of a verb. You will learn more about this in your later study of Latin.
Remember, the **-t ending can mean "he," "she," or "it," depending on who is doing the action.

3. When you have any job to do, what do you do? laboro

4. When you see something dirty, what should you do? lavo

III. Label each picture with the Latin word that best describes it.

lavo	purgo	coquo	pasco	laboro

IV. Practice writing the **laudo** chant without the meanings.

Laudo Chant	
laudo	laudamus
laudas	laudatis
laudat	laudant

V. Write the singular forms of **laudo** with their meanings.

Laudo Chant: Singular Meanings	
Laudo Forms	Meanings
laudo	I praise
laudas	you praise
laudat	he/she/it praises

Show What You Know

I. Circle the correct meaning for each Latin word.

1. **laboro**	a. I clean	b. I wash	c. I cook	d. I work
2. **lavo**	a. I feed	b. I wash	c. I cook	d. I clean
3. **coquo**	a. I clean	b. I cook	c. I work	d. I feed
4. **pasco**	a. I clean	b. I wash	c. I feed	d. I work
5. **purgo**	a. I feed	b. I cook	c. I wash	d. I clean

II. Write the meaning, in English, of the famous saying from this chapter: **Ora et labora**.

Pray and work!

III. Write out the singular forms of the **laudo** chant, with the meanings.

Laudo Chant: Singular Meanings	
Laudo Forms	Meanings
laudo	I praise
laudas	you praise
laudat	he/she/it praises

Chapter 9

Communicating with Others

Words to Learn

1. **dico** I speak, say
2. **clamo** I shout
3. **susurro** I whisper
4. **scribo** I write
5. **oro** I pray

Review Words

1. **sede**	sit
sedete	sit (to more than one person)
2. **surge**	rise, stand up
surgite	rise, stand up (to more than one person)
3. **scribe**	write
scribite	write (to more than one person)
4. **repete**	repeat
repetite	repeat (to more than one person)

Chapter Song

<u>Speaking and Writing Song</u> [Track 10(C)/40(E)]

I **dico, dico, dico,**
I love to speak, speak, speak!
I **clamo, clamo, clamo,**
I shout from mountain peak!

And when my mom is sleeping, I whisper, oh, so soft!
Susurro, yes, I whisper,
Susurro, oh, so soft!

I **scribo, scribo, scribo,**
I write to friends away;
And **oro** when I talk to God,
I **oro** all the day.

Dico, clamo,
Susurro, oh, so soft.
Scribo, oro
Oro all the day.

Famous Saying

Scribere est cogitare. = To write is to think.

You have probably learned that writing takes much thinking. It's easy to say things without thinking about them, but writing takes more effort. Writing your thoughts down on paper makes you think more carefully about the words you use. Sometimes, writing even helps your thinking to be more organized and clear.

Chapter Lesson◊

By now, you should know the chant and conjugation for **laudo** very well! You have also learned how to create conjugation charts for other verbs. In chapter 8 you studied the chart for **lavo** (I wash) and earlier you studied one for **do** (I give), too. In this lesson we will create a new conjugation chart for **clamo**. Here it is:

Clamo Chant◊◊			
Singular		Plural	
clam*o*	I shout	**clama*mus***	we shout
clama*s*	you shout	**clama*tis***	you all shout
clama*t*	he/she/it shouts	**clama*nt***	they shout

<u>Sample Sentences</u>

Now let's create some sample sentences to study using the endings you have learned:

Clamo.	I shout.
Marcus clamat.	Mark shouts.
Julia clamat.	Julia shouts.
Marcus et (and) Julia clamant.	Mark and Julia shout.*

◊ You might note that all the conjugations (verb families) that we list in this book are from the first conjugation. This is because we don't want to confuse young students at this point with the different patterns they would see if we conjugated verbs from other conjugations. For example, scribo is from the third conjugation and would be listed with different connecting or stem vowels (i and u). See the introduction to the teacher's edition for more information about how we treat verbs in this book.

◊◊ If your students are a bit more advanced and you think they'd be up for a challenge, share the following with them: Clamo, clamatis, omnes clamamus pro glace lactis! Do you know what that means? It's the Latin translation of a saying that is famous in English: "I scream, you scream, we all scream for ice cream!" Which endings were used to show *who* is doing the screaming?

The endings used to show "who" in this saying are: -o, -s, and -mus. Clamo, clamatis, omnes clamamus pro glacie lactis! can be literally translated as "I shout, you all shout, we all shout for ice of milk (or ice made of milk)." Note these Latin words that are unfamiliar to students. You will most likely need to define these words to help your students understand this sentence: omnis, omne (all); glacies, glaciei (ice); lac, lactis (milk).

*Since Marcus and Julia are more than one person, we use **clamant** for "they shout." We could translate the sentence as: Marcus and Julia—they shout.

Grow Your English

When a very small child tries to write, what does his writing usually look like? Think about the Latin word for "write"! Besides the word "scribble," some other words that come from **scribo** are *scribe*, *inscribe*, and *inscription*. See if you can figure out how each of these words relate to **scribo** in meaning.◊◊◊

Now, think of another one of your new words: **dico**. A *dictator* is someone who *tells* other people what to do. Lastly, think about the word ***exclamation*** and tell your teacher which Latin word it came from!

The word "exclamation" comes from the Latin clamo, "I shout."

Practice Your Latin

◊◊◊ **Should you need to give your students hints to direct their reasoning regarding the scribo derivatives mentioned above, here are some pointers:**

Scribe: a person who *writes*. Often the job of a scribe in ancient Roman times was simply copying down what someone else had already written, or what someone else said. They were professional "writers," not authors.

Inscribe: This word literally means to "write into" something, as you can see from its roots. Inscribing is commonly used to refer to writing that is actually carved or engraved into a surface, but also is used when referring to a note at the beginning of a book or a similar short bit of writing that carries some significance.

Inscription: You have to take apart the word a bit to see the scribo root, and it may link more directly to scriptio, but there is definitely a relationship between the two words. An inscription is the words, the writing that is inscribed (see above). An inscription usually refers to a few significant words placed on a gravestone, plaque, award, jewelry, or document. The connection to the Latin word in form and meaning should be fairly easy to point out from here.

I. Practice your new words by tracing the dots.

dico clamo oro

susurro scribo

II. In each box, draw a picture that illustrates the Latin word.

dico
I speak, say

clamo
I shout

susurro
I whisper

I write

scribo

I pray

oro

III. Draw a line from each Latin word to the situation in which you might do that action.

1. **susurro** — telling a secret
2. **clamo** — warning someone about danger
3. **dico** — talking at the dinner table
4. **oro** — before eating
5. **scribo** — making a note in a book

(Choices: warning someone about danger; before eating; making a note in a book; telling a secret; talking at the dinner table)

IV. On the lines provided, write the meanings for each form of the **clamo** chant. Practice saying the chant aloud, with the meanings.

Clamo Chant	
Clamo Forms	Meanings
clamo	I shout
clamas	you shout
clamat	he/she/it shouts

Clamo Chant	
CLAMO FORMS	MEANINGS
clamamus	we shout
clamatis	you all shout
clamant	they shout

◊◊◊◊ Be sure to use Latin in the classroom during routines and transitions, including commands such as the above. You may want to send a note home to the parents of your students and encourage them to incorporate as much Latin as possible into conversations.

V. Write, in Latin, the days of the week and then provide their translations in English. Once you have written them down, chant the days of the week in Latin! ◊◊◊◊

1. Dies Solis — Sunday
2. Dies Lunae — Monday
3. Dies Martis — Tuesday
4. Dies Mercurii — Wednesday
5. Dies Iovis — Thursday
6. Dies Veneris — Friday
7. Dies Saturni — Saturday

Show What You Know

I. Draw lines to match the Latin words to their meanings.

1. **oro**	whisper
2. **dico**	pray
3. **susurro**	shout
4. **scribo**	speak
5. **clamo**	write

II. Write the meaning of the Latin saying: **Scribere est cogitare.** To write is to think.

III. Simeon got all jumbled up as he was saying the meanings of the **laudo** chant! Help him out by writing the correct number of the form in the blank provided.

4 we praise

2 you praise

6 they praise

1 I praise

3 he/she/it praises

5 you all praise

1. **laudo**
2. **laudas**
3. **laudat**
4. **laudamus**
5. **laudatis**
6. **laudant**

Words/Phrases to Learn

1. **ambulo**	I walk
2. **curro**	I run
3. **equito**	I ride a horse
4. **volo**	I fly
5. **navigo**	I sail
6. **vehor in vehiculo**	I ride in a car

Review Words/Phrases

1. **audi**	listen
audite	listen (to more than one person)
2. **tace**	be quiet
tacete	be quiet (to more than one person)
3. **attolle manum**	raise your hand
attollite manus	raise your hands (to more than one person)
4. **Qui mensis est?**	What month is it?
5. **Martius**	March

Chapter Song

Walk and Ride Song [Track 11(C)/41(E)]

I walk, I **ambulo**, I walk far up the hill.
Then I run, I **curro, curro, curro** down the hill.
I run to the ship at bay, I **navigo** the seas.
Navigo, yes, off I go, and sail with the breeze.

I ride, I **equito** on my horse named Captain Pie.
When I have far to go, I **volo** in the sky.
Still, I am happiest when I **navigo** the seas.
Navigo, yes, off I go, and sail with the breeze.

I walk, I **ambulo**, I walk far up the hill.
Then I run, I **curro, curro, curro** down the hill.
I run to the ship at bay, I **navigo** the seas.
Navigo, yes, off I go, and sail with the breeze.

I ride, I **equito** on my horse named Captain Pie.
But when I have far to go, I **volo** in the sky.
Still, I am happiest when I **navigo** the seas.
Navigo, yes, off I go, and sail with the breeze.

Famous Saying

Verba volant, littera manet. = Words fly away, the letter remains.

This Latin saying means that sometimes it is easy to forget words that people say, but words that are written may last for thousands of years. Therefore, learn to write well, and be careful what you write!

Which word in this saying comes from this chapter's Words to Learn? volant (comes from volo)

Chapter Lesson

Do you remember the verb endings and forms you have been learning? Take a minute to review the **o-s-t** chant with the meanings. Then review the **clamo** chant that you learned last week. Both the **o-s-t** chant and the **clamo** chant are listed below.

O-S-T Chant				
PERSON	SINGULAR		PLURAL	
First Person	**-o**	I	**-mus**	we
Second Person	**-s**	you	**-tis**	you all
Third Person	**-t**	he/she/it	**-nt**	they

Clamo Chant			
SINGULAR		PLURAL	
clam*o*	I shout	**clama*mus***	we shout
clama*s*	you shout	**clama*tis***	you all shout
clama*t*	he/she/it shouts	**clama*nt***	they shout

Sample Sentences

This week let's study how verbs with a **-t** attached to the end work. We will focus on the activity of a **puella** and **frater**. You learned the word **puella** in *SSL1*—it means "girl." You also learned that **frater** means "brother." Study the following sentences about a **puella** and **frater** and see how the verbs all end with a **-t**.

Puella clamat. The girl shouts.*
Frater laudat. The brother praises.

We know that the **-t** ending means "he, she, or it." Since **puella** is a "she," we use the **-t** ending with the verb, as you see with **clamat** in the first sample sentence. Since **frater** is a "he," we use the **-t** ending with the verb, as you see with **laudat** in the second sample sentence.

*There is no specific word for the word "the" in Latin, so you often need to add it in the English when you translate.

Now let's try to make a sentence using a new verb—**laboro**. **Laboro** means "I work." If we add a **-t** to **laboro,** we will get **laborat**. Remember, we also change the vowel to the connecting vowel **a** right before the **-t**. Let's use **laborat** in two sentences:

Puella laborat. The girl works.
Julia laborat. Julia works.

Now see if you can translate the following sentences:

Canis laborat. The dog works.

Frater clamat. The brother shouts.

Julia laudat. Julia praises.

Grow Your English

There are quite a few interesting English words that originate from words in this chapter. See if you can find an English derivative from this hint: If someone feels too sick to *walk*, a vehicle (**vehiculo**) called an ambulance might come to pick him up. Some other derivatives of the Latin word **ambulo** include *amble*, which is to walk slowly, and ambulatory, which is what a person is called when he is able to walk.

Think of a river running. If it is running fast, the *current* is strong, but if it is running slowly, the *current* is weak. What Latin word does *current* come from? curro

Navigo gives us the words *navigate* and *navy*. What connections do you see between these words and the Latin word **navigo**? Discuss with your teacher and/or classmates. Navigo means "I sail." The navy is the part of an army that sails. When you're sailing, you have to *navigate* the water, which means you sail your ship from where you are to where you want to go.

Practice Your Latin

I. Practice writing your new words on the lines.

ambulo curro equito

volo navigo

vehor in vehiculo

II. On a separate piece of paper, draw a picture of yourself traveling by your favorite mode of transportation and label it in Latin.

III. Simeon has a long trip home. Help him figure out how to navigate each stretch of the journey! Using the words from the word bank, write the best choice for travel on the line under each part of Simeon's journey.

Word Bank:	
volo	**navigo**
equito	**ambulo**
curro	**vehor in vehiculo**

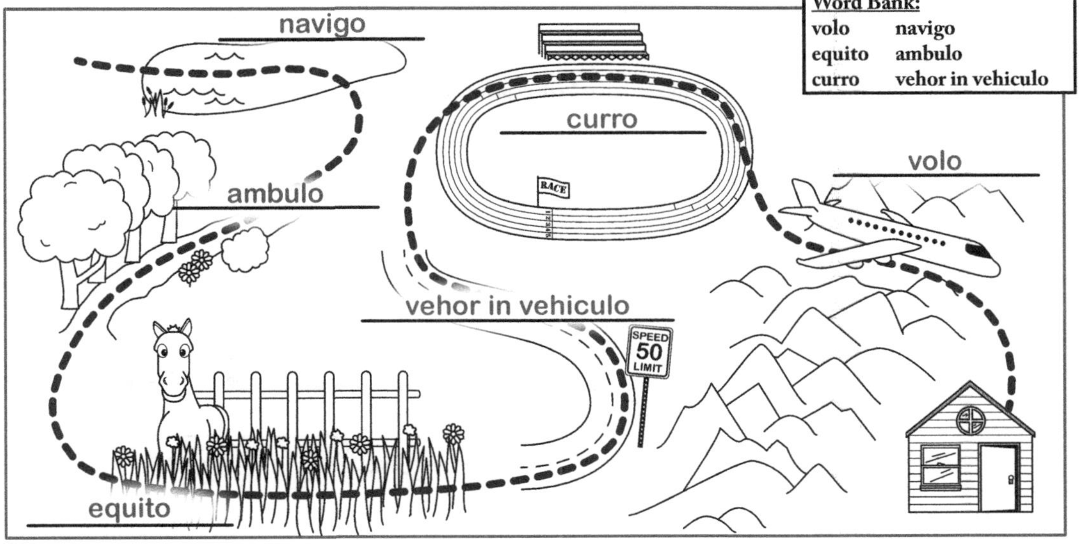

IV. In the blanks provided, write in Latin the answers to the questions.

1. If you were being chased by a bee, would you rather **curro** or **ambulo**? curro
2. If you were traveling down the Mississippi River, would you **navigo** or **curro**? navigo
3. If you were crossing the desert, would it work better to **navigo** or **equito**? equito
4. If you are carrying a heavy box of fragile things, should you **ambulo** or **curro**? ambulo
5. If you go to visit your grandmother at Thanksgiving, would you rather **ambulo** or **vehor in vehiculo**?
   Answers may vary, depending on how close students live to their grandmothers.
6. If your grandmother lives on the other side of the country from you, would it be faster to **vehor in vehiculo** or **volo** to go see her? volo

Show What You Know

I. Draw lines to match the Latin words to their English meanings.

1. **ambulo**	I ride in a car
2. **curro**	I ride a horse
3. **equito**	I fly
4. **navigo**	I sail
5. **vehor in vehiculo**	I walk
6. **volo**	I run

II. Let's do some translating!

1. On the lines provided, write the translations of the following Latin sentences. Don't forget that you may need to add the word "the" to your English translation.

   a. **Simeon laborat.** Simeon works.

   b. **Frater laudat.** The brother praises.

   c. **Puella laborat.** The girl works.

2. Fill in your name and translate the sentence into English. Names will vary. **laudat.**

   Translation: ________ praises.

3. Translate the famous Latin saying from this chapter: **Verba volant, littera manet.**

   Words fly away, the letter remains.

Chapter 11

Things to Learn in School

Words to Learn

1. **mathematica** math
2. **grammatica** grammar, language arts
3. **lectio** reading
4. **scriptio** writing
5. **physica** science
6. **historia** history

Review Words/Phrases

1. **amabo te** please
2. **tibi gratias ago** thank you
3. **ignosce mihi** excuse me
4. **Maius** May
5. **Iunius** June

Chapter Song

The Subjects Song [Track 12(C)/42(E)]

We need to learn our numbers, **mathematica**!
To add, subtract, and multiply, **mathematica**!
And to write our words and letters and sounds,
Scriptio helps us write them down.
So, let's learn **scriptio** and **mathematica**!

◊ The following are some thoughts and questions to guide discussion of this famous saying.

Students, can you think of how knowledge might give you more power as a student? What about knowledge in the subjects you are learning? The more you know about reading and writing, the better you will become at doing those things. The more knowledge you have about science, the more power you have, for example, to build a strong tower or bridge, grow a healthy plant, or be healthy yourself. The more knowledge you have in math, the more power you have to figure out difficult math problems and solve problems in real life, such as how best to spend your money or how to properly follow a recipe. How do you think your parents' knowledge gives them power in how they do their jobs and run your home? Do you think your teacher has power given by knowledge? Knowledge about circumstances can help you understand how to speak to someone or handle a situation. What about in war? How can knowledge of what your enemy is doing give you power? There are so many applications of this famous saying that we will not think of them all today, but just think how valuable knowledge is to you!

Historia tells me what has happened a hundred years ago,
Famous men in battles and war—tales of weal and woe!
Physica speaks of planets and snakes,
Rocks and trees and big earthquakes.
Historia and **physica** are wonderful things to know.

To learn these things we need to read, and read aloud and clear,
And **lectio**, our favorite friend, brings stories very near.
Grammatica is the way we know
The rules of words and sentence flow.
Grammatica and **lectio** are subjects we revere.

Famous Saying

Scientia potentia est. = Knowledge is power. (Sir Francis Bacon)

This saying can encourage you to work hard to gain knowledge! In what ways do you think it is true that knowledge is power?◊

Chapter Lesson

Translating Latin into English can be challenging at times, but you have already studied some short Latin sentences and have done a little translating yourself. Now we will practice translating some sentences that have singular Latin verbs—verbs ending in **-o**, **-s**, or **-t**. Later, we will practice translating sentences that have plural Latin verbs—verbs ending in **-mus**, **-tis**, or **-nt**.

Verbs Have "Person"

You have learned that verbs can be singular or plural. That means that singular verbs (such as I walk, you walk, or he/she/it walks) only have one single person doing the action. Plural verbs (such as we walk, you all walk, and they walk) all have two or more people doing the action. Well, verbs also have "person," which means that they show which person is doing the action. First person means "I" am doing the action; for example, "I walk." Second person is when the person you are talking *to* is doing the action; for example, "you walk." Third person is when *someone else* is doing the action, someone you are talking *about*; for example, "he walks" or "she walks." The following is a summary of the persons that do the action of a verb:

First Person: *I* walk (**ambulo**)
Second Person: *you* walk (**ambulas**)
Third Person: *he*, *she*, or *it* walks (**ambulat**)

Third-Person Pronouns

The third-person pronouns for a single person are *he*, *she*, and *it*. These pronouns take the place of a noun such as Mark or Julia. Look at the following sentences:

Mark walks.	**Marcus ambulat.**
He walks.	**Ambulat.**
Julia washes.	**Julia lavat.**
She washes.	**Lavat.**

Do you see how "he" takes the place of "Mark" and "she" takes the place of "Julia"? Notice also that in Latin the pronouns "he" and "she" are built right into the Latin verb. We can translate **ambulat** by itself as "he walks," "she walks," or even "it walks." The **-t** ending tells us that a he, she, or it is doing the action.◊◊

◊◊ We will cover all of the pronouns in the next chapter.

Let's look at some more examples.

Canis ambulat.	The dog walks.
Ambulat.	It walks.
Femina ambulat.	The woman walks. /A woman walks.*
Ambulat.	She walks.
Vir laborat.	The man works. /A man works.*
Laborat.	He works.

Do you see how you can translate **ambulat** in three different ways depending on who or what is doing the action?

Try using some other nouns you know to complete these Latin sentences:

Answers will vary. **ambulat.**

________________ **lavat.**

________________ **clamat.**

*Remember that there is no word for "the" or "a" in Latin, so you could choose to translate sentences such as these with either "the" or "a."

For each pair of the following sentences, study the first one, then complete the second one using a noun of your choice. Then translate your sentence. Remember, you can add "the" or "a" if it sounds better in English.

1. **Flumen susurrat.** The river whispers.
2. Answers will vary. **susurrat.** Answers will vary.
3. **Feles clamat.** The cat shouts.
4. Answers will vary. **clamat.** Answers will vary
5. **Discipulus laborat.** The student works.
6. Answers will vary. **laborat.** Answers will vary.

Grow Your English

You can see the roots of English words in all of the new words in this chapter. For example, our English words *physical* and *physician* come from the Latin word **physica**. Can you think of some obvious derivatives of **historia**? **Scriptio** gives us many words, such as *script* and *inscription*. Be sure to be ***grammatical*** when you write letters and ***mathematical*** when you go shopping!

Historian, historical, and history are some derivatives of historia.

Practice Your Latin

I. Practice writing your new words by tracing the dots.

mathematica grammatica

lectio scriptio physica

historia

II. What is your favorite subject in school? On a separate piece of paper draw a picture that relates to it, and label it with the Latin word. (If your favorite subject is Latin, you can write **Latina**.)

III. In the blank provided, write the Latin word that fits the description.

1. In scriptio, you learn to write good paragraphs.
2. In mathematica, you learn your times tables.
3. In this subject, you learn about the world around you. physica
4. Grammatica teaches you how to make words plural.
5. In lectio, your teacher listens to you read aloud.
6. Historia teaches you about the past.

IV. **Color by Subject!** Read the words inside each mosaic tile and, using the color coding, color them according to the subject to which they are related.

Mathematica = red
Grammatica = purple
Physica = green
Scriptio = blue
Lectio = orange
Historia = yellow

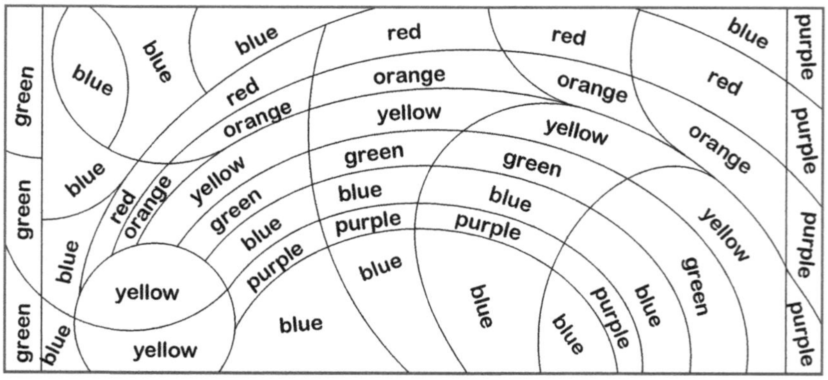

Show What You Know

I. Circle the meaning for each Latin word.

1. **mathematica** — a. writing — b. reading — c. math (circled)
2. **scriptio** — a. reading — b. writing (circled) — c. grammar
3. **physica** — a. science (circled) — b. math — c. grammar
4. **lectio** — a. writing — b. reading (circled) — c. math
5. **grammatica** — a. math — b. science — c. grammar (circled)

II. Let's do some more translating!

1. On the lines provided, write the translations of the following Latin sentences. Don't forget that you may need to add the word "the" to your English translation.

   a. **Simeon navigat.** Simeon sails.

   b. **Mater laudat.** The mother praises.

   c. **Vir laborat.** The man works.

2. Fill in your name and translate the sentence into English. Answers will vary. **lavat.**

   Translation: ________ washes.

3. Translate the famous Latin saying from this chapter: **Scientia potentia est.**

   Knowledge is power.

Chapter 12

Celebration

Words to Learn

1. **epulae** — feast
2. **familia** — family
3. **celebratio** — celebration
4. **ludus** — game, school, play
5. **musica** — music
6. **amicus** — male friend
   amica — female friend

Review Words

1. **canis** — dog
2. **feles** — cat
3. **pisces** — fish
4. **quattuor** — four
5. **quinque** — five

Chapter Song

<u>Celebratio Song</u> [Track 13(C)/43(E)]

Time to **cel-e-bra-ti-o**!
Fa-mi-li-a will gather.
Invite your favorite **a-mi-cae**
To a tasty **e-pu-lae**.

Celebratio, celebratio, amici, musica, familia.
Rejoice, sing **musica**!

Birthdays, holidays, and fun,
The season has begun.
Bring another dear **amica**.
The girls will play **musica**!

Celebratio, celebratio, amici, musica, familia.
Rejoice, sing **musica**!

Prepare a tasty **epulae**.
Familia will drop by!
Gear up for a rowdy **ludus**,
Don't forget your **amicus**!

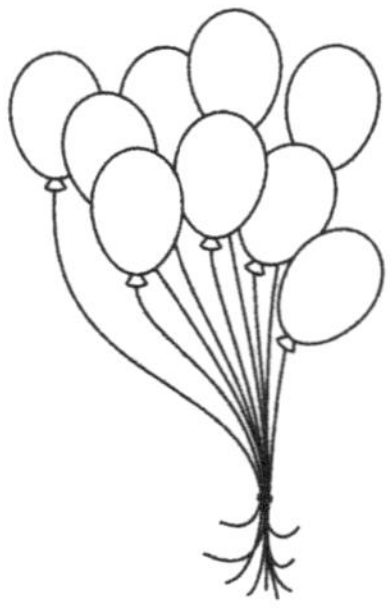

Celebratio, celebratio, amici, musica, familia.
Rejoice, sing **musica**!

Famous Saying

Ab initio = from the beginning

What is the best way to tell a story? **Ab initio!** What is the best way to learn a language? **Ab initio!** When is the best time to try your hardest? **Ab initio!** What else is best **ab initio**?◊

◊ Suggested answers: reading a book, making a recipe, playing a game, watching a movie. Find ways to validate every creative answer students give.

Chapter Lesson

Did you wonder why the new vocabulary list has two forms for "friend"? In English, you can call any friend "friend," but in Latin you have to be careful who you call a friend! **Amic*a*** is a female friend, and **amic*us*** is a male friend. As you continue studying Latin, you will learn that many word endings change to be masculine or feminine (masculine words are boy-related words and feminine words are girl-related words). If you look closely at the song for this chapter, you will see some slightly different endings also: **amic*ae*** is the plural form of female friend, and **amic*i*** is the plural of male friend. You can also say **amici** when you are talking about a mixed group of male and female friends. Study the following chart:

Singular		Plural	
amic*us*	friend (male)	**amic*i***	friends (male)
amic*a*	friend (female)	**amic*ae***	friends (female)
discipul*us*	student (male)	**discipul*i***	students (male)
discipul*a*	student (female)	**discipul*ae***	students (female)
lud*us*	game	**lud*i***	games
famili*a*	family	**famili*ae***	families

Just as we add *s* to English nouns to make them plural, Latin often uses **i** or **ae**.

<u>Sample Sentences</u>

Now let's study some sentences that use plural Latin nouns. You will see that these sentences are using the plural endings.

Laboramus.	We work.
Laboratis.	You all work.
Amici laborant.	The friends (male) work.
Laborant.	They work.
Amicae equitant.	The friends (female) ride.
Equitant.	They ride.
Discipulae sussurant.	The students (female) whisper.
Familiae clamant.	The families shout.

Plural Nouns with Plural Verbs

Take another look at this:

Amici laborant.

Notice that the noun **amici** (friends) is plural and the verb **laborant** (they work) also has one of the plural endings—**-nt**. Plural nouns are always matched with plural verbs. You will learn more about this as you continue your study of Latin.

Third-Person Plural Pronoun

In some of the sentences above, notice that we use the word "they" in the place of "friends." The word "they" is a pronoun that we can use in English to take the place of two or more people doing the action of a verb. So, instead of only saying, "The friends work," we can also say, "They work."

All the Pronouns!

Pronouns are little words we use all the time. Study the chart below—the pronouns are in bold print.

	Person	Explanation	Pronoun(s)
Singular (when one person does the action)	First Person	When I am the one doing the action	**I**
	Second Person	When the person you are talking *to* is doing the action	**you**
	Third Person	When the person you are talking *about* is doing the action	**he, she, it**
Plural (when two or more people do the same action)	First Person	When the people you are *with* are doing the action	**we**
	Second Person	When the people who you are talking *to* are doing the action	**you all or you***
	Third Person	When the people you are talking *about* are doing the action	**they**

*"You" in English can be either singular or plural—just like the English word "fish."

Now try translating the following Latin sentence into English:

Amici equitant. The friends (male) ride.

Now, translate the following English sentence into Latin. (Remember, there is no Latin word for "the.")

The friends (female) wash. Amicae lavant.

Grow Your English

It's easy to see how the words *celebration* and *family* come from their Latin roots, isn't it? They're spelled almost the same as their Latin roots. The Latin word **ludus** gives us some interesting words, such as *ludicrous*. Ludicrous means "silly or unbelievable." So, if you say something somebody says to you is *ludicrous*, it's like you're saying, "You must be playing games with me." The word *elude*, another derivative of **ludus**, means "to get away/keep away from someone." When you play hide-and-seek and you're the person hiding, your goal is to *elude* the person doing the seeking. An *amicable* person is a friendly person. Do you know what Latin word *amicable* is derived from? amicus

Practice Your Latin

I. Practice writing your new Latin words by tracing the dots.

epulae familia

celebratio ludus musica

amicus amica

II. Label the pictures with the correct Latin words from the word bank.

Word Bank:	musica	ludus	amicus	celebratio	epulae	familia

familia

amicus

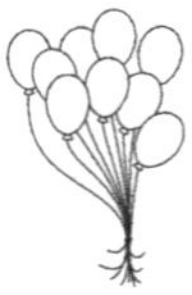

celebratio

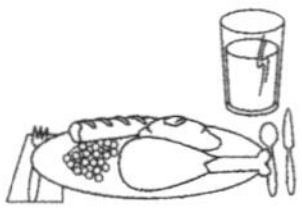

epulae

ludus

musica

III. Draw a picture of **quattuor feles** having an **epulae** with **tres canes** and **quinque pisces**.

Students should draw a picture of four cats, three dogs, and five fish having a feast.

IV. Fill in the blanks of this invitation with the appropriate Latin words from the word bank. (Note: One of the words will be used more than once.)

Word Bank:	amici	amicus	ludus	celebratio	familia	epulae	musica

Dear Amici & Familia,

You are invited to a celebratio in honor of our mutual amicus, Simeon. Come hungry and enjoy a tasty epulae! Bring your favorite ludus for a night of fun. Simeon himself will play musica for us on his lute. His entire familia will be there, so don't be late!

Date: November 12
Time: 7 p.m.
Place: Simeon's **casa**

You're Invited!

Show What You Know

I. Draw lines to match the Latin words to their English meanings.

1. **ludus**	celebration
2. **amicus**	game, school
3. **musica**	feast
4. **amica**	music
5. **familia**	male friend
6. **celebratio**	family
7. **epulae**	female friend

(Answer lines drawn: 1. ludus – game, school; 2. amicus – male friend; 3. musica – music; 4. amica – female friend; 5. familia – family; 6. celebratio – celebration; 7. epulae – feast)

Master Your Words

Disciplui, you have now learned another twenty-eight Latin words! Now it is time once again to make sure you have mastered all of your words. Can you give the correct English word for each of the following Latin words?

Chapter 8 New Words

1. **laboro** ____ I work ____
2. **lavo** ____ I wash ____
3. **coquo** ____ I cook ____
4. **pasco** ____ I feed ____
5. **purgo** ____ I clean ____

Chapter 8 Review Words/Phrases

1. **casa** ____ house ____
2. **porta** ____ door, gate ____
3. **murus** ____ wall ____
4. **fenestra** ____ window ____
5. **Qui dies est?** ____ What day is it? ____
6. **Hodie est ______.** ____ Today is ______. ____

Chapter 9 New Words

1. **dico** ____ I speak, say ____
2. **clamo** ____ I shout ____
3. **susurro** ____ I whisper ____
4. **scribo** ____ I write ____
5. **oro** ____ I pray ____

Chapter 9 Review Words

1. **sede** ____ sit ____
   sedete ____ sit (to more than one person)
2. **surge** ____ rise, stand up ____
   surgite ____ rise, stand up (to more than one person)
3. **scribe** ____ write ____
   scribite ____ write (to more than one person)
4. **repete** ____ repeat ____
   repetite ____ repeat (to more than one person)

Chapter 10 New Words/Phrases

1. ambulo — I walk
2. curro — I run
3. equito — I ride a horse
4. volo — I fly
5. navigo — I sail
6. vehor in vehiculo — I ride in a car

Chapter 10 Review Words/Phrases

1. audi — listen
   audite — listen (to more than one person)
2. tace — be quiet
   tacete — be quiet (to more than one person)
3. attolle manum — raise your hand
   attollite manus — raise your hands (to more than one person)
4. Qui mensis est? — What month is it?
5. Martius — March

Chapter 11 New Words

1. mathematica — math
2. grammatica — grammar, language arts
3. lectio — reading
4. scriptio — writing
5. physica — science
6. historia — history

Chapter 11 Review Words/Phrases

1. amabo te — please
2. tibi gratias ago — thank you
3. ignosce mihi — excuse me
4. Maius — May
5. Iunius — June

Chapter 12 New Words

1. epulae — feast
2. familia — family
3. celebratio — celebration

4. **ludus** game, school, play

5. **musica** music

6. **amicus** male friend

amica female friend

Chapter 12 Review Words

1. **canis** dog
2. **feles** cat
3. **pisces** fish
4. **quattuor** four
5. **quinque** five

Master Your Songs

The Working Song [Track 9(C)/39(E)]

Laboro, laboro, I work with my family,
Work with my family, work with my family.
Purgo, purgo, I clean up the dirty things,
Clean them happily.

Work with my family,
Work with my family,
Laboro, laboro, I work with my family,
Work with them happily.

Coquo, coquo, I help cook the food we eat,
Help cook the food we eat, help cook the food we eat.
Pasco, pasco, I feed the cat and parakeet,
Feed them happily.

I work with my family,
I work with my family,
Laboro, laboro, I work with my family,
Work with them happily.

Lavo, lavo, I wash dishes while I sing,
Wash dishes while I sing, wash dishes while I sing.
Purgo, purgo, I clean up everything,
Clean up happily.

Work with my family,
Work with my family,
Laboro, laboro, I work with my family,
Work with them happily.

Speaking and Writing Song [Track 10(C)/40(E)]

I **dico, dico, dico,**
I love to speak, speak, speak!
I **clamo, clamo, clamo,**
I shout from mountain peak! (*shout*)

And when my mom is sleeping, I whisper, oh, so soft!
Susurro, yes, I whisper,
Susurro, oh, so soft! (*whisper last line*)

I **scribo, scribo, scribo,**
I write to friends away;
And **oro** when I talk to God,
I **oro** all the day.

Dico, clamo,
Susurro, oh, so soft.
Scribo, oro
Oro all the day.

<u>Walk and Ride Song</u> [Track 11(C)/41(E)]

I walk, I **ambulo**, I walk far up the hill.
Then I run, I **curro**, **curro**, **curro** down the hill.
I run to the ship at bay, I **navigo** the seas.
Navigo, yes, off I go, and sail with the breeze.

I ride, I **equito** on my horse named Captain Pie.
When I have far to go, I **volo** in the sky.
Still, I am happiest when I **navigo** the seas.
Navigo, yes, off I go, and sail with the breeze.

I walk, I **ambulo**, I walk far up the hill.
Then I run, I **curro**, **curro**, **curro** down the hill.
I run to the ship at bay, I **navigo** the seas.
Navigo, yes, off I go, and sail with the breeze.

I ride, I **equito** on my horse named Captain Pie.
But when I have far to go, I **volo** in the sky.
Still, I am happiest when I **navigo** the seas.
Navigo, yes, off I go, and sail with the breeze.

<u>The Subjects Song</u> [Track 12(C)/42(E)]

We need to learn our numbers, **mathematica**!
To add, subtract, and multiply, **mathematica**!
And to write our words and letters and sounds,
Scriptio helps us write them down.
So, let's learn **scriptio** and **mathematica**!

Historia tells me what has happened a hundred years ago,
Famous men in battles and war—tales of weal and woe!
Physica speaks of planets and snakes,
Rocks and trees and big earthquakes.
Historia and **physica** are wonderful things to know.

To learn these things we need to read, and read aloud and clear,
And **lectio**, our favorite friend, brings stories very near.
Grammatica is the way we know
The rules of words and sentence flow.
Grammatica and **lectio** are subjects we revere.

<u>Celebratio Song</u> [Track 13(C)/43(E)]

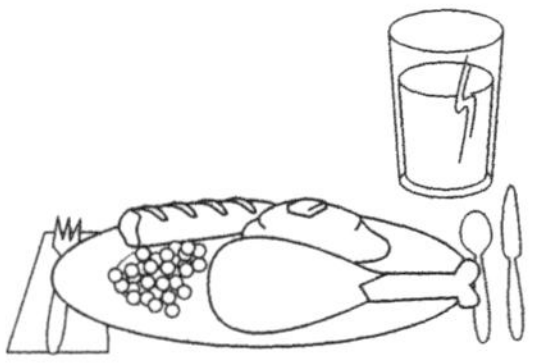

Time to **cel-e-bra-ti-o**!
Fa-mi-li-a will gather.
Invite your favorite **a-mi-cae**
To a tasty **e-pu-lae**.

Celebratio, celebratio, amici, musica, familia.
Rejoice, sing **musica**!

Birthdays, holidays, and fun,
The season has begun.
Bring another dear **amica**.
The girls will play **musica**!

Celebratio, celebratio, amici, musica, familia.
Rejoice, sing **musica**!

Prepare a tasty **epulae**.
Familia will drop by!
Gear up for a rowdy **ludus**,
Don't forget your **amicus**!

Celebratio, celebratio, amici, musica, familia.
Rejoice, sing **musica**!

Word Review Activities

I. **Word Search:** Fill in the blanks with the Latin words that match the meanings of the following words. Then, find and circle the Latin words in the word search.

I work	laboro	I wash	lavo	I cook	coquo
I say	dico	I shout	clamo	I write	scribo
I pray	oro	I walk	ambulo	I run	curro
I fly	volo	math	mathematica	grammar	grammatica
history	historia	family	familia	game	ludus
friend	amicus	music	musica		

A	X	O	R	I	A	K	V	N	P	L	F	N	Q	U	X	D	M	G	C	A	D	A
Q	M	K	L	C	O	L	A	B	O	R	O	U	C	U	R	R	O	U	I	Y	I	J
C	V	I	I	J	L	T	M	X	I	Q	L	U	D	U	S	F	E	R	C	T	C	W
B	O	S	C	M	A	T	H	E	M	A	T	I	C	A	E	L	O	S	U	L	O	M
D	U	Q	V	U	A	Q	U	O	C	Y	V	A	O	L	B	T	V	O	L	O	M	A
M	J	H	U	G	S	B	M	E	S	C	R	I	B	O	S	H	L	A	V	O	Y	F
X	I	O	L	O	L	A	D	C	U	E	P	E	R	I	Q	E	T	R	Z	S	O	W
U	Z	R	S	E	L	O	F	B	W	R	F	J	H	E	T	F	A	M	I	L	I	A
A	N	O	A	C	K	E	A	M	B	U	L	O	S	Q	U	R	E	S	J	B	V	O
C	J	G	R	A	M	M	A	T	I	C	A	I	D	V	J	M	R	Y	N	O	E	Z

II. **Story Time:** Complete these mini-stories by circling the correct Latin words. You will notice a few other Latin words that you learned in *Song School Latin Book 1.* ◊ See p. 56 for this note.

1. Simeon and his friend Justus are planning a _______ (**celebratio** / **hiems**). They need to buy **cibus**, such as **lac** and
celebration winter food milk
crustula, at the store. But how will they get there?
cookies
"My **equus** is here," said Simeon. "_______ (**Volo** / **Equito**) to the store."
horse I fly I ride a horse
"I'm afraid of horses," said Justus. "_______ (**Navigo** / **Ambulo**) to the store on my own two feet all the time."
I sail I walk
"_______ (**Dico** / **Lavo**)!" said Simeon. "That will take too long! _______ (**Coquo** / **Curro**) fast and you
I say I wash I cook I run
_______ (**coquas** / **curras**) fast, too! Let's see who can get there first!"
you cook you run
The **equus** said, "I will come, too, even if no one will ride me!"
horse
2. When it was time for the _______ (**lectio** / **celebratio**), Justus's best _______ (**amicus** / **musica**) and _______
reading celebration friend music
(**familia** / **ludus**) arrived at the **casa**.
family school house.
"We brought our instruments to play some _______ (**mathematica** / **musica**)!" said Simeon's _______ (**epulae** / **amicus**).
math music feast friend
"I brought my favorite _______ (**ludus** / **sella**) to play," said Justus's other _______ (**amicus** / **canis**).
game chair friend dog
Another of Justus's friends likes to sit and read. He said, "Since _______ (**susurro** / **lectio**) is my favorite activity, I
I whisper reading
brought a **liber**. Does anyone want to enjoy some _______ (**lectio** / **vehor in vehiculo**) with me?" Soon, everyone was
book reading ride in a car
having fun!

3. In the following mini-story, you will have to think about the endings on the verbs. When you choose your answer, pay attention the ending (**-o, -s, -t, -mus**) as well as the meaning.

Simeon and Justus were building a fort in the **silva**. "_______ (**Laboramus** / **Ambulat**) very hard on this fort!" said Justus.
forest — We work — We walk

"Justus!" Simeon _______ (**clamat** / **ambulo**). "I see bear tracks!"
shouted — walked

"Bear tracks?" **dicit** Justus. "_______ (**Scribo** / **Susurro**) very softly around bears! Why do _______ (**volo** / **clamas**) so loudly?"
says — I write — I whisper — I fly — you shout

Simeon said, "_______ (**Pasco** / **Volo**) berries to bears. I read in my _______ (**physica** / **historia**) book that bears eat berries."
I feed — I fly — science — history

Justus said, "_______ (**Dico** / **Navigo**)! These are just **canis** tracks. I know from my _______ (**mathematica** / **historia**) book that the **canis** has been **vir**'s best _______ (**amicus** / **panis**) for thousands of **anni**."
I say — I sail — dog — math — history — dog — man — friend — bread — years

"Look out!" said Simeon. "We were both wrong! Those are **elephantus** tracks, and that **elephantus** _______ (**ambulat** / **navigo**) straight for our fort!"
elephant — elephant — he walks, is walking — I sail

◊ After your students have filled in the blanks in each story, read the story aloud to them, using the correct Latin words. If you have confident readers, you can have students participate. Then do a reading in all English, followed by one more reading with the Latin words in place.

III. Below you will see several pairs of activities. On the lines provided, translate the Latin words or phrases. Then, for each pair of activities, circle the activity you would most enjoy doing. With each of your choices, you will be earning points for either Simeon or Justus. When you finish circling your answers, use the chart in between Simeon and Justus to figure out each point. Here's how it works: If you chose number 1 over number 2, circle the number 1 under Simeon's name and he gets the point. If you chose number 3 over number 4, circle the number 3 under Justus's name and he gets the point. Once you've circled all the numbers that you chose, count up the number of circles under each person's name and write their final scores in the space on the front of their podiums. Who will the winner be? ◊◊

Simeon	Justus
1	2
4	3
5	6
7	8
10	9
11	12
14	13
16	15
17	18

◊◊ This exercise requires that students translate each phrase in pairs before they can choose their preferred or favorite activity. Most of the phrases feature a verb, thus reviewing many of the verbs students have learned thus far. Note that we have not put the nouns in the accusative case—even though Latin verbs do take nouns in the accusative case. We will mention to students this use of the accusative case in chapter 21, but the study of the accusative case used with verbs will be the focus of later Latin study. Finally, some of the nouns actually are in the accusative case (such as **feles** and **flumen**) because in the case of these nouns the nominative and accusative cases are identical.

1. **purgo** or
I clean

2. **pasco feles**
I feed a cat

3. **laboro in hortus** or
I work in a garden

4. **laboro in nix**
I work in the snow

5. **navigo** on a **flumen** or
I sail — river

6. **vehor in vehiculo**
I ride in a car

7. do a problem in **mathematica** or math

8. study **grammatica** grammar

9. **lavo fenestera** or I wash a window

10. **coquo cena** I cook dinner

11. **curro** in a race or I run

12. **cano musica** sing music

13. **coquo pullus** or I cook a chicken

14. **coquo panis** I cook bread

15. **scribo** a letter or I write

16. **dico** to **amici** I talk friends

17. **edo** a(n) **epulae** or I eat feast

18. **susurro** a secret I whisper

Master Your Famous Sayings

Write the English translation of each of the following famous sayings.

1. **Ora et labora** Pray and work!
2. **Scribere est cogitare.** To write is to think.
3. **Verba volant, littera manet.** Words fly away, the letter remains.
4. **Scientia potentia est.** Knowledge is power.
5. **Ab initio** From the beginning

Master Your Derivatives

Draw lines from the Latin words to their English derivatives. If you do it correctly, you will see your favorite constellations taking shape!

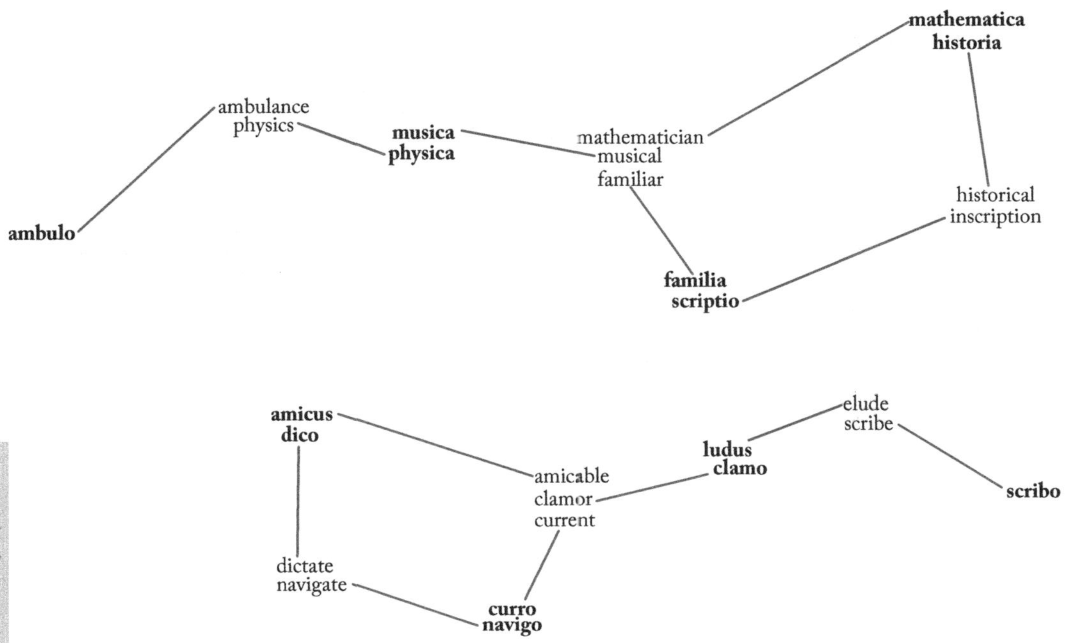

Chapter 14

Words to Learn

1. **rex** king
2. **regina** queen
3. **corona** crown
4. **patria** country, fatherland
5. **populus** people
6. **rego** I rule, direct

Review Words

1. **leo** lion
2. **avis** bird
3. **ursa** bear
4. **septem** seven
5. **decem** ten

Chapter Song

Rex and Regina Song [Track 14(C)/44(E)]

We are the **populus** here in the land,
This is our **patria**, the fatherland.
Our king is just and has sworn to us all,
"I **rego** the land and I'm servant of all."

The **rex** and **regina**, they sit on gold thrones,
They wear gold **coronas** with beautiful stones.
The **populus** love them and frequently say,
"They've brought the land peace and a new
dawning day."

Famous Saying

Regnat populus. = The people rule.

Most of you are blessed to live in America, a country in which everyone has a part in ruling, not just the rulers. When people are allowed to vote and to speak their opinions, they are helping to rule.

Chapter Lesson

You've already learned a lot about verbs. Can you remember one way to describe them? Verbs usually describe things that you can *do*. This kind of verb is called an *action verb*. There is another kind of verb that we use quite often, which is called a *being verb*. Verbs can show action, but they can also show that something *is*. When you use the words "am," "is," or "are," you are using being verbs.* Here are some example sentences that use being verbs (in italics):

I *am* tall.
He *is* smart.
The weather *is* cold.
You *are* wet.
The students *are* helpful.◊

◊ Please note that these are specifically *present tense* being verbs. Future and past tense being verbs will be introduced later, but to keep it simple for students, we are only dealing with present tense being verbs for now.

You can see that although no specific actions are taking place in these sentences, the sentences still contain verbs—being verbs.

Circle the following sentences that include being verbs.

Jack ran up the hill.
I am tired.
The hill is steep.
She loves brownies.
Jill carried her pail.
The brownies are warm.
Mother is watchful.

Now, take turns with your classmates making up and sharing your own sentences that include being verbs.

*Sometimes being verbs are called linking verbs, because they "link" the subject to information about the subject.

Sample Sentences

Now look at these sample sentences that have being verbs in Latin:

Julia est puella. Julia is a girl.
Julia est regina. Julia is a queen.

Can you guess what **est** means in Latin? That's right, it means "is"! You will learn more about the word **est** in the next chapter.

Grow Your English

As you can probably tell, several of the Latin words in this chapter's Words to Learn are related. The **reg-** part of words such as **regina** and **rego** is related to royalty and ruling. The word *regal* means "royal, king-like." Lions are often described as regal. Can you think of other things that are regal? ◊◊

If an area is *populous*, that means it is full of many people. If many people like you, you are *popular*. From what Latin word did these words come? populus

A *coronation* is a special ceremony that takes place when the **corona** (crown) is placed on the head of a new king or queen.

Practice Your Latin

I. Practice writing your new Latin words by tracing the dots.

rex regina
corona patria
populus rego

> ◊◊ Get creative when describing or evaluating "regal" examples. Regal can be just an attitude or style, such as a queenly pose, a kingly gesture, or a composed and gracious demeanor. You might say that a fancy robe is regal or that the furnishings of a fancy house or a large, fancy car are regal. You can even call grand mountains "regal." The word can apply to pretty much anything that reflects nobility, dignity, or grandeur.

II. Draw a line to match each description with the correct image. (Hint: Some of the images are described more than once, so they will have more than one line drawn to them.)

1. I am a male ruler.
2. We love our **rex** and **regina**!
3. I wear a crown and a pretty gown.
4. I sit on the heads of royalty.
5. We are a married, ruling couple.
6. Those who wear me have great power.
7. According to the famous saying in this chapter, we should help rule.

III. On a separate piece of paper draw a picture of a **rex** and **regina** wearing **coronas**.

IV. Pretend you are a **populus** looking for a **rex**. Write a job description for a good **rex**. Try to use three words from this chapter, and any other Latin words that will fit.

Answers will vary.

Show What You Know

I. Write the English translations on the lines provided.

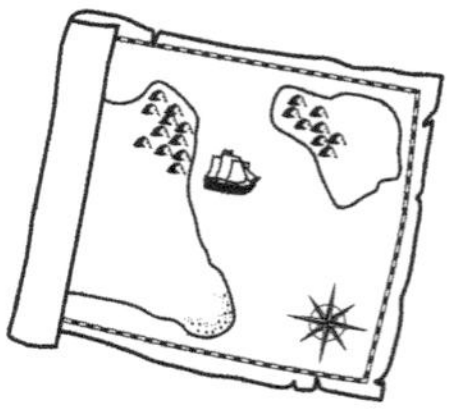

1. **rego** I rule/direct
2. **rex** king
3. **populus** people
4. **regina** queen
5. **corona** crown
6. **patria** country/fatherland

II. Complete the following sentences with English *being verbs*:

1. Marcus is a very fast runner.
2. All the boys are outside.
3. It is time for school!
4. We are tan from playing in the sun.
5. Father is a hard worker.

III. **Derivatives:**

1. Write one English derivative of **rego**: Answers will vary, but some examples include regal, regulate, regular, region, and direct.
2. Write one English derivative of **populus**: Answers will vary, but some examples include popular, population, populate, populous, people.

Chapter 15

Military Matters

Words to Learn

1. **miles**	soldier
2. **gladius**	sword
3. **bellum**	war
4. **pugno**	I fight
5. **vinco**	I conquer
6. **video**	I see

Review Words

1. **agnus**	lamb
2. **infans**	baby
3. **lavo**	I wash
4. **coquo**	I cook
5. **pasco**	I feed

Chapter Song

The Mighty Miles Song [Track 15(C)/45(E)]

I'm a mighty **miles,** I can swing a sword.
My **gladius** is my best friend when I go off to war.
I fight to save my **patria, pugno** to keep it free,
Pugno for liberty!

Video many enemies, and **vinco** all I see,
To see and conquer enemies, courageous I must be.
A **bellum** is a tragedy, but a **miles** still must go
Pugno in rain or snow!

Famous Saying

◊ Being verbs are sometimes called linking verbs.

The present tense being verbs are "am," "is," "are." Here are some examples of sentences containing being verbs (the being verbs are underlined):

I am happy. Simeon is funny. You are smart. The boys are tall.

Veni, vidi, vici. = I came, I saw, I conquered.

This is a famous saying by Julius Caesar, a powerful Roman **miles** and ruler. He said this when reporting one of his many victories. You will often see this phrase used in different ways or used with a different ending word. This would be a fun way to report a job accomplished or a test aced to your parents!

Chapter Lesson

Do you remember that in the previous chapter, we talked about verbs of being, or being verbs? (What is the other name they are sometimes called?) Take a minute to recall what the being verbs are, and to share examples of sentences containing being verbs.◊

In this chapter, you are going to learn the conjugation of the Latin being verb **sum. Sum** means "I am." So, **sum discipulus** means "I am a student." When we conjugate most regular, present tense verbs, we add the endings **-o, -s, -t, -mus, -tis**, or **-nt. Sum** does not completely follow this pattern, but it is not too hard to learn. Look at the forms of **sum** below.◊◊

Person	Singular	Plural
First Person	**sum** (I am)	**sumus** (we are)
Second Person	**es** (you are)	**estis** (you all are)
Third Person	**est** (he/she/it is)	**sunt** (they are)

One funny thing you might notice is that the first form does not end in **-o**—it ends in **-m**! Also, the beginning part of the word changes. It goes back and forth between **su-** and **es-**. This is quite unusual, but easy to memorize. Some verbs do not follow the normal rules, and they are called "irregular." **Sum** is an example of an irregular verb. You can chant the **sum** conjugation just like the other verb endings and forms you have learned. This week, don't worry about learning the meanings of the forms of **sum**, just focus on learning the forms themselves.

Chant **sum** like this:

Sum, es, est! (clap, clap) **Sumus, estis, sunt!** (clap, clap)

◊◊ As you can see, sum is not a typical verb. Most verbs have a standard stem to which different endings are added. This irregular verb stem changes back and forth between su and es in the present tense. That is why this verb must be taught and memorized individually. Please note that this chapter lesson only references regular, present tense verb forms.

Sample Sentences

The following are some more sentences that use the singular and plural forms of **sum**.

Singular	
Puella ***est*** discipula.	The girl is a student.
Sum **ursa.**	I am a bear.
Es **stella.**	You are a star.
Est **vir.**	He is a man.
Est **femina.**	She is a woman.
Plural	
Sumus **amici.**	We are friends.
Estis **discipuli.**	You are students.
Sunt **viri.**	They are men.
Marcus et Davus *sunt* viri.	Mark and Dave are men.

Notice that we use plural forms of the nouns with the plural forms of **sum**. For example, since **sumus** (*we* are) is plural, we use the plural word "friends" (**amici**), not the singular word for "friend" (**amicus**).

Grow Your English

Wouldn't you like to be *invincible*! No one can conquer someone who is invincible. What is the Latin root of this word? vinco

A *pugnacious* person loves to fight, and a *belligerent* person can cause a war. Do you know from what Latin words these English words are derived? pugno and bellum

Video is both an English word and a Latin word. In which language do you think it first appeared? Latin

Practice Your Latin

I. Practice writing your new Latin words by tracing the dots.

miles gladius bellum

pugno vinco video

◊◊◊ Here are the translations for the body parts listed in the word bank: **manus** (hand), **pes** (foot), **caput** (head), **corpus** (body), **auris** (ear), **nares** (nose), **oculus** (eye), **os** (mouth).

II. **Equip the *Miles*:** Cut out the **miles** and the pieces of his armor on page 293. Next, label the parts of the soldier's body using the following list. (Hint: You learned the Latin names for body parts in *Song School Latin Book 1*, chapters 19 and 20.) Once you have labeled the soldier, dress him in the pieces of armor you cut out.

manus	pes	caput	corpus	auris	nares	oculus	os

◊◊◊

III. Take a look at the two soldiers below and pick which one is your favorite. Then, fill in the blanks and help your favorite **miles** win all six points! For every correct answer, your **miles** gets a point.

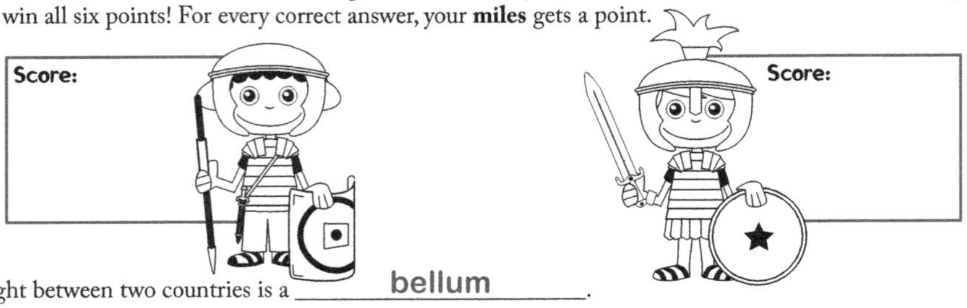

1. A fight between two countries is a ____bellum____.
2. A ____miles____ marched onto the field.
3. Through my spyglass (small telescope), ____video____ the enemy approaching over the hill.
4. My best weapon is the ____gladius____.
5. ____Pugno____ against the enemies of my **patria**.
6. With the help of my fellow **miles**, ____vinco____ our enemies!

Show What You Know

I. Draw lines to match the Latin words to their English translations.

1. **bellum**	I conquer
2. **pugno**	sword
3. **miles**	war
4. **video**	soldier
5. **vinco**	I see
6. **gladius**	I fight

II. Write out the six Latin forms of **sum**.

Singular	Plural
sum	sumus
es	estis
est	sunt

Everyday Actions

Words to Learn

1. **porto** I carry
2. **specto** I look at
3. **narro** I tell
4. **vivo** I live
5. **amo** I love
6. **voco** I call

Review Words

1. **cano** I sing
2. **laudo** I praise
3. **do** I give
4. **dico** I speak, say
5. **scribo** I write

Chapter Song

<u>Porto-Amo Song</u> [Track 16(C)/46(E)]

Porto—carry,
Porto—carry,
Porto books!
Porto rocks!
Specto at the horses,*
Specto at the blue sky,*
Look around,
Look up high.

Amo pater,
Amo amicus,
I love you,
Yes, you, too!
Vivo in the city,
Vivo in the country,
I live high,
I live free.

Narro stories,
Narro stories,
I tell tales!
Tall, tall tales!
Voco all my best friends,
I call all my neighbors,
"Come see me,
Come to tea."

*The word **specto** means "I look at," so including the English word "at" in these two lines of the song repeats the idea that's already included in the Latin word.

Famous Saying

Labor omnia vincit. = Work conquers all.

◊ Encourage a little discussion about work here. If nothing else, students' school tasks or chores at home could be used as examples. If you have students who are learning an instrument or sport, this is highly applicable as well.

Sometimes we are given tasks or problems that seem very challenging. One secret weapon is good, persistent work! You can accomplish more than you think you can by diligent, ongoing work—even by working in small amounts every day. What are some things in your life that can be conquered by daily, diligent work? ◊

Chapter Lesson

In the previous chapter, you started learning the forms of **sum**, a Latin being verb. In this chapter, you will review **sum**, and focus on learning the meanings.

PERSON	SINGULAR	PLURAL
First Person	**sum** (I am)	**sumus** (we are)
Second Person	**es** (you are)	**estis** (you all are)
Third Person	**est** (he/she/it is)	**sunt** (they are)

Now practice the **sum** chant:

Sum, es, est! (clap, clap) **Sumus, estis, sunt!** (clap, clap)

You can also chant the meanings like this:

<u>Bonus Chant: Being Chant</u> [Track 17(C)/47(E)]

Sum, "I am." **Sum**, "I am."
And **es**, "you are." **Es**, "you are."
Est, "he, she, it is." **Est**, "he, she, it is."

Sumus, "we are." **Sumus**, "we are."
Estis, "you all are." **Estis**, "you all are."
Sunt, "they are." **Sunt**, "they are."

Sample Sentences

Study the following sentences that show you how to use **sum** in both its singular and plural forms.

Singular

***Sum* discipulus.**	I am a student (male).
***Sum* discipula.**	I am a student (female).
***Es* discipulus.**	You are a student (male).
Marcus *est* discipulus.	Marcus is a student.
Julia *est* discipula.	Julia is a student.

Plural

***Sumus* discipuli.**	We are students.*
***Estis* discipuli.**	You are students.*
Marcus et Davus *sunt* discipuli.	Mark and Dave are students.
Julia et Rosa *sunt* discipulae.	Julia and Rose are students.
Amici *sunt* discipuli.	The friends are students.*
Amicae *sunt* discipulae.	The friends are students (female).

Notice how we change to the plural form of the noun when using **sumus**, **estis**, and **sunt**. **Discipulus** means "student (male)," but **discipuli** means "students." **Discipula** means "student (female)," but **discipulae** means "students (female)."

Now see if you can complete the following sentences by filling in the blank with the correct form of **sum**.

Julia et Rosa ____sunt____ **amicae.** Julia and Rose are friends.

Marcus ____est____ **rex.** Mark is a king./Mark is the king.

Grow Your English

What does it mean to sur*viv*e? It means to live through something difficult, right? To re*viv*e someone is to bring them back to life or to consciousness. *Viv*acious means "full of life"! Do you see that sneaky Latin root hiding in these words? What is it?

Porto gives us many words, such as *portable* (carry-able), *export*, *important*, *port*, *airport*, *transport*, and *import*!

The Latin root hiding in the words "survive," "revive," and "vivacious" is viv-.

*Latin uses the masculine (male) plural form (such as **discipuli**) for both a group of males and for a combined group of males and females.

From **voco**, we get *vocal*, *vocation* (a calling), and *evoke* (to call forth). Can you think of any other words that contain the **voc-** or **vok-** root? Some examples include revoke and invoke.

You can probably think of English words that come from **specto** without any help. What do you call someone who is watching, but not participating? A *spectator*! What other words have **spect-** in them?
Examples include: inspection, spectacles, spectacle, respect, suspect, and expect.

A *narrator* is someone who tells the story, and a story can be called a *narrative*. What is the Latin root in these words?
The Latin root is narro.

Practice Your Latin

I. Practice writing your new words by tracing the dots.

porto specto narro

vivo amo voco

II. **What Should You Do?** The following statements present different situations in which you might find yourself. Read each statement and then circle the word that would be the best thing for you to do in each situation.

1. You are standing in a stream with your canoe, looking at a beaver dam that is in your way.

porto (circled)	**amo**	**pasco**
I carry	I love	I feed

2. You are sitting next to a friend in a library and remind your friend to be quiet.

susurro (circled)	**specto**	**vivo**
I whisper	I look at	I live

3. You are sitting by a campfire with friends when someone asks you to tell a story.

pugno	**narro** (circled)	**clamo**
I fight	I tell	I shout

4. You are standing in front of a beautiful painting in a museum.

specto	porto	lavo
I look at	I carry	I wash

5. Your car has a flat tire.

specto	amo	voco
I look at	I love	I call

III. Using words from the word bank, complete the sentences with the correct Latin verbs. Be careful: The sentences may need a being verb to complete them properly! (Hint: One of the verbs will be used more than once.)

Word Bank: voco amo specto sede est sum es vivo porto

1. ___Amo___ my family and my dog!
2. The **pullus** ___est___ loud.
3. ___Sum___ ready for school.
4. ___Voco___ my friends to see if they can play.
5. ___Vivo___ in a small house in a big field.
6. ___Specto___ the snow falling from the window.
7. ___Sede___ in my seat, waiting for the teacher.◊◊
8. ___Es___ very brave, my friend.
9. ___Porto___ heavy bags for my mother.
10. Simeon ___est___ brown and fuzzy.

◊◊ **Sede should look and sound very familiar to your students if you are using common Latin classroom commands. You might ask them what ending should be added to it to make it mean "I sit" instead of just "sit" and see if they can come up with -o, producing the form sedeo.**

Show What You Know

I. Circle the correct English translations of these Latin words.

1. **vivo**	a. I call	b. I live	c. I look at	d. I love
2. **voco**	a. I carry	b. I love	c. I call	d. I live
3. **porto**	a. I look at	b. I port	c. I am	d. I carry
4. **narro**	a. I tell	b. I say	c. I call	d. I love
5. **amo**	a. I call	b. I carry	c. I love	d. I look at
6. **specto**	a. I call	b. I look at	c. I carry	d. I tell

II. Write the Latin words from which these English words are derived.

1. spectator ___specto___
2. survive ___vivo___
3. portable ___porto___
4. narrator ___narro___

III. Provide the English translation of this famous Latin saying: **Labor omnia vincit.** ___Work conquers all.___

IV. Provide the English meanings for the conjugation of **sum**.

Person	Singular	Plural
First Person	**sum** (I am)	**sumus** (we are)
Second Person	**es** (you are)	**estis** (you all are)
Third Person	**est** (he/she/it is)	**sunt** (they are)

Chapter 17

Adverbs: How We Do Things

Words to Learn

1. **nunc** now
2. **numquam** never
3. **saepe** often
4. **cito** fast, quickly
5. **lente** slowly
6. **semper** always

Review Words

1. **manus** hand
2. **pes** foot
3. **caput** head
4. **corpus** body
5. **ambulo** I walk

Chapter Song

Cito-Lente Song [Track 18(C)/48(E)]

Put out the fire! **Cito**!
How should I do it? **Cito**!
Put out the fire, not slow.
Put out the fire, **cito**!

Walk very slowly, **lente**!
Creep up the stairs, **lente**!
Sneak around the corner, all day.
Take your time, **lente**!

Semper, always! I always do!
Saepe, often, and you, too!
Always or often, tie your shoe.
Semper, **saepe**, tie your shoe!

Nunc or **numquam**, now or never!
Nunc or **numquam**, don't wait forever!
Let's play **nunc** and play forever.
Let's play **nunc** and forever!

Famous Saying

Nunc aut numquam! = Now or never!

You have almost certainly heard this saying in English, probably many times. Sometimes the person saying it just means, "Hurry up, I'm tired of waiting!" The saying can also be applied to more important things. It is often true that many opportunities and responsibilities do not wait for us for very long. You either have to do it now or give up the chance. So, eat your ice cream before it melts, do your chores and studying on time, and be bold to try new things! And next time you need to get a friend to hurry up, tell them, "**Nunc aut numquam!**"

Chapter Lesson

Review the **sum** chant and the "Being Chant."

Bonus Chant: Being Chant [Track 17(C)/47(E)]

Sum, I am. **Sum**, I am.
Es, you are. **Es**, you are.
Est he, she, it is. **Est** he, she, it is.

Sumus, we are. **Sumus**, we are.
Estis you are. **Estis** you are.
Sunt they are. **Sunt** they are.

Person	Singular	Plural
First Person	**sum** (I am)	**sumus** (we are)
Second Person	**es** (you are)	**estis** (you all are)
Third Person	**est** (he/she/it is)	**sunt** (they are)

In the previous chapter, you looked at sentences that used singular forms of **sum**. In this chapter, you will see more of such sentences, but also sentences with plural forms of **sum**.

Do you remember that the purpose of action verb endings, such as the **o-s-t** endings you learned earlier, is to show *who* is doing the action? Well, that's still true, but sometimes you don't translate the meaning of that verb ending in a sentence. For example, in the sentence "**Vir videt**," you do not need to translate it as "The man he sees," but just "The man sees." You don't have to translate the verb ending because a noun in the sentence takes care of telling who is doing the action. The same is true with forms of being verbs, such as **sum**. Read the example sentence, and then translate the others.

Example: **Puellae sunt amicae.** The girls are friends.

1. **Sumus amici.** We are friends.

2. **Estis discipuli.** You all are students.

3. **Sum puer.** I am a boy.

4. **Sunt feminae.** They are women.

5. **Estis puellae.** You all are girls.

6. **Est ludus.** It is a game.

7. **Reginae sunt feminae.** The queens are women.

8. **Vir est rex.** The man is a king.

9. **Sum miles.** I am a soldier.

Grow Your English

The following English derivatives are a little harder to see than others you have learned, but they're still very important! The forms of **sum** with **es** in them give us words such as *pr<u>es</u>ence* and *<u>es</u>sence* and many others. If you think about the meanings of these words, you can see the connection to the idea of "being."

Practice Your Latin

I. Practice writing your new words by tracing the dots.

nunc numquam saepe

cito lente semper

II. Fill in the forms of **sum**, including the correct meanings.

Person	Singular	Plural
First Person	sum (I am)	sumus (we are)
Second Person	es (you are)	estis (you all are)
Third Person	est (he/she/it is)	sunt (they are)

III. Look at the pictures and label each one with the Latin word that best describes *when* or *how* these events should happen.

numquam

semper

saepe

cito

lente

IV. On a separate piece of paper, draw a picture of what you are doing or look like right **nunc**.

V. Circle *T* if the statement is true and *F* if it is false.

1. You should **semper** go to bed at night. (T) F
2. Simeon likes to eat bananas **saepe**. (T) F
3. You should **numquam** brush your teeth. T (F)

4. A cheetah can run **cito**. (T) F

5. Your teacher is sleeping right **nunc**. T (F)

6. Compared to an airplane, a train moves **lente**. (T) F

Show What You Know

I. Fill in the missing forms and meanings of **sum**.

Person	Singular	Plural
First Person	sum (I am)	sumus (we are)
Second Person	es (you are)	estis (you all are)
Third Person	est (he/she/it is)	sunt (they are)

II. Draw lines to match the Latin words to their English translations.

1. **saepe**	never
2. **semper**	quickly
3. **lente**	always
4. **nunc**	now
5. **numquam**	slowly
6. **cito**	often

III. Provide the English translation of the following famous Latin saying: **Nunc aut Numquam!**

Now or never!

Chapter 18

More Adverbs

◊ The words **bene**, **optime**, and **pessime** appeared as new vocabulary words in chapter 3 of *SSL1* and as review vocabulary in chapter 4 of this book. We are including them in the new vocabulary list here (rather than in the review vocabulary list) because we have incorporated them into the chapter song and they were not part of a song in *SSL1*.

Words to Learn

1. **non** not
2. **forte** bravely
3. **pessime** badly, terrible◊
4. **diligenter** carefully
5. **bene** well, fine◊
6. **optime** best◊

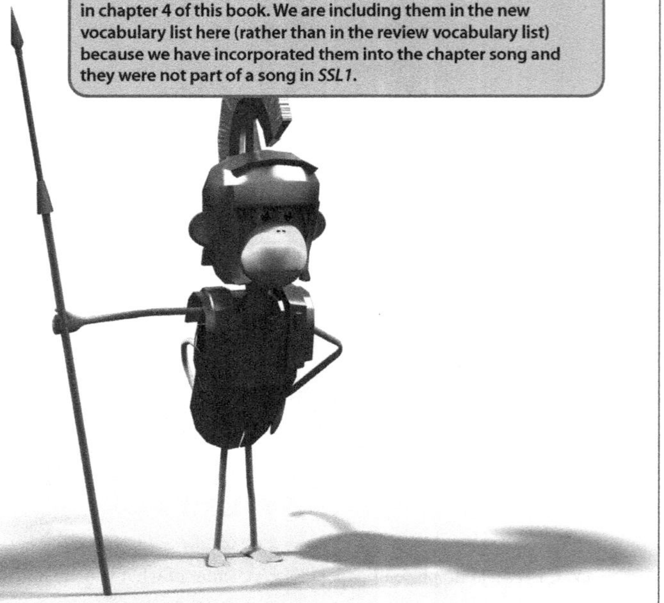

Review Words

1. **auris** ear
2. **oculus** eye
3. **os** mouth
4. **grammatica** grammar, language arts
5. **physica** science

Chapter Song

Forte Song [Track 19(C)/49(E)]

When you're scared, just face it bravely!
Like a soldier—**forte**!
And work **diligenter**—carefully!
Forte, diligenter!

Bene, do well, give your best,
Or you'll do **pessime** on your test!
Pessime—badly, **optime**—best!
Now let's give it your best!

Optime is **non pessime**,
and **pessime** is **non optime**.
Mice live in fear, **non forte**.
The word **non** means "not"!

Famous Saying

Semper fidelis = always faithful

◊◊ Ideas for discussion: These words are pulled from a dictionary definition of "faithful": reliable, loyal, trusted, true to your word, true to duty. You might use these words to discuss "faithful" with your students, and then ask if they can think of people who are faithful in what they do. You can guide students to answers such as parents, mailman, emergency personnel, ministers, teachers, military, and government rulers. You might also want to discuss this from the other side, asking students what it would be like if these people were *not* **semper fidelis**. Then turn it around and (continued below)

This is the motto of the U.S. Marine Corps, and a great goal for everyone. What does it mean to be **semper fidelis**? ◊◊

see if they can think of ways to be **semper fidelis** themselves, to their duties, to their parents, to their friends, to their sports teams, etc.

Chapter Lesson

All of the verb forms you have learned so far are in the *present tense*. Do you know what that means? Verbs in the present tense show action that is happening right now. But what about something that happened in the past? You would use a verb that is in the *past tense*, which means that the verb is talking about something that happened in the past. You have already learned the present tense forms of the being verb **sum**. In this chapter, you're going to be introduced to past tense forms of **sum**. Look at the chart below.◊◊◊

Person	Singular	Plural
First Person	**era*m*** (I was)	**era*mus*** (we were)
Second Person	**era*s*** (you were)	**era*tis*** (you all were)
Third Person	**era*t*** (he/she/it was)	**era*nt*** (they were)

◊◊◊ You might want to explain to your students that the English word "tense" (in this context) means "time." The word "tense" here is derived from the Latin word **tempus**, which means "time." There is another English word "tense" derived from the Latin verb **tendere**, which means "to stretch."

Notice how similar these forms are to the present tense forms of **sum**! It is easy to memorize these new forms when you see that these forms still include the endings **-s**, **-t**, **-mus**, **-tis**, and **-nt**! The only one that's different is the **-m** where you're used to seeing the **-o**. Practice chanting the past tense forms of sum just like you did the present tense **sum** chant.

Translating sentences with the past tense forms of **sum** is just like using the present tense forms, except you use "was" and were" instead of "is" and "are." Take a look at the following sentences.

Pater erat magister.	Father was a teacher.
Erant puellae.	They were girls.
Erat saxum.	It was a rock.*
Eram discipulus.	I was a student.

*(You know it wouldn't be "he" or "she" was a rock!)

Now, try translating the following sentences.

Erat canis. It was a dog.

Eras puer. You were a boy.

Erant discipuli. They were students.

Eram puer. I was a boy.

Grow Your English

A *pessimist* is a person who always expects the worst to happen. An *optimist* expects good things! From which Latin words are these words derived? pessime, optime

From which Latin word do you think the English word *none* came? That's right, **non**! You can hear the Latin word **non** in many English words. When someone says "That's *non*sense!" they are saying, "That does *not* make sense!" You can easily guess what these words mean: *nontoxic*, *nondairy*, *nonfiction*. Anytime you hear **non** in a word, you can think "not" or "no" and it will help you figure out what the word means. Can you think of other words that have **non** in them?

Practice Your Latin

I. Practice writing your new words by tracing the dots.

non forte pessime

diligenter bene optime

II. Write the past tense forms of **sum** with their meanings in the chart below. (The first one is done for you.) After you have filled in the chart, chant the forms.

Person	Singular	Plural
First Person	**eram** (I was)	eramus (we were)
Second Person	eras (you were)	eratis (you all were)
Third Person	erat (he/she/it was)	erant (they were)

III. Label the following pictures with Latin adverbs that describe how the action is or was done.

pessime

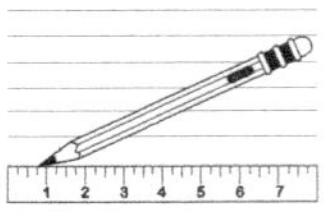

diligenter

optime

forte

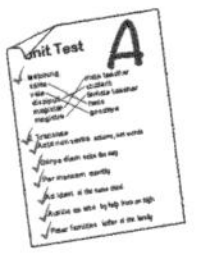

bene

IV. **Word Scramble:** Write the Latin word beside the scrambled versions of them and then draw lines to match them to their meanings.

1. onn non	well, fine
2. fetro forte	ear
3. emssepi pessime	eye
4. gretenildi diligenter	bravely
5. enbe bene	badly, terrible
6. mitpoe optime	mouth
7. rsaiu auris	grammar/language arts
8. scluuo oculus	carefully
9. so os	best
10. catmgrmaia grammatica	science
11. hsyiacp physica	not

Show What You Know

I. Circle the correct meaning of each word:

1. **non**	a. badly	b. well	c. bravely	d. not
2. **pessime**	a. badly, terrible	b. well	c. bravely	d. carefully
3. **bene**	a. not	b. best	c. well, fine	d. quickly
4. **optime**	a. carefully	b. best	c. often	d. not
5. **forte**	a. well	b. always	c. bravely	d. badly
6. **diligenter**	a. carefully	b. bravely	c. not	d. slowly

II. Write the translation of the famous Latin saying: **semper fidelis.**

always faithful

III. Finish the chart by writing in the missing past tense forms of **sum** and/or their meanings.

PERSON	SINGULAR	PLURAL
First Person	eram (I was)	eramus (we were)
Second Person	**eras** (you were)	eratis (you all were)
Third Person	erat (he/she/it was)	erant (they were)

Chapter 19 Review

Master Your Words

You have learned thirty more Latin words! Now it is time once again to make sure you have mastered all of these newest words. Can you provide the correct English translation for each of the following Latin words?

Chapter 14 Words

1. **rex** king
2. **regina** queen
3. **corona** crown
4. **patria** country, fatherland
5. **populus** people
6. **rego** I rule, direct

Chapter 14 Review Words

1. **leo** lion
2. **avis** bird
3. **ursa** bear
4. **septem** seven
5. **decem** ten

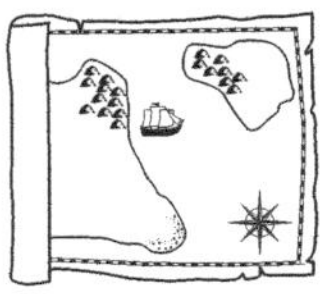

Chapter 15 New Words

1. miles — soldier
2. gladius — sword
3. bellum — war
4. pugno — I fight
5. vinco — I conquer
6. video — I see

Chapter 15 Review Words

1. agnus — lamb
2. infans — baby
3. lavo — I wash
4. coquo — I cook
5. pasco — I feed

Chapter 16 New Words

1. porto — I carry
2. specto — I look at
3. narro — I tell

4. vivo — I live
5. amo — I love
6. voco — I call

Chapter 16 Review Words

1. cano — I sing
2. laudo — I praise
3. do — I give
4. dico — I speak, say
5. scribo — I write

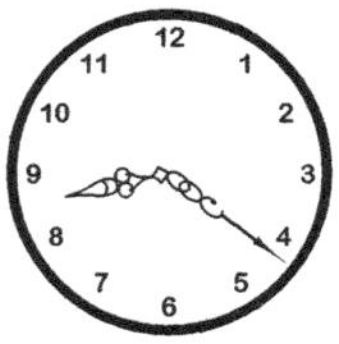

Chapter 17 New Words

1. nunc — now
2. numquam — never
3. saepe — often
4. cito — fast, quickly
5. lente — slowly
6. semper — always

Chapter 17 Review Words

1. **manus** hand
2. **pes** foot
3. **caput** head
4. **corpus** body
5. **ambulo** I walk

Chapter 18 New Words

1. **non** not
2. **forte** bravely
3. **pessime** badly
4. **diligenter** carefully
5. **bene** well, fine
6. **optime** best

Chapter 18 Review Words

1. **auris** ear
2. **oculus** eye
3. **os** mouth

4. **grammatica** grammar, language arts
5. **physica** science

Master Your Songs

Rex and Regina Song [Track 14(C)/44(E)]

We are the **populus** here in the land,
This is our **patria**, the fatherland.
Our king is just and has sworn to us all,
"I **rego** the land and I'm servant of all."

The **rex** and **regina**, they sit on gold thrones,
They wear gold **coronas** with beautiful stones.
The **populus** love them and frequently say,
"They've brought the land peace and a new dawning day."

The Mighty Miles Song [Track 15(C)/45(E)]

I'm a mighty **miles**, I can swing a sword.
My **gladius** is my best friend when I go off to war.
I fight to save my **patria, pugno** to keep it free,
Pugno for liberty!

Video many enemies, and **vinco** all I see,
To see and conquer enemies, courageous I must be.
A **bellum** is a tragedy, but a **miles** still must go
Pugno in rain or snow!

Porto-Amo Song [Track 16(C)/46(E)]

Porto—carry,
Porto—carry,
Porto books!
Porto rocks!
Specto at the horses,
Specto at the blue sky,
Look around,
Look up high.

Amo pater,
Amo amicus,
I love you,
Yes, you, too!
Vivo in the city,
Vivo in the country,
I live high,
I live free.

Narro stories,
Narro stories,
I tell tales!
Tall, tall tales!
Voco all my best friends,
I call all my neighbors,
"Come see me,
Come to tea."

Bonus Chant: Being Chant [Track 17(C)/47(E)]

Sum, "I am." **Sum**, "I am."
And **es**, "you are." **Es**, "you are."
Est, "he, she, it is." **Est**, "he, she, it is."

Sumus, "we are." **Sumus**, "we are."
Estis, "you all are." **Estis**, "you all are."
Sunt, "they are." **Sunt**, "they are."

Cito-Lente Song [Track 18(C)/48(E)]

Put out the fire! **Cito**!
How should I do it? **Cito**!
Put out the fire, not slow.
Put out the fire, **cito**!

Walk very slowly, **lente**!
Creep up the stairs, **lente**!
Sneak around the corner, all day.
Take your time, **lente**!

Semper, always! I always do!
Saepe, often, and you, too!
Always or often, tie your shoe.
Semper, **saepe**, tie your shoe!

Nunc or **numquam**, now or never!
Nunc or **numquam**, don't wait forever!
Let's play **nunc** and play forever.
Let's play **nunc** and forever!

Forte Song [Track 19(C)/49(E)]

When you're scared, just face it bravely!
Like a soldier—**forte**!
And work **diligenter**—carefully!
Forte, **diligenter**!

Bene, do well, give your best,
Or you'll do **pessime** on your test!
Pessime—badly, **optime**—best!
Now let's give it your best!

Optime is **non pessime**,
and **pessime** is **non optime**.
Mice live in fear, **non forte**.
The word **non** means "not"!

Word Review Activities

I. **Word Search:** Find and circle the Latin words that match the English meanings listed below. (Hint: You may want to write down the Latin words next to their English meanings before you do the word search.)

king rex
crown corona
people populus
war bellum
I conquer vinco

soldier miles
I look at specto
I tell narro
I call voco
never numquam

slowly lente
often saepe
bravely forte
carefully diligenter
best optime

A	T	D	K	O	U	E	Z	F	X	E	Q	U	M	F	W	I	O	R	Z	P	C	S
P	Y	H	Z	C	O	R	O	N	A	K	R	A	N	O	S	B	U	V	E	J	U	G
O	J	T	B	Q	W	X	P	I	T	B	D	K	X	R	J	E	J	M	X	X	N	Q
P	N	L	V	D	U	C	T	K	M	V	L	D	Y	T	H	Z	A	L	D	W	N	O
U	G	E	F	M	K	D	I	L	I	G	E	N	T	E	R	U	I	V	F	Y	C	T
L	R	N	L	P	X	R	M	Q	L	U	C	M	Y	B	Q	S	B	M	E	N	A	V
U	W	T	Y	J	V	N	E	U	E	J	A	F	V	M	P	I	K	E	I	P	N	H
S	P	E	C	T	O	B	P	G	S	W	H	Z	U	O	G	U	T	V	C	J	A	S
D	H	C	R	K	C	Z	E	L	V	D	M	N	K	F	B	E	L	L	U	M	Q	V
I	N	A	R	R	O	A	O	S	A	E	P	E	I	W	E	R	P	Y	C	X	K	U

◊ Please note that this exercise utilizes different verb endings, such as **-nt** on **voco** and **-mus** on **rego.** You may want to call attention to each of these verbs and have students identify the endings and what they mean, and figure out the whole meaning of the word from there.

II. **Story Time:** Read the story aloud (or read along quietly while your teacher reads) and circle the Latin words when you come to them. Then go through and write the English meanings underneath the Latin words. Once you have done that, read the story again completely in English.◊

Simeon was very tired one afternoon and decided to take a nap. Soon, he was fast asleep and dreaming.

The rex and regina vocant for Simeon and Justus unus day. "Regimus the patria diligenter, but we are worried about a
king queen call one We rule country/fatherland carefully

bellum," they say. "Many populi vident enemy milites* around the borders, and the populi are scared. If we do not think
war people see soldiers people

diligenter and act cito and forte, the patria may be in trouble."◊◊
carefully quickly bravely country/fatherland

◊◊ Note that in our diglot (two languages) stories featuring Latin and English, we do not put the Latin nouns in the (continued below) accusative case when they are the object of verbs. This is to keep the emphasis on vocabulary practice rather than on introducing the grammar of verb-noun agreement in Latin. For example, **"Regimus the patria"** would normally be rendered **"Regimus the patriam,"** putting **patriam** in the accusative case.

Simeon and Justus say, "Amamus our patria! Let us vocamus many milites together and then pugnamus the enemies."
We love country/fatherland We call soldiers we fight

"How soon can you do this?" asks the rex.
king

"Give us tres hours," says Justus. "Videtis many milites gathering, each portat a gladius, ready to fight a bellum."
three We see soldiers carries sword war

Simeon says, "Laboramus optime for the patria and corona!"
We work best country/fatherland crown

"Our populi are the optime!" says the regina.
people best queen

Simeon and Justus each get on their equus and equitant around the patria. Narrant many populi about the enemy.
horse ride country/fatherland they tell people

Some do non believe them and say, "Narratis a crazy fabula! Non pugno a bellum. Pugnamus numquam a bellum." ◊◊◊
not You tell story I do not fight war we never fight war

◊◊◊ You may need to help students figure out a natural-sounding translation for **non pugno** and **pugnamus numquam.** For these phrases to be acceptable in English, the adverb really needs to be inserted between the action and the pronoun, making **non pugno** "I do not fight" and **pugnamus numquam** "we never fight." Push students toward this translation, assuring them that it really is OK (and necessary) to move the words around like that.

*__Milites__ is the plural form of **miles** (soldier).

But more than one miles forte follows them with a gladius. Simeon and Justus's army grows, and soon they are
soldier bravely sword

heading back to the rex and regina, shouting, "Semper fidelis!"
king queen Always faithful

Simeon woke up lente and looked around. The sol was shining through the fenestra. He heard his mater vocat, as she
slowly sun window mother call

saepe did, "Come and eat before the cibus gets cold!"
often food

III. **Matching:** Help each **miles** find his **equus** by drawing lines to match the Latin words to their English meanings.

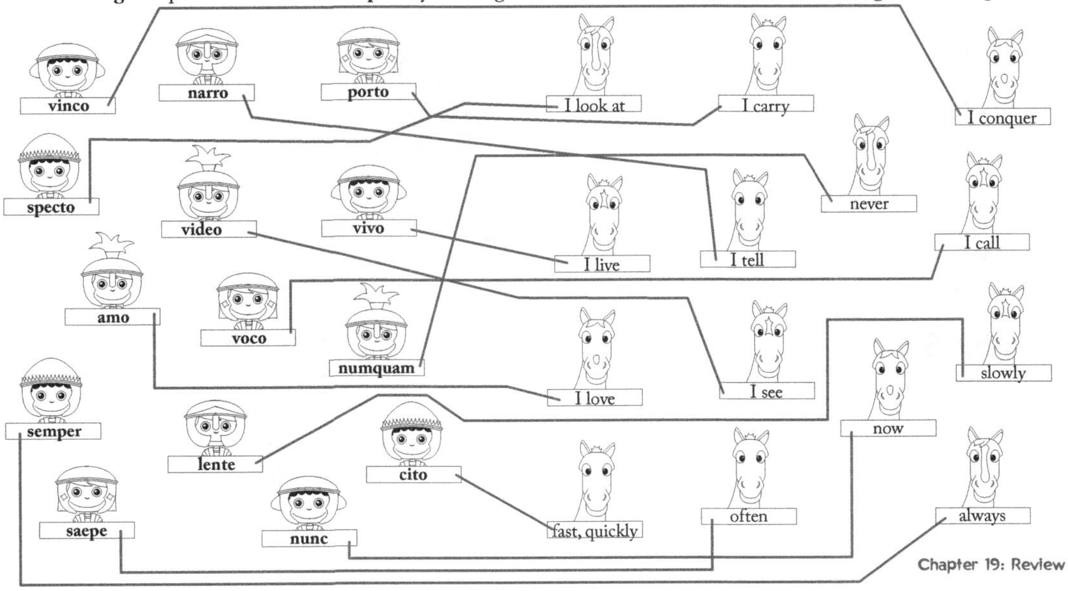

Master Your Famous Sayings

On the lines provided, write the English translations of the famous Latin sayings.

1. **Regnat populus.** The people rule.
2. **Veni, vidi, vici.** I came, I saw, I conquered.
3. **Labor omnia vincit.** Work conquers all.
4. **Nunc aut numquam!** Now or never!
5. **Semper fidelis** always faithful

Master Your Derivatives

Draw lines to match the Latin words to their English derivatives. If you do it correctly, you will see a familiar shape. Once the shape is revealed, label it with the correct Latin word and color it!

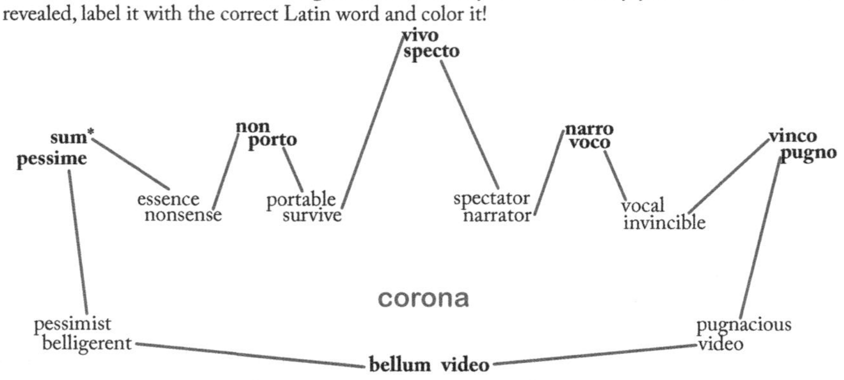

*Finding the derivative of **sum** might be a little tough, so here's a hint: The second-person singular of **sum** is **es**. Is there a word in the derivative list that has **es** in it and seems to be related to the meaning of **sum** ("I am"—a state of being)?

Chapter 20 When I Grow Up, Part I

Words to Learn

1. **negotium** job, occupation
2. **poeta** poet
3. **vigil** guard, policeman, fireman
4. **tabernarius** shopkeeper
5. **architectus** architect
6. **artifex** artist
7. **medicus** doctor

Review Words

1. **cibus** food
2. **cena** dinner
3. **edo** I eat
4. **familia** family
5. **ludus** game, school, play

Chapter Song

<u>The Negotium Song, Part I</u> [Track 20(C)/50(E)]

There's lots of things that you could do
When you grow tall and strong.
The **negotium** that's right for you,
That you'll love all day long!

When Jack fell down and broke his crown
His mother called the doctor
And the **medicus** made Jack lay down
And soon Jack felt much better.

When you see a **vigil** who guards your town,
A **vigil** strong and brave,
Make sure you thank him for his work,
Give him a smile and wave.

An **architectus** draws designs
For buildings tall and bold.
An **artifex** is glad, I'm told
When his artwork is all sold.

When you walk into the general store,
Say, "Hello, **Tabernarius**!"
And buy a book of **poeta***
And read the poems to us!

◊ Examples to cite or elicit include Da Vinci's *Mona Lisa* and *The Last Supper* and Michelangelo's frescoes in the Sistine Chapel and statue of *David*, all of which are around 500 years old. You may wish to mention performing arts as well and how beauty that is choreographed and composed can last a very long time. Note as well that the Latin word "est" (is) is absent in this saying. In Latin, sometimes the verb for being is assumed.

Famous Saying

Ars longa, vita brevis. = Art is long, life is brief.

Why is this a true saying? Can art last longer than life? Can you think of any famous works of art? The majority of famous art was not created in your lifetime or even in your parents' lifetime. The beauty that an artist captures may last for hundreds of years and give joy to many.◊

*The phrase "of **poeta**" can mean "of a poet" or "of the poet." Remember that in Latin there is no word for "a" or "the," so **poeta** by itself could be translated "the poet" or "a poet."

Chapter Lesson

◊◊ Some examples of English being verbs are "am," "is," "are," "was," and "were."

You know by now what a verb of being is. Try to think of two examples of English being verbs right now.◊◊ Now, think of two examples in Latin!◊◊◊You should be able to think of **sum** with its six present tense forms and the past tense form **eram**. In this chapter, you will learn the future tense form of **sum**. The future tense is what we use to talk about things that haven't happened yet. This means that with the future tense form of **sum** you can talk about something that *will be* in the future. An example of a sentence that uses the future tense is: I *will be* eight years old in April. Here's another example: He *will be* a great basketball player! You will find it very easy to learn the Latin future tense forms of **sum** because they are very similar to the past tense forms. Look at the following chart for the future tense of **sum**:

◊◊◊ Some examples of Latin being verbs are **sum, es, sumus, and sunt.**

Person	Singular	Plural
First Person	**ero** (I will be)	**erimus** (we will be)
Second Person	**eris** (you will be)	**eritis** (you all will be)
Third Person	**erit** (he/she/it will be)	**erunt** (they will be)

Look at the forms and find the similarities and differences between these forms and the past tense forms. Then, practice chanting the future tense forms many times.◊◊◊◊

◊◊◊◊ Notice that the stem is -er for both the future and imperfect tense and that the endings are very regular: -o, -s, -t, -mus, -tis, -nt. Allow students to look through and point out characteristics that they recognize and then give them the big picture as stated above (stem is -er, regular endings are added).

<u>Sample Sentences</u>

It should be easy for you to understand the following sentences, which feature the future forms of **sum**.

<u>Singular</u>

Ero architectus.	I will be an architect.
Eris poeta.	You will be a poet.
Marcus erit medicus.	Mark will be a doctor.
Julia erit artifex.	Julia will be an artist.
Erit artifex.	She (or he) will be an artist.

Plural

Erimus medici.	We will be doctors.
Erimus amici.	We will be friends.
Eristis tabernarii.	You all will be shopkeepers.
Julia et Rosa erunt poetae.	Julia and Rose will be poets.
Erunt poetae.	They will be poets.

Verbs at the End of the Sentence

In Latin, it is common to put the verbs at the end of sentence, like this:

Architectus ero.	I will be an architect.
Julia artifex erit.	Julia will be an artist.

In the sentences below, fill in the blank with the correct future form of **sum**.

Davus ____erit____ **artifex.**
(David will be an artist.)

Julia et Rosae ____erunt____ **medici.**
(Julia and Rose will be doctors.)

◊◊◊◊◊ Some animals that could be considered vigilant include dogs (watchdogs), cats (watching for mice and insects), birds (who scold when you get close to a nest), mother lions and most animals with their young!

Grow Your English

You probably noticed right away that the Latin words **architectus** and **poeta** are almost exactly like the English words *architect* and *poet*. What about **medicus**—what English words does it remind you of? Your list could include *medical*, *medicine*, and *medic* and you could probably think of a couple more! The Latin word **vigil** gives us the English word *vigil*, which means "a time to watch and guard." A *vigilant* person is watchful and careful. Can you think of an animal that might be vigilant? ◊◊◊◊◊

Practice Your Latin

I. Practice writing your new Latin words by tracing the dots.

negotium poeta vigil

tabernarius architectus

artifex medicus

II. Practice writing (and chanting) the future tense forms of **sum** with the meanings.

Person	Singular	Plural
First Person	ero (I will be)	erimus (we will be)
Second Person	eris (you will be)	eritis (you all will be)
Third Person	erit (he/she/it will be)	erunt (they will be)

III. In the circles, draw a picture of a person doing the **negotium** with which the circle is labeled.

guard, policeman, fireman

vigil

shopkeeper

tabernarius

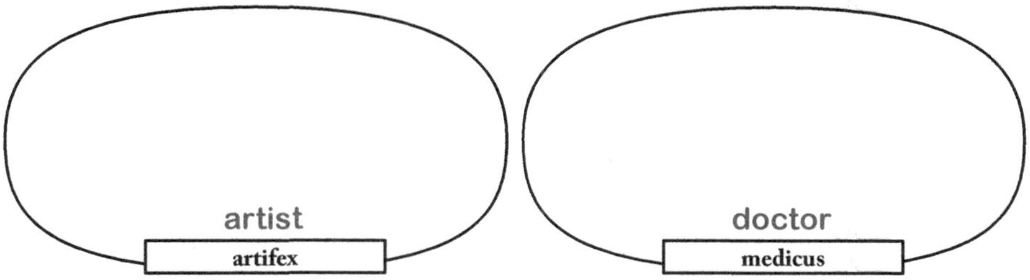

IV. Read the following clues and, in the spaces provided, write the job names in Latin. (Hint: Some job names may be used more than once.)

1. I fight fire! I am a(n) ____vigil____.
2. I create lines, verses, and rhythms with words. I am a(n) ____poeta____.
3. I keep the shelves filled with all sorts of good things and keep them tidy so people can find what they need. I am a(n) ____tabernarius____.
4. I love to create beauty. I am a(n) ____artifex____.
5. I draw plans for tall buildings and bridges. I am a(n) ____architectus____.
6. My job is help people get well. I am a(n) ____medicus____.
7. I protect my town from bad people. I am a(n) ____vigil____.
8. I can sell you the things you need! I am a(n) ____tabernarius____.
9. I use tools such as paints and pencils to do my job. I am a(n) ____artifex____.

Show What You Know

I. Write the meaning, in English, of the famous saying from this chapter: **Ars longa, vita brevis.**

____Art is long, life is brief.____

II. Draw lines to match the Latin words to their meanings.

1. **artifex**	poet
2. **architectus**	doctor
3. **medicus**	shopkeeper
4. **negotium**	artist
5. **vigil**	job, occupation
6. **poeta**	architect
7. **tabernarius**	guard, policeman, fireman

III. In the following table, fill in the future tense forms and/or the meanings of **sum**.

Person	Singular	Plural
First Person	ero (I will be)	erimus (we will be)
Second Person	eris (you will be)	eritis (you all will be)
Third Person	erit (he/she/it will be)	erunt (they will be)

Chapter 21

When I Grow Up, Part II

Words to Learn

1. **agricola** farmer
2. **structor** builder
3. **nauta** sailor
4. **venator** hunter
5. **athleta** athlete
6. **musicus** male musician
   musica female musician
7. **scriptor** writer
8. **senator** senator, politician

Review Words

1. **panis** bread
2. **crustulum** cookie
3. **lac** milk
4. **patria** country, fatherland
5. **populus** people

Chapter Song

The Negotium Song, Part II [Track 21(C)/51(E)]

An **agricola** on a summer day
Went out to plant some hay.
A **venator** shot down a deer
While the **nauta** sailed away!

The **musicus** played a pretty song,
And a **scriptor** wrote a book,
The **senators** passed a brand-new law,
And locked up every crook.

An **athleta** and a mouse did race.
The mouse, he took first place.
A **structor** built a fancy house
With lots of rooms and space.

◊ You may want to explain to students that a state seal is a symbol that represents qualities and/or ideals that a state's government believes to be representative of that state's unique attributes. You may also want to explain that the word tyrannus can also be translated as "tyrant," which is a type of ruler or dictator who exercises power harshly or cruelly. In chapter 29, students will learn the word tyrannus translated as "ruler, dictator."

◊◊ The Latin present tense can be translated in three different forms of the English present—the simple present (I carry), the progressive present (I am carrying), and the emphatic present (I do carry). In this book we will translate the Latin present in the English simple and progressive present tenses to aid students in understanding that either of these translations is appropriate. The sentence "Specto coronam" (on p. 147) is rendered with both translations (I am looking/I look) so that students can see that either is acceptable.

Famous Saying

Sic semper tyrannis! = Thus always to tyrants!

Sic semper tyrannis was adopted as the motto for the state of Virginia in 1776. The phrase can be translated as "thus always to tyrants," which means that tyrants should be removed from power (and possibly even killed). The seal of the state of Virginia illustrates this idea with a picture of a warrior (Virtue) standing over a subdued tyrant, with the tyrant's crown lying on the ground.◊

Chapter Lesson

You have started learning about Latin verbs of being in three different tenses. What are they? That's right, they're the present, future, and past tenses. See if you can chant the forms for **sum**, **eram**, and **ero** now without thinking about them too hard!

In this chapter, you are going to learn endings that can go on almost any verb to change it into the past tense. That means that if you add these endings to a verb, the endings change the verb so it is talking about action that has already happened. For example, in English: "I am looking at the crown" is in the present (or "right now") tense.◊◊ If you said, "Five hours ago, I was looking at the crown," that would be in the past tense. This past tense is also called the *imperfect* tense, and that is what we will call this tense and its endings from now on—imperfect tense and imperfect tense endings.

Take a look at the endings in the following table and notice how similar they are to the imperfect forms of *sum*. Remember, these endings are *added* to verbs; they are not words that can stand-alone. (Hint: That little dash [-] in front of the endings indicates that these are endings and not stand-alone words.)

PERSON	SINGULAR	PLURAL
First Person	**-bam**	**-bamus**
Second Person	**-bas**	**-batis**
Third Person	**-bat**	**-bant**

Practice chanting these endings with the same rhythm as the o-s-t chant. They are fun to say!

Sample Sentences

To add an ending to a Latin verb, we take the stem of the verb then add the ending. For instance, the stem of **specto** is **specta**.* Now that we know the stem, we add the imperfect endings to **specta**, like this:

specta + **-bam** = **spectabam** (I was looking at)
specta + **-bas** = **spectabas** (you were looking at)
specta + **-bat** = **spectabat** (he/she/it was looking at)
specta + **-bamus** = **spectabamus** (we were looking at)
specta + **-batis** = **spectabatis** (you all were looking at)
specta + **-bant** = **spectabant** (they were looking at)

◊◊◊ The Latin imperfect tense can be translated in two different forms of the English past—the simple past (I carried) and the progressive past (I was carrying). The simple past should be used rarely, as the imperfect generally means ongoing, past (progressive) action. The word "imperfect" literally means "not complete," so the imperfect indicates incomplete action. In this book we will generally translate the imperfect as the English progressive past tense, but occasionally use the simple past when the context makes it clear the action is ongoing.

Now take a look at the following sentences:

Specto coronam.** I am looking at the crown./I look at the crown.
Spectabam coronam. I was looking at the crown.◊◊◊
Spectabas coronam. You were looking at the crown.
Marcus spectabat coronam. Mark was looking at the crown.

◊◊◊◊ Students should not worry about the form of **coronam** in the accusative case, as they will be studying this case and its meaning in later study (e.g., *Latin for Children, Primer A*). We use it here to show them how the new verb forms work.

*You will learn more about verb stems later in your study of Latin. For now, know that verb stems will usually end in **a** (like **specta**) or **e**.
Note that we placed an **m at the end of **corona** (making it **coronam**). This is because nouns that take the action of a verb are in the accusative case in Latin. You will learn more about this in your later study of Latin.◊◊◊◊

Grow Your English

The Latin word for "farmer," **agricola**, gives us a big word that has to do with farming in general: *agriculture*! The Latin word for "sailor," **nauta**, gives us the English word *nautical*, which we use to describe things that are related to sailing or the ocean. You can also see how **structor** is in the English words *construction* and *structure*. Can you think of other words that have *struct* in them? Examples include destruct, destruction, instruct, and reconstruction.

Which one of the words in this chapter did not change even one letter when it transferred into English? Which one only changed one letter? Which one is an English word if you take away only two letters?◊◊◊◊◊

◊◊◊◊◊ **senator**
athleta
musicus

Practice Your Latin

I. Practice writing your new Latin words by tracing the dots.

agricola structor nauta
venator athleta musicus/a
scriptor senator

II. Practice writing (and chanting) the imperfect tense verb endings.

PERSON	SINGULAR	PLURAL
First Person	-bam	-bamus
Second Person	-bas	-batis
Third Person	-bat	-bant

III. Help each person do his or her work! Draw a line to match the tool or item to the person labeled with the correct corresponding job.

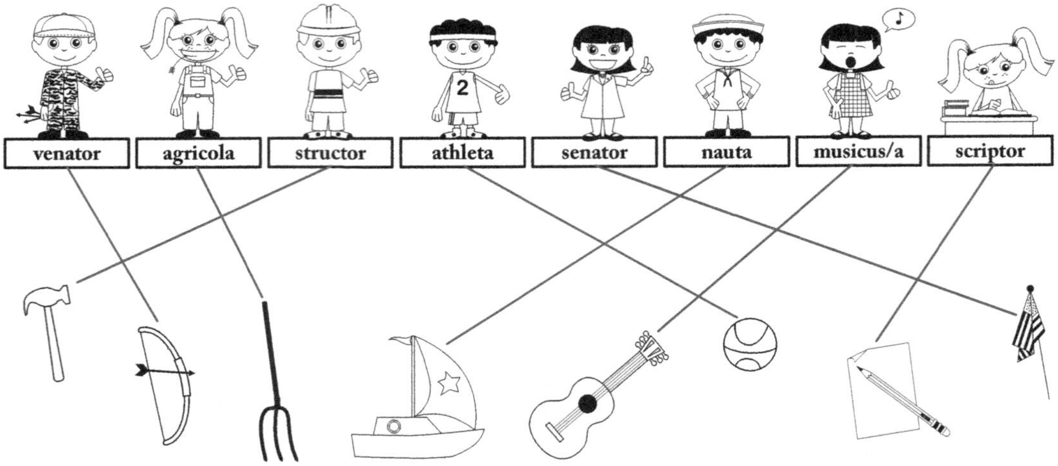

IV. Listen as your teacher reads the following problems out loud, then write the Latin name of at least one kind of person who could help. You may be able to think of two or more for some of them! (Hint: Some of the words will come from the previous chapter.)

1. Poor Simeon has a sore throat and a cough. Who can help him? ____medicus____

2. Uh-oh! A **venator** came on the **agricola**'s land and shot a cow. The **venator** claims that there is no law against shooting cows, only dogs. Can you think of two people who might help in this situation?

____senator____ ____vigil____

3. The **rex** wishes to build a summer palace on a beautiful island. He cannot get there or build it by himself, though! What three people might help him get to the island and build a beautiful palace?

____architectus____ ____nauta____ ____structor____

4. Once the palace is complete, who can help entertain the **rex** and **regina**? Name two or three people who would be good at this.

____musicus____ ____poeta____ ____athleta____

5. Marcus's kitten climbed up a tree and can't get down. Marcus can't reach her either! Who can come help rescue the kitten?

____vigil____

6. Now that Simeon is feeling better, he is going to go out for his morning run! He gets lonely when he runs by himself, though. He needs a friend who can run as fast as he does. What kind of person would be a good running buddy for Simeon?

____athleta____

V. **Draw Your Thoughts!** What is your favorite **negotium** of all the ones that you have learned in Latin? Draw a picture of yourself doing it, and label it with the Latin word. (You can use a future tense form of **sum**: **Ero** __________!)

Show What You Know

I. Write the meaning, in English, of the famous saying from this chapter: **Carpe diem!** Seize the day

II. Circle the correct meaning for each Latin word.

1. **agricola**	a. sailor	b. farmer	c. writer	d. athlete
2. **musicus**	a. hunter	b. builder	c. musician	d. sailor
3. **athleta**	a. athlete	b. senator	c. hunter	d. farmer
4. **scriptor**	a. hunter	b. builder	c. senator	d. writer
5. **nauta**	a. writer	b. sailor	c. guard	d. farmer
6. **structor**	a. doctor	b. writer	c. sailor	d. builder
7. **senator**	a. sailor	b. senator	c. fireman	d. farmer
8. **venator**	a. hunter	b. artist	c. poet	d. musician

III. In the following table, write out the imperfect tense verb endings.

Person	Singular	Plural
First Person	-bam	-bamus
Second Person	-bas	-batis
Third Person	-bat	-bant

Chapter 22 Where Things Are, Part I

Words to Learn

1. **sub** under
2. **supra** over, above, on top of
3. **prope** near
4. **trans** across
5. **ex** out of
6. **ad** to, toward
7. **circum** around
8. **pone** behind

Review Words

1. **nix** snow
2. **imber** rain
3. **nimbus** cloud
4. **arcus** rainbow
5. **vinco** I conquer

Chapter Song

<u>The Shoe Song</u> [Track 22(C)/52(E)]

"It's time to go," Dad says.
I look under and near the bed.
I look for my shoes, which I always lose,
Sub and **prope** the bed!

"Please hurry, or we'll be late.
We must drive across the state.
Trans the whole state, **ad** grandma's house,
To grandmother's house by eight!"

I look behind the chairs.
I look above the stairs.
Pone the chairs, **supra** the stairs,
Can't find them anywhere.

Our dog strolls into the house
With one of my shoes in his mouth
We circled him—**circum**—and saw
My shoe locked tight in his jaw.

> **◊ You may want to explain to the students that a motto is "a sentence, phrase, or word that expresses the spirit or purpose of a person, organization, city, etc."**
>
> **◊◊ You can take this idea wherever is most appropriate for your class, or leave it as an open-ended question that students can think about on their own.**

Famous Saying

Ad astra per aspera! = To the stars through difficulties!

This is the Kansas state motto. It reminds us to work hard to achieve, even though we may have great difficulties.◊ "To the stars" means to try to achieve your very best, even beyond what you think is possible. If you are striving for something beyond what you can reach, you will likely achieve things that you never would with less effort. We all benefit from people who have made this their motto. We enjoy modern inventions, medicine, art, and more because of those who reach for the stars! How can you strive to go "to the stars" this week?◊◊

Chapter Lesson

All of words in this chapter's vocabulary list are *prepositions.* Do you know what prepositions are? They are words that show the location of things or make connections between words. For example: The ant is *on* the bowl. "On" is a preposition that shows where the ant is. Another example: The girl is the daughter *of* the teacher—"of" is a preposition that shows the connection between the girl and the teacher. Here is an example in Latin using one of your new vocabulary words: **sub aqua** (under the water).

Future Tense

In the last chapter, you learned a new set of endings for verbs. Those endings show action happening in the past. Do you remember what those endings are called? The imperfect tense! Now that you've learned how to talk about the past, you're going to learn how to talk about the future, about things that *will* happen. Here are a couple of examples of the future tense in English: "Next week we *will* go to the museum!" "Tomorrow, I *will* look at the crown."

The Latin endings that show future action are called the future tense endings. Study the following chart.

Person	Singular	Plural
First Person	**-bo**	**-bimus**
Second Person	**-bis**	**-bitis**
Third Person	**-bit**	**-bunt**

Did you notice that these endings rhyme with the future tense of **sum** (**ero, eris, erit, erimus, eritis, erunt**)? Practice chanting these new endings.

Sample Sentences

To add the future endings to a Latin verb, we take the stem of the verb, then add the ending. Do you remember the stem of **specto**? That's right, it's **specta**. We use that same stem to form the future tense by adding the future endings, like this:

specta + **-bo** = **spectabo** (I will look at)
specta + **-bis** = **spectabis** (you will look at)
specta + **-bit** = **spectabit** (he/she/it will look at)
specta + **-bimus** = **spectabimus** (we will look at)
specta + **-bitis** = **spectabitis** (you all will look at)
specta + **-bunt** = **spectabunt** (they will look at)

Now let's look at some sentences that use all of the tenses that you've learned so far.

Specto coronam. I look at the crown. (present tense)
Spectabam coronam. I was looking at the crown. (past tense)
Spectabo coronam. I will look at the crown. (future tense)
Spectabis coronam. You will look at the crown. (future tense)
Julia spectabit coronam. Julia will look at the crown. (future tense)
Marcus et Davus spectabunt coronam. Mark and Dave will look at the crown. (future tense)

Now complete the following sentences by adding the correct future tense ending for **specto**.

Marcus specta____bit____ **coronam.** (Mark will look at the crown.)
Julia et Rosa specta____bunt____ **coronam.** (Julie and Rose will look at the crown.)

Grow Your English

Your *circumstances* include the things, events, and people *around* you. Magellan *circumnavigated* the earth! Can you see what Latin word these English words come from? circum

To *transport* something is to carry it across a distance. Can you think of other words that have **trans** in them?
Some examples include transition, translate, transmit, transmission, translucent, and transect.

Practice Your Latin

I. Practice writing your new Latin words by tracing the dots.

sub supra prope trans

ex ad circum pone

II. Practice writing (and chanting) the future tense verb endings:

Person	Singular	Plural
First Person	-bo	-bimus
Second Person	-bis	-bitis
Third Person	-bit	-bunt

III. Fill in the blanks with the correct Latin prepositions.

1. Simeon is ice skating ____trans____ (across) the lake.
2. There is a dust bunny ____sub____ (under) the bed.
3. I like to sit ____prope____ (near) my grandma when she visits.

4. We held lanterns high ____supra____ (above) our heads and walked ____circum____ (around) our campsite.
5. My brother sneaked up ____pone____ (behind) me and scared me!
6. Simeon hiked ____ad____ (to) the waterfalls with us.
7. A fish jumped ____ex____ (out of) the water.

IV. Help Simeon reach the market from his house! Look at the map below and number the directions in order from 1 to 6.

__3__ Walk **pone** the pond. behind
__1__ Walk **trans** the horse pasture. across
__2__ Go **sub** the bridge. under
__6__ The market is just **circum** the corner! around
__5__ Look for the flag **supra** the door, and turn left. over, above, on top of
__4__ When you are **prope** the church, turn right. near

V. **Show It!** Choose three of the words from this chapter, and draw pictures in the boxes that illustrate the word meanings. Write a sentence underneath each that includes a Latin preposition.◊◊◊

◊◊◊ Encourage use of other Latin words in sentences when possible.

Answers will vary.
The following are some examples of the types of sentences students should be producing:

The tree is supra the water.

The girl is running circum the pond.

Show What You Know

I. Write the meaning, in English, of the famous saying from this chapter: **Ad astra per aspera!**

To the stars through difficulties!

II. Draw lines to match the Latin words with their meanings.

1. **pone**	around
2. **ad**	under
3. **ex**	across
4. **supra**	near
5. **sub**	behind
6. **circum**	to, toward
7. **trans**	out of
8. **prope**	over, above, on top of

III. Write out the future tense verb endings.

Person	Singular	Plural
First Person	-bo	-bimus
Second Person	-bis	-bitis
Third Person	-bit	-bunt

Chapter 23

Words to Learn

1. **contra** against
2. **dum** while
3. **extra** outside of
4. **inter** between, among
5. **ante** before
6. **post** after
7. **cum** with
8. **sursum** up
9. **de** down from, concerning, about

Review Words

1. **hiems** winter
2. **ver** spring
3. **autumnus** fall
4. **aestas** summer

Chapter Song

Visiting Song [Track 23(C)/53(E)]

I ran up the hill with my friend,
Cum amicus, my best friend.
Sursum the hill, then **de** the hill,
Up and down the hill we went.

◊ Students can provide examples from the objects surrounding them and the actions they currently are doing and seeing. Ensure that students identify their examples as nouns and verbs. If students start offering Latin examples, that is great, as long as they are sticking with nouns and verbs.

We went to visit the goat,
He lives **extra**, outside of a moat.
Between the trees, among the bees,
He paddles around in his boat!

After dinner, **post** eating, we went
To visit the cow in a tent.
He was building a stall, **contra** the wall,
And hoping to charge us rent.

While walking home in the dark,
Dum walking, we went through the park.
Ante we got home, we heard a big boom!
Ran all the way home in the dark.

Famous Saying

Dum spiro, spero. = While I breathe, I hope.

Cicero, a famous Roman philosopher, originally came up with this phrase. Many people and organizations have adopted it as a motto, including the state of South Carolina. The idea is that things can always improve, and so you should never give up hope. As long as there is a breath of possibility, there is always a reason to have hope!

Chapter Lesson

In the last several chapters you have learned a lot of endings for Latin verbs. (Be sure to keep practicing your chants so that you can chant all of the verb endings you've learned from memory.) Early in this book you also learned that nouns could have endings, such as singular and plural endings. For example, you may remember that **amicus** means "friend" but **amici** means "friends." Now you will be learning more endings that go with nouns. Before we start, however, let's review what a noun is. *A noun is a word that usually names a person, place, or thing.* Take a minute to name some specific verbs and nouns.◊

We have seen that both verbs and nouns can be either singular or plural. Look at the following sentence:

Amicus clamat. The friend shouts.

In this sentence, both **amicus** and **clamat** are singular. **Amicus** means "friend (singular)" (that's just one single friend), and **clamat** has the **-t** ending which lets us know that it means "*he, she, or it* shouts."

Now study the following sentence:

Amici clamant. The friends shout.

In this sentence, both **amicus** and **clamant** are plural. **Amici** means "friends (plural)" (that's two or more friends), and **clamant** has the **-nt** ending that tells us it means "*they* shout."

Not only do nouns have singular or plural endings (which we can call *number*), but they also have another feature called *case*. The case of a noun helps us to know what job a noun does in a sentence. In the future, you will learn more about the noun cases and how they work, but for now, you get to learn their names and some of their endings. Here are the names of the noun cases: nominative, genitive, dative, accusative, and ablative.◊◊

Aren't those words long and fun to say? You can remember their order by memorizing the following sentence. Each of the words in this sentence starts with the same letter as one of the noun cases:

Never **G**ive **D**avus **A**ny **A**pples!

Practice chanting the noun cases, starting with the memory sentence.

Grow Your English

You probably know that when something happens at 8:00 a.m. it is happening at 8 o'clock in the morning. But did you that the little "a.m." following the time comes from the Latin **ante meridiem**, which means "before noon." Can you guess what "p.m." means? It stands for **post meridiem**, which means "*after* noon," of course! These are Latin words that are part of our everyday English language.

Post is often used with a hyphen or as a prefix to simply mean "after." One example is *postgame* (after the game). The Latin word **de** is used as a prefix in many English words, such as *descend* (come *down*) and depend.

Practice Your Latin

I. Practice writing your new Latin words by tracing the dots.

contra dum extra inter

ante post cum de

II. Circle the best Latin word to complete each sentence. You will have to remember some of the words you learned in chapter 22!

1. The bear must stay __________ (**inter** / **supra** / **extra**) the house!
2. Simeon, please carry the dishes __________ (**pone** / **ad** / **ex**) the table.
3. __________ (**Dum** / **Contra** / **Post**) you are at the fair, stay __________ (**trans** / **ante** / **cum**) your sister at all times!
4. You may have your dessert __________ (**dum** / **post** / **sursum**) you eat your dinner.
5. I like to read books __________ (**pone** / **de** / **ante**) I go to bed.
6. The detective found the clue __________ (**contra** / **inter** / **dum**) the pages of a huge book.
7. My horse ran __________ (**trans** / **sub** / **prope**) the pasture __________ (**ex** / **pone** / **ad**) me when I called him.
8. My dog hid his bone __________ (**pone** / **ex** / **sursum**) the couch.
9. I had to stand on my tiptoes so that I could pull a book __________ (**extra** / **ante** / **de**) the top shelf.
10. __________ (**Post** / **Circum** / **Prope**) I ate breakfast, I went to watch two soccer teams playing __________ (**dum** / **pone** / **contra**) each other.

◊◊ Curious students might want to know more about these mysterious cases. Depending on the amount of time you have and the ability and past training of your students, you may want to give a brief explanation of the noun jobs that these cases perform. The following is a brief rundown of the noun jobs. The nominative case does the work of a subject noun; the genitive case shows possession (possessive noun adjective); the dative case is used for indirect objects; the accusative case is used for direct objects and the objects of prepositions; the ablative case is used with objects of prepositions. Here are the Latin roots for these words: nomen (name): nominative ; genitus (begotten): genitive; datus (given): dative; accusativus (pointing to the origin, accused): accusative; ablatus (carried away): ablative.

III. Each of the following boxes is labeled with a preposition. On the blank provided, write the English translation of the preposition. Then draw a picture in each box that illustrates the preposition.◊◊◊

◊◊◊ **Drawings will vary, but a suggested idea for each preposition has been supplied. The suggestions feature a dog, but obviously pretty much any animal, or even a person, could be used. Suggestions: cum (with): a boy walking with his dog; extra (outside of): a dog sitting outside of its doghouse; sursum (up): a dog jumping up; inter (between, among): a dog sitting between two cats.**

cum with

extra outside of

sursum up

inter between, among

Show What You Know

I. Write the meaning, in English, of the famous saying from this chapter: **Dum spiro, spero.**

While I breathe, I hope.

II. Circle the correct meaning for each of the following Latin words.

1. **extra**	a. near	(b. outside)	c. under	d. over
2. **cum**	(a. with)	b. behind	c. beside	d. after
3. **ante**	a. while	b. against	(c. before)	d. down from, concerning, about
4. **sursum**	a. around	(b. up)	c. above	d. between
5. **post**	a. while	b. near	(c. after)	d. down from, concerning, about
6. **contra**	a. between	b. after	(c. against)	d. behind
7. **inter**	a. with	b. before	c. behind	(d. between)
8. **dum**	a. after	(b. while)	c. under	d. across
9. **de**	a. against	b. between	c. up	(d. down from, concerning, about)

III. Write out the sentence that helps you remember the names of the noun cases. Then, on the blanks provided, write out the names of the noun cases. The first letter of each noun case has been provided for you.

Memory Sentence: Never Give Davus Any Apples

Nominative

Genitive

Dative

Accusative

Ablative

◊ You may want to explain to your students that a virtue is a positive character trait that has to be learned, trained, and cultivated.

Chapter 24

Growing Virtues◊

Words to Learn

1. **fortis, forte** — brave, strong*
2. **fidelis, fidele** — faithful
3. **humilis, humile** — humble
4. **diligens, diligentis** — careful, attentive**
5. **sapiens, sapientis** — wise
6. **oboediens, oboedientis** — obedient
7. **verax, veracis** — truthful, honest
8. **beneficus, benefica, beneficum** — kind, generous***
9. **studiosus, studiosa, studiosum** — eager to learn
10. **virtus** — virtue, courage, excellence****

Review Words

1. **caelum** — sky
2. **stella** — star
3. **sol** — sun
4. **saepe** — often
5. **cito** — fast, quickly

*Adjectives in Latin come in three main groups. First there is a group of adjectives that have the endings **-is** and **-e** (such as **fortis, forte** and **fidelis, fidele**).
Then there is a group that has the endings **-ns and **-is** (such as **diligens, diligentis**). **Verax, veracis** is an irregular example from this second group.
***Finally there is a group that has the endings **-us**, **-a**, **-um** (such as **beneficus, benefica, beneficum**). These different endings are used when the adjectives describe nouns of different gender—mainly masculine and feminine, but also neuter. You will learn more about how Latin adjectives (and their endings) work with Latin nouns later in your study of Latin. For now, be sure to memorize all of the forms of these words—doing this will come in very handy later!
****Note: In this list, the word **virtus** is a noun meaning "virtue, courage, excellence," and not an adjective. Because it is a noun we only show it with one form. The other words in the list are all adjectives which will have different forms for different genders.

◊◊ We have listed or spelled out the complete "dictionary form" (the way adjectives are listed in a Latin dictionary) of the adjectives in this week's vocabulary list in order to prevent future confusion when we occasionally show adjectives combined with nouns in this book. Since students will be learning the gender of nouns, we think it is worth showing them the dictionary forms for adjectives that contain the gender endings. At this point in their study, students should not be concerned with the various forms and endings that different adjectives have, but should still memorize the dictionary forms, knowing that they will learn the details of how they function in later study (i.e., in *Latin for Children, Primer A*).

Chapter Song

Grow My Virtus [Track 24(C)/54(E)]

I'm gonna grow my **virtus** every day, uh-huh,
Grow **virtus** as I work and play, uh-huh.
Verax, truthful words I'll say, truthful words will win the day,
Be **fortis**, brave and strong, along the way.

Fidelis, faithful, that's what I should be,
Diligens, working carefully!
Oboediens, doing what's asked of me, obedient to my family,
And **humilis**, with humility, uh-huh.

Beneficus, helping family and friends,
Studiosus, learning my numbers, chants, and blends!
I'm going to work to be wise or **sapiens**, I'll thank my parents, teachers, and friends.
I'm gonna grow my **virtus** every day, uh-huh.

Famous Saying

Fortes fortuna iuvat! = Fortune favors the brave!

This famous saying may have been said first by the playwright Terence, but it has been quoted many times throughout history to encourage acts of bravery. It carries the idea that those who step out in bravery and do things that are frightening or difficult are often blessed with good results, or good "fortune."

Chapter Lesson◊◊

Adjectives

Do you know what an adjective is? An adjective is a word that tells you something about a noun. We sometimes say that an adjective *describes* a noun. An adjective always answers a question such as What kind? Which one? or How many? Take a look at the phrase below:

The kind queen. **Benefica regina.**

Can you tell which word is the adjective? It is the word "kind" (**benefica**). The word "kind" (**benefica**) is telling us something about the queen—that she is kind. The adjective "kind" is answering the question: What kind? In other words, it's asking, "What kind of queen?" The answer is: a kind queen.

Because adjectives describe nouns, adjectives will have the same kind of endings that nouns have. Notice that **benefica** and **regina** both have the same ending—**-a.** You will learn more about how the endings of adjectives and nouns work together as you continue your study of Latin.

More About Nouns

In the last lesson, you learned that Latin nouns have different endings called cases. Can you say the names of the cases? Take a minute to review them. **The cases are nominative, genitive, dative, accusative, ablative.**

There are five different families of nouns, called *declensions.* These five families, or declensions, may have different endings, but the endings for nominative, genitive, dative, accusative, and ablative all perform the same noun jobs! Later in your study of Latin you will learn what these jobs are, but for now just enjoy memorizing the endings of each family or declension. Here are all the endings for the first declension:

Case	Singular	Plural
Nominative	**-a**	**-ae**
Genitive	**-ae**	**-arum**
Dative	**-ae**	**-is**
Accusative	**-am**	**-as**
Ablative	**-a**	**-is**

I bet you already guessed that you will be chanting these fabulous endings! It's easy to find a good rhythm to use for them! You can also sing the following song to help you learn them.

Bonus Chant: First Declension Endings Chant [Track 25(C)/55(E)]

-a, -ae, -ae, -am, -a
-ae, -arum, -is, -as, -is

-a, -ae, -ae, -am, -a
-ae, -arum, -is, -as, -is

Grow Your English

The Latin word **fortis** gives us some wonderful English words related to strength. To *fortify* is to make something stronger or better. A *fort* is a strong place of protection! *Fortitude* means strength and courage.

If you think about the Latin word **diligens**, you can see a connection between it and the English word *diligent. Veracity* means truthfulness. What Latin word do you think the word *veracity* came from? **verax, veracis**

Practice Your Latin

I. Practice writing your new Latin words by tracing the dots.

fortis forte fidelis fidele
diligens diligentis sapiens
sapientis humilis humile
verax veracis beneficus
benefica beneficum studiosus
studiosa studiosum oboediens
oboedientis virtus

II. Help these lost Roman soldiers find their way to the virtue they need.

To make each path easier to follow, encourage your students to use a different color for each word.

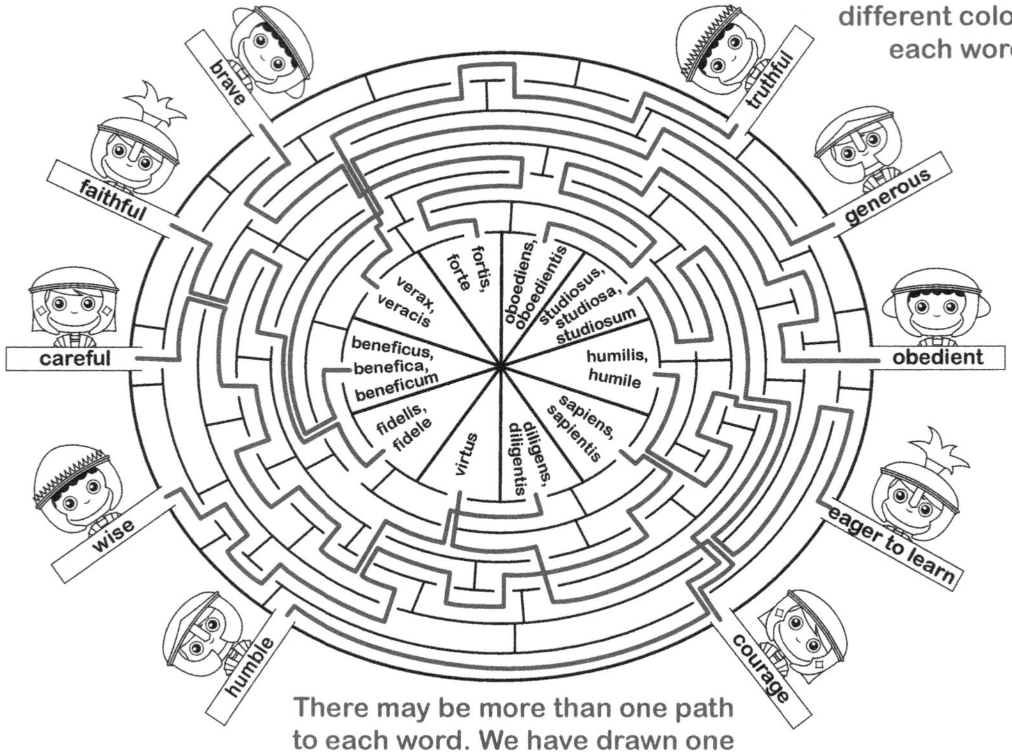

There may be more than one path to each word. We have drawn one option for each.

III. **Grow Your Virtues:** Plant the seeds (Latin words) to grow the plants (English words). Draw lines to plant your seeds in the correct pots.

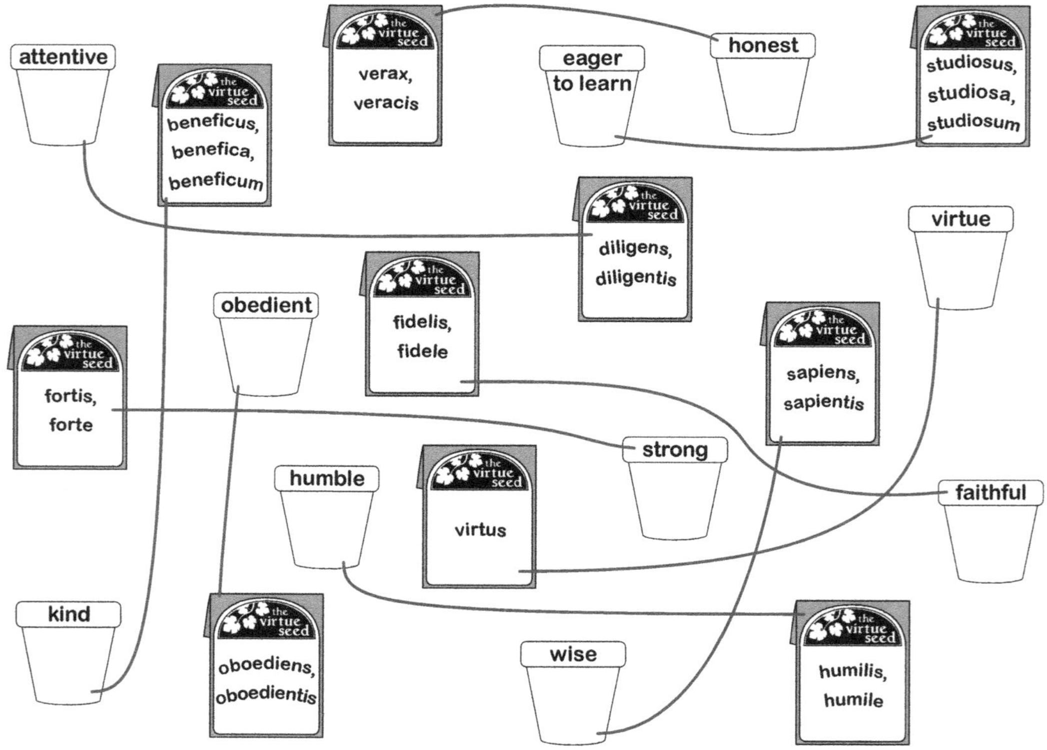

IV. Can you think of animals that we associate with some of the virtues that you have learned in this chapter? In each of the following boxes, draw a picture of an animal that may show the virtue with which the box is labeled.

Answers will vary. The following are ideas for the three virtues. Fortis: lion, dog, horse. Sapiens: fox, owl, ant. Oboediens: dog, horse, cow, dolphin, sheep, trained lions, etc. Some students may offer unexpected answers, but if they can make a case for them, it shows they are thinking about the words.

fortis	**sapiens**	**oboediens**

Show What You Know

I. Draw lines to match each Latin word with the correct English meaning.

1. **fortis, forte**	obedient
2. **humilis, humile**	brave, strong
3. **oboediens, oboedientis**	humble
4. **studiosus, studiosa, studiosum**	careful, attentive
5. **fidelis, fidele**	wise
6. **diligens, diligentis**	eager to learn
7. **sapiens, sapientis**	truthful, honest
8. **virtus**	kind, generous
9. **verax, veracis**	faithful
10. **beneficus, benefica, beneficum**	virtue, courage, excellence

II. Write the meaning, in English, of the famous saying from this chapter: **Dum spiro, spero.**

While I breathe, I hope.

III. In the following table, write out the first declension endings.

Case	Singular	Plural
Nominative	-a	-ae
Genitive	-ae	-arum
Dative	-ae	-is
Accusative	-am	-as
Ablative	-a	-is

IV. **Review:** Write out names of the noun cases.

Nominative

Genitive

Dative

Accusative

Ablative

Master Your Words

In this unit you learned more than forty new words! It's time once again to make sure you have mastered all of these newest words. Provide the correct English translation for each of the following Latin words.

Chapter 20 New Words

1. **negotium** job, occupation
2. **poeta** poet
3. **vigil** guard, policeman, fireman
4. **tabernarius** shopkeeper
5. **architectus** architect
6. **artifex** artist
7. **medicus** doctor

Chapter 20 Review Words

1. **cibus** food
2. **cena** dinner
3. **edo** I eat
4. **familia** family
5. **ludus** game, school, play

Chapter 21 New Words

1. **agricola** farmer
2. **structor** builder
3. **nauta** sailor
4. **venator** hunter
5. **athleta** athlete
6. **musicus** male musician
   musica female musician
7. **scriptor** writer
8. **senator** senator, politician

Chapter 21 Review Words

1. **panis** bread
2. **crustulum** cookie
3. **lac** milk
4. **patria** country, fatherland
5. **populus** people

Chapter 22 New Words

1. sub — under
2. supra — over, above, on top of
3. prope — near
4. trans — across
5. ex — out of
6. ad — to, toward
7. circum — around
8. pone — behind

Chapter 22 Review Words

1. nix — snow
2. imber — rain
3. nimbus — cloud
4. arcus — rainbow
5. vinco — I conquer

Chapter 23 New Words

1. contra — against
2. dum — while
3. extra — outside of
4. inter — between, among
5. ante — before
6. post — after
7. cum — with
8. sursum — up
9. de — down from, concerning, about

Chapter 23 Review Words

1. hiems — winter
2. ver — spring
3. autumnus — fall
4. aestas — summer

Chapter 24 New Words

1. **fortis, forte** — brave, strong
2. **fidelis, fidele** — faithful
3. **humilis, humile** — humble
4. **diligens, diligentis** — careful, attentive
5. **sapiens, sapientis** — wise
6. **oboediens, oboedientis** — obedient
7. **verax, veracis** — truthful, honest
8. **beneficus, benefica, beneficum** — kind, generous
9. **studiosus, studiosa, studiosum** — eager to learn
10. **virtus** — virtue, courage, excellence

Chapter 24 Review Words

1. **caelum** — sky
2. **stella** — star
3. **sol** — sun
4. **saepe** — often
5. **cito** — fast, quickly

Master Your Songs

<u>**The Negotium Song, Part I**</u> [Track 20(C)/50(E)]

There's lots of things that you could do
When you grow tall and strong.
The **negotium** that's right for you,
That you'll love all day long!

When Jack fell down and broke his crown
His mother called the doctor
And the **medicus** made Jack lay down
And soon Jack felt much better.

When you see a **vigil** who guards your town,
A **vigil** strong and brave,
Make sure you thank him for his work,
Give him a smile and wave.

An **architectus** draws designs
For buildings tall and bold.
An **artifex** is glad, I'm told
When his artwork is all sold.

When you walk into the general store,
Say, "Hello, **Tabernarius**!"
And buy a book of a **poeta**
And read the poems to us!

<u>**The Negotium Song, Part II**</u> [Track 21(C)/51(E)]

An **agricola** on a summer day
Went out to plant some hay.
A **venator** shot down a deer
While the **nauta** sailed away!
The **musicus** played a pretty song,
And a **scriptor** wrote a book,
The **senators** passed a brand-new law,
And locked up every crook.

An **athleta** and a mouse did race.
The mouse, he took first place.
A **structor** built a fancy house
With lots of rooms and space.

The Shoe Song [Track 22(C)/52(E)]

"It's time to go," Dad says.
I look under and near the bed.
I look for my shoes, which I always lose,
Sub and **prope** the bed!

"Please hurry, or we'll be late.
We must drive across the state.
Trans the whole state, **ad** grandma's house,
To grandmother's house by eight!"

I look behind the chairs.
I look above the stairs.
Pone the chairs, **supra** the stairs,
Can't find them anywhere.

Our dog strolls into the house
With one of my shoes in his mouth
We circled him—**circum**—and saw
My shoe locked tight in his jaw.

Visiting Song [Track 23(C)/53(E)]

I ran up the hill with my friend,
Cum amicus, my best friend.
Sursum the hill, then **de** the hill,
Up and down the hill we went.

We went to visit the goat,
He lives **extra**, outside of a moat.
Between the trees, among the bees,
He paddles around in his boat!

After dinner, **post** eating, we went
To visit the cow in a tent.
He was building a stall, **contra** the wall,
And hoping to charge us rent.

While walking home in the dark,
Dum walking, we went through the park.
Ante we got home, we heard a big boom!
Ran all the way home in the dark.

Grow My Virtus [Track 24(C)/54(E)]

I'm gonna grow my **virtus** every day, uh-huh,
Grow **virtus** as I work and play, uh-huh.
Verax, truthful words I'll say, truthful words will win the day,
Be **fortis**, brave and strong, along the way.

Fidelis, faithful, that's what I should be,
Diligens, working carefully!
Oboediens, doing what's asked of me, obedient to my family,
And **humilis**, with humility, uh-huh.

Beneficus, helping family and friends,
Studiosus, learning my numbers, chants, and blends!
I'm going to work to be wise or **sapiens**, I'll thank my parents, teachers, and friends.
I'm gonna grow my **virtus** every day, uh-huh.

Bonus Chant: First Declension Endings Chant [Track 25(C)/55(E)]

-a, -ae, -ae, -am, -a
-ae, -arum, -is, -as, -is

-a, -ae, -ae, -am, -a
-ae, -arum, -is, -as, -is

Word Review Activities

I. **Crossword Puzzle:** Use the English clues to fill in the puzzle with Latin words.

Across

2. Come play _______ me!
8. We will read a book _______ dinner.
9. Climb _______ the ladder to pick apples.
11. It takes a _______ soldier to fight the enemy!
13. The chipmunk popped _______ his hole.
15. The _______ mother bird fed her chicks.
16. A leader must have ______ to set a good example.
17. I arrange words in patterns.
18. Start each school day with a _______ attitude!

Down

1. Ants are _______ because they gather food for winter.
3. The scarecrow is standing _______ two cornstalks.
4. Come play _______ me!
5. Listen, and I'll play you a song.
6. My job is to capture beauty.
7. Look _______ the bed.
10. Be _______ because pride goes before a fall!
12. The _______ dog lay down immediately.
14. I put stories on paper.
17. Look _______ the door for the broom.
19. I climbed _______ the highest branch of the tree.

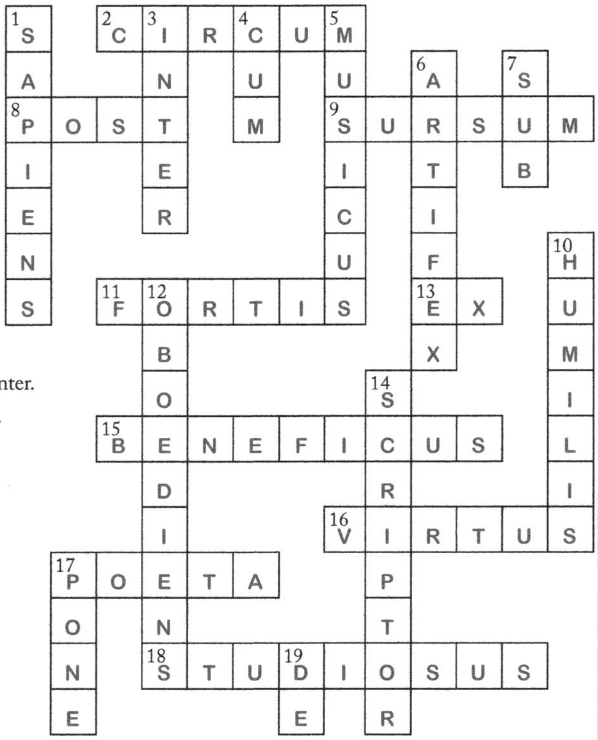

II. **Sample Sentences:** Study the sentences below and then answer the questions that follow each one.

1. **Fortis ursa ambulat pone virum***. The brave bear walks behind the man.

   What kind of word is **fortis**? ______ adjective ______

   What kind of word is **pone**? ______ preposition ______

2. **Venator spectat ursam***. The hunter looks at the bear.

   Is the verb **spectat** in the past, present, or future tense? ______ present ______

3. **Verax senator laudabit medicum***. The truthful/honest senator will praise the doctor.

   Is the verb **laudabit** in the past, present, or future tense? ______ future ______

4. **Vir erit verax tabernarius.** The man will be a truthful/honest shopkeeper.

   Is the verb **erit** a being verb? ______ yes ______

   Is the verb **erit** in the past, present, or future tense? ______ future ______

5. **Marcus est diligens discipulus.** Mark is a diligent student.

   What kind of word is **diligens**? ______ adjective ______

6. **Scriptor et musicus sunt amici.** The writer and musician are friends.

   Is the noun **amici** singular (meaning one person) or plural (meaning two or more)? ______ plural ______

7. **Puella erat studiosa musica.** The girl was an eager musician.

   Is the being verb **erat** in the past, present, or future tense? ______ past ______

*Note that often nouns that are receiving the action of the verb (or that follow certain prepositions) end with an **m** and are in the accusative case.

III. **Matching:** Draw lines to help each worker find his **negotioum**!

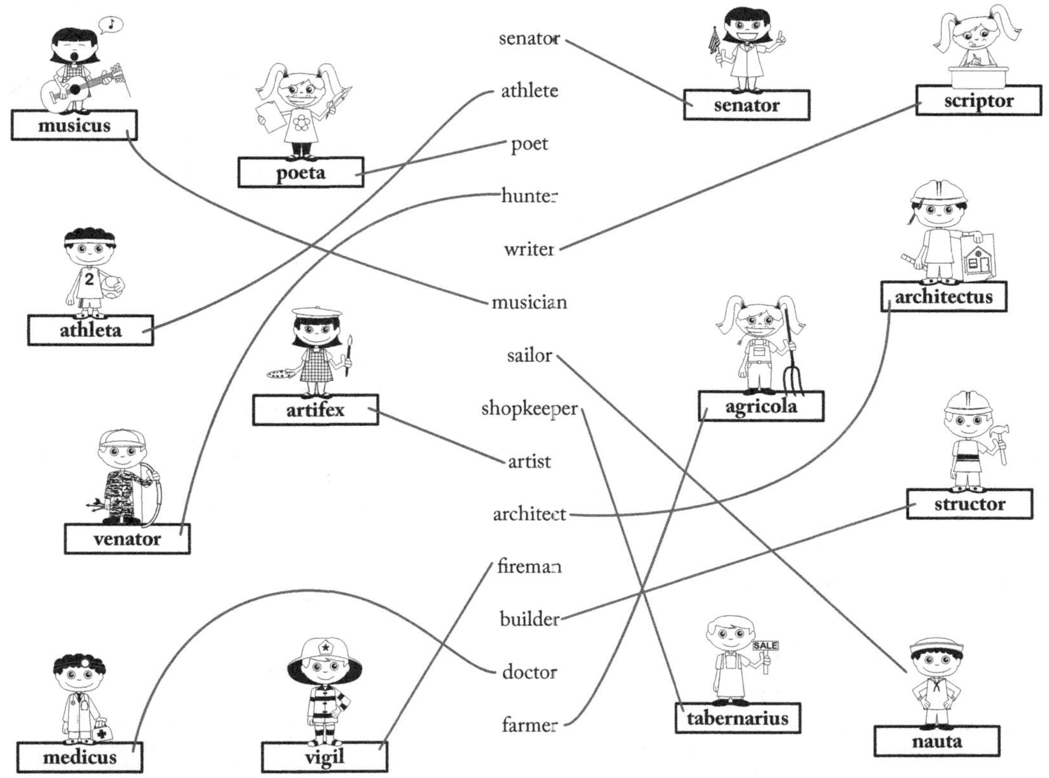

IV. **Write!** Choose four of your favorite workers from the previous exercise and write sentences about them or what they do. You can use forms of **sum** or other verbs you know. You can also use English words along with the Latin words you know. Try to use some future or imperfect endings on the verbs. If you need ideas for words, look at the review chapters and also the following word bank. Here are a couple of examples to get you started:

Poeta scribebit saepe.	The poet will write often.
Tabernarius portabat feles.	The shopkeeper was carrying the cat.

1. Answers will vary.______________________

2. ____________________________________

3. ____________________________________

4. ____________________________________

Word Bank:

laborat he/she works/is working	**humilis** humble
laudat he/she praises	**pater** father
ambulat he/she walks	**miles** soldier
currit he/she runs	**lente** slowly
clamat he/she shouts	**saepe** often
videt he/she sees	**numquam** never
scribit he/she writes/is writing	**magister** teacher
equitat he/she rides	**puella** girl
portat he/she carries	**equus** horse
narrat he/she says/tells	**feles** cat
amat he/she loves	**casa** house
spectat he/she looks at	**liber** book
vincit he/she conquers	**herba** plant/herb
vocat he/she calls	**leo** lion
bonus, -a good	**frater** brother

V. **Simeon Says!** Listen carefully to the instructions your teacher gives. *Only* follow the instructions if your teacher first says, "Simeon says." If you follow the directions when your teacher does not say, "Simeon says," you will be eliminated from the game. You will need to do your best listening and remember your Latin prepositions! ◊

◊ **Review prepositions by giving commands in Latin. The following is a sampling of commands; feel free to mix them up and also to make up your own. Use more or less Latin in each command depending on the confidence of your students.**

1. Put your **manus supra** your **caput.** Put your hand above your head.
2. Put your right **pes pone** your left **pes.** Put your right foot behind your left foot.
3. Stand **prope** the **porta.** Stand near the door/gate.
4. Rub your **manus trans** your stomach. Rub your hand across your stomach.
5. Take your **pes** out of your shoe. Take your foot out of your shoe.
6. Walk **ad** the front of the classroom. Walk to the front of the classroom.
7. Push **contra** the wall **dum** counting to **decem** in Latin. Push against the wall while counting to ten in Latin
8. Walk **circum** your **sella.** Walk around your chair.
9. Pull your **auris de** (gently!). Pull your ear down (gently!).
10. Roll your **oculi sursum** and **de.** Roll your eyes up and down.
11. Push your **nares contra a liber post** putting your **manus circum** your neck. Push your nose against a book after putting your hand around your neck.
12. **Ante** placing your **corpus** in your **sella,** walk **inter** the **magister/a** and the desk/chair/bookcase **cum** your classmates. Before placing your body in your chair, walk between the teacher and the desk/chair/bookcase with your classmates.

Master Your Chants◊◊

Future Tense of Sum

Person	Singular	Plural
First Person	**ero** (I will be)	**erimus** (we will be)
Second Person	**eris** (you will be)	**eritis** (you all will be)
Third Person	**erit** (he/she/it will be)	**erunt** (they will be)

Imperfect (Past) Tense of Sum

Person	Singular	Plural
First Person	**era*m*** (I was)	**era*mus*** (we were)
Second Person	**era*s*** (you were)	**era*tis*** (you all were)
Third Person	**era*t*** (he/she/it was)	**era*nt*** (they were)

Imperfect Tense Verb Endings

Person	Singular	Plural
First Person	**-bam**	**-bamus**
Second Person	**-bas**	**-batis**
Third Person	**-bat**	**-bant**

◊◊ **Students should take the time to review the following chants until they can recite them from memory without looking at them. For additional practice, you may want to have students write out these chants from memory on a whiteboard or separate piece of paper.**

Future Tense Verb Endings

Person	Singular	Plural
First Person	**-bo**	**-bimus**
Second Person	**-bis**	**-bitis**
Third Person	**-bit**	**-bunt**

Noun Cases:

Never Give Davus Any Apples!
Nominative
Genitive
Dative
Accusative
Ablative

First Declension Noun Endings

Case	Singular	Plural
Nominative	**-a**	**-ae**
Genitive	**-ae**	**-arum**
Dative	**-ae**	**-is**
Accusative	**-am**	**-as**
Ablative	**-a**	**-is**

Master Your Famous Sayings

On the lines provided, write the English translations of the famous Latin sayings.

1. **Ars longa, vita brevis.** Art is long, life is brief.
2. **Carpe diem!** Seize the day!
3. **Ad astra per aspera!** To the stars through difficulties!
4. **Dum spiro, spero.** While I breathe, I hope.
5. **Fortes fortuna iuvat!** Fortune favors the brave!

Master Your Derivatives

Draw lines to match the Latin words to their English derivatives. If you do it correctly, you will see a familiar shape. Once the shape is revealed, label it with the correct Latin name for the person who uses it, and then color the shape in.

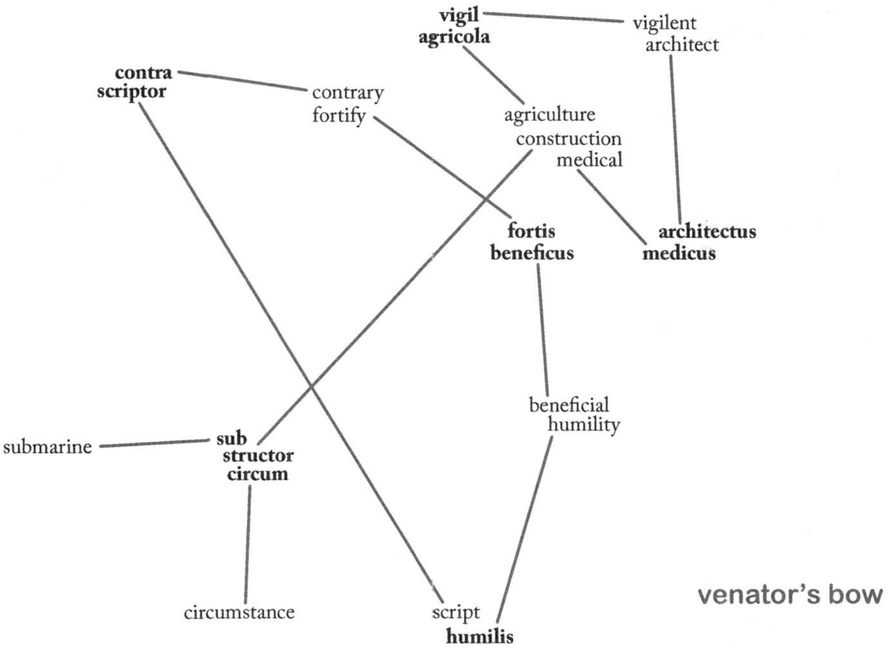

Chapter 26

Time for Bed!

Words to Learn

1. **dormio**	I sleep
2. **fessus, fessa, fessum**	tired*
3. **lectus**	bed
4. **fabula**	story
5. **balneum**	bath
6. **prex**	prayer
7. **stratum**	blanket
8. **lux**	light
9. **nox**	night
10. **carmen**	song

Review Words

1. **unda**	wave
2. **lacus**	lake
3. **flumen**	river
4. **diligenter**	carefully
5. **forte**	bravely

*Remember, when we list multiple endings for words that's so that you can see the genders that the word can take. For instance, **fessus** is masculine, **fessa** is feminine, and **fessum** is neuter.

Chapter Song

<u>Bedtime Song</u> [Track 26(C)/56(E)]

First a bath, **balneum**,
Then I tidy my bedroom,
Then my **pater** tucks me in,
In my fuzzy blue **stratum**.

A **fabula**,
A bedtime tale,
Makes me sleepy, without fail. *(x2)*

I say a **prex**, say a prayer,
Sing a **carmen** with my **mater**,
But she tells me that time flies
So I close my **fessus** eyes.

Nox brings rest
For a new day,
Strength for work and for play. *(x2)*

Dormio, I sleep tight
In my **lectus**, through the **nox**, night
With my **nox lux**, shining bright light,
Keeping company tonight.

Dormio, sweetly sleep
In my **lectus**, counting sheep. *(x2)*

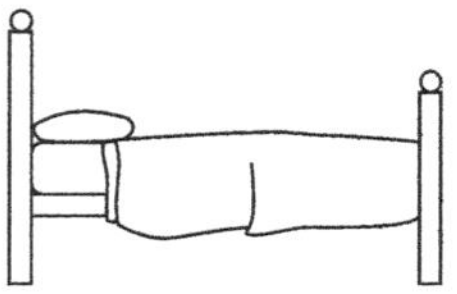

Famous Saying

Fiat lux! = Let there be light!

These words were spoken at the beginning of creation, and the sun, moon, and stars came into being to light our universe. You can also think of **fiat lux** as gaining new information or wisdom that "lights" up a puzzle or problem. When you suddenly understand something, it feels like someone said, "**Fiat lux**!"

Chapter Lesson

You have mastered the first declension noun endings now, so it is time to move on to second declension nouns. The nouns in this family are listed in a dictionary (and your vocabulary list) with the endings **-us** or **-um**. The endings you see below are for the words that end in **-us**. Words that end in **-us** are masculine, so these are *second declension masculine endings*. Every noun is masculine, feminine, or neuter. Sometimes it is very obvious why a word might be masculine or feminine, such as when one names a male or female, but often it is not so obvious. Take a look at the endings below and practice chanting them.

<u>Second Declension Masculine Endings</u>

Case	Singular	Plural
Nominative	**-us**	**-i**
Genitive	**-i**	**-orum**
Dative	**-o**	**-is**
Accusative	**-um**	**-os**
Ablative	**-o**	**-is**

You can chant these endings with a rhythm pattern like this: quick-quick-slow, slow, slow, quick-quick-slow, slow, slow.

Now here is a chart showing **lectus** (bed) with all of these endings attached:

Case	Singular	Plural
Nominative	**lect-us**	**lect-i**
Genitive	**lect-i**	**lect-orum**
Dative	**lect-o**	**lect-is**
Accusative	**lect-um**	**lect-os**
Ablative	**lect-o**	**lect-is**

Sample Phrases and Sentences

The following are some phrases that feature **lectus**, **lacus**, and **medicus**, all of which are second declension masculine nouns because they end in **-us**. Note that in the plural nominative form they end in **-i**. Note the use of the past, present, and future forms of **sum**!◊

Unus lectus.	One bed.
Duo lecti.	Two beds.
Unus lacus.	One lake.
Tres laci.	Three lakes.
Marcus est medicus.	Mark is a doctor.
Marcus et Julia sunt medici.	Mark and Julia are doctors.
Marcus eram medicus.	Mark was a doctor.
Marcus erit medicus.	Mark will be a doctor.
Eramus medici.	We were doctors.
Erant medici.	They were doctors.
Erimus medici.	We will be doctors.

◊ Students may need to review the forms of **sum** in the past, present, and future tenses. **Medicus** (from chapter 20) is a masculine noun but can be changed into a feminine form for females (**medica, -ae**) or stay in the masculine but nonetheless be used for females. The masculine plural (**medici**) is used with a mixed group of males and females.

Grow Your English

Fabula is a fabulous word, so good you would think it's just a fable! What are the two derivatives in that sentence? **Dormio** gives us sleepy words, such as *dormant* and *dormitory*. **Stratum** is used to name certain clouds that are stretched out over the sky like a blanket—*stratus* clouds. **Lux** gives us many words related to light, such as *lucid*, *elucidate*, and *translucent*. *Nocturnal* is an English word that comes from **nox** and can refer to creatures that are awake at night and sleep during the day, such as cats and opossums. **Fabulous and fable are two derivatives of fabula.**

Practice Your Latin

I. Practice writing your new Latin words by tracing the dots.

dormio fessus fessa prex

lectus fabula balneum

stratum lux nox carmen

II. Simeon is a **fessus** monkey and he needs to go home to sleep. Help Simeon make it to his **casa** by discovering the secret password to get through each gate. To do so, supply the Latin translation of each of the English words.

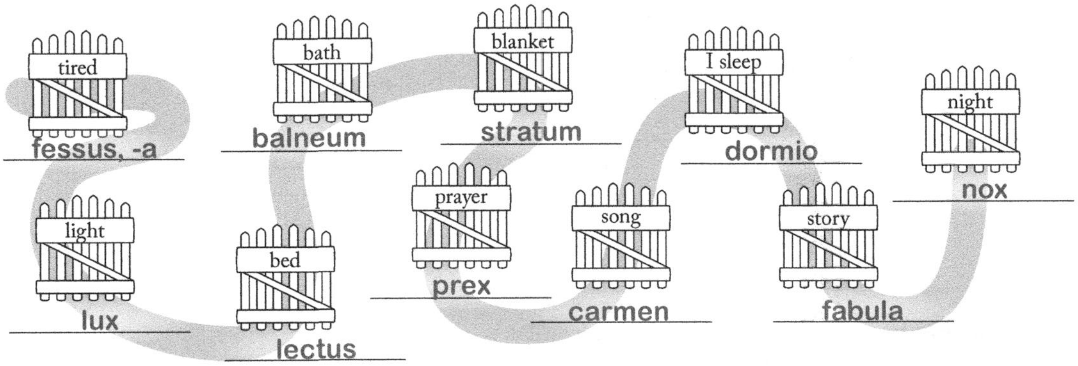

III. Fill in the blanks with Latin words.

The whole **familia** is yawning! It's time to go to **lectus**. **Nox** is here, and it is dark now. Earlier in the evening, **post cena**, we played outside while it was still **lux**. Each of us took a **balneum** so we could go to **lectus** clean and fresh. **Pater** told us a **fabula**, **Mater** sang us a **carmen**, and we climbed under the warm **stratum**. Turn out the **lux**! **Dormite bene**, everyone! (Sleep well!)

IV. Look at the picture and label everything you can with Latin words!

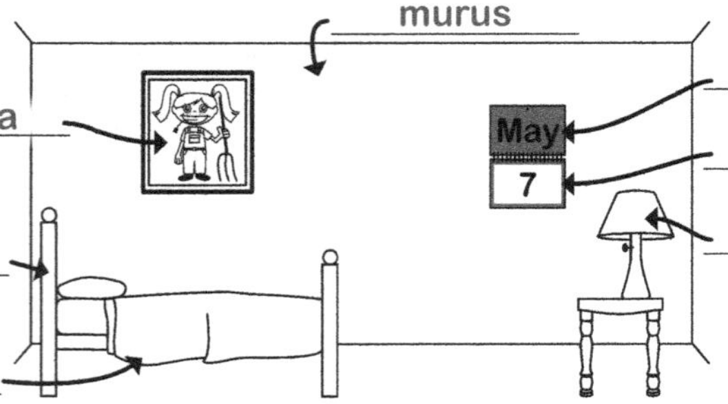

Show What You Know

I. Write the meaning, in English, of the famous saying from this chapter: **Fiat lux!**

Let there be light!

II. Circle the correct meaning for each of the following words.

1. **nox**	light	sleep	dark	(night)
2. **dormio**	(I sleep)	prayer	bed	blanket
3. **prex**	night	bath	(prayer)	story
4. **lux**	bed	night	tired	(light)
5. **fessus**	song	(tired)	story	bath
6. **stratum**	(blanket)	bed	prayer	I sleep

7. **lectus**	light	story	(bed)	blanket
8. **balneum**	song	(bath)	story	light
9. **fabula**	blanket	I sleep	night	(story)
10. **carmen**	(song)	light	tired	blanket

III. Fill in the second declension masculine endings.

Case	Singular	Plural
Nominative	**-us**	-i
Genitive	-i	-orum
Dative	-o	-is
Accusative	-um	-os
Ablative	-o	-is

IV. **Derivatives:** Write the Latin word from which each English word is derived.

1. dormant dormio
2. fable fabula
3. nocturnal nox
4. stratus stratum

Chapter 27

A Time for Everything

Words to Learn

1. **tempus** time
2. **hora** hour
3. **aurora** dawn, morning
4. **vesper** evening
5. **dies** ◊ day
6. **meridies** noon
7. **septimana** week
8. **mensis** ◊ month
9. **annus** year

◊ Students may notice that they have encountered the words **dies** and **mensis** earlier in chapters 2 and 3. Since these words were taught only as part of phrases in those chapters, we thought they deserved separate emphasis in this chapter.

Review Words

1. **flos** flower
2. **hortus** garden
3. **folium** leaf
4. **negotium** job, occupation
5. **tabernarius** shopkeeper

Chapter Song

Grand Old Father Time [Track 27(C)/57(E)]

The grand old Father Time,
He marches every day.
The **Pater Tempus** chimes
Every **hora**, while we play.

Each **dies**, day, he calls,
As **aurora** breaks the sky,
And then as evening, **vesper**, falls
He bids **dies** good-bye.

Each **septimana** is a week,
Five days for work and school,
Then two days for rest and play
But remember your lunch at **meridies**
Each day when you're at school.

Each **mensis** a new moon comes
For **nox** to light the night.
Every **annus**, every night,
Pater Tempus brings us light.

The grand old Father Time,
He marches every day.
The **Pater Tempus** chimes
Every **hora**, while we play.

Famous Saying

Tempus fugit! = Time flees (flies)!

What do you think "time flees" means? We usually say "Time flies" and we mean that it passes very quickly. Sometimes it feels as though time moves very slowly, but every minute that slips by is a minute that can't be used again. Use the minutes of your days wisely, because they do not come back!

Chapter Lesson

In the previous chapter, you learned the chant for **lectus**, which showed **lectus** with all of the endings attached. In this chapter, you will learn a new chant that uses endings you already know—the first declension noun endings. You can add these endings to any first declension noun (most nouns that end in **-a**) following the example of your new chant: **hora**! Before you learn your new chant, review the first declension noun endings by chanting them.

First Declension Noun Endings

Case	Singular	Plural
Nominative	**-a**	**-ae**
Genitive	**-ae**	**-arum**
Dative	**-ae**	**-is**
Accusative	**-am**	**-as**
Ablative	**-a**	**-is**

The following is the chant and chart for **hora**:

Case	Singular	Plural
Nominative	**hora**	**horae**
Genitive	**horae**	**horarum**
Dative	**horae**	**horis**
Accusative	**horam**	**horas**
Ablative	**hora**	**horis**

Sample Sentences

Following are some sentences that feature the first declension nouns **hora**, **regina**, and **corona**. Did you notice how each of those words ends in **-a**? Note that **corona** appears in the accusative case (**coronam**—accusative singular; **coronas**—accusative plural) because it is receiving the action of a verb. You will learn more about the accusative case in your later study of Latin.◊◊

Unus lectus.	One bed.
Una hora.	One hour.*
Tres horae.	Three hours.
Julia est regina.	Julia is a queen.
Julia et Rosa sunt reginae.	Julia and Rose are queens.
Julia spectat coronam.	Julia looks at the crown.
Rosa et Julia portant coronas.	Rose and Julia carry crowns.
Rosa portat tres coronas.	Rose carries three crowns.

◊◊ As noted in chapter 26, students may need to review the use of **sum**. They should be able to recognize that **est** means "is" and **sunt** means "they are." You may want to conjugate **specto** and **porto** in the present tense so that students can see that **spectat** (third person, present, singular) means "he/she/it looks at," **portat** (third person, present, singular) means "he/she/it carries," and that **portant** (third person, present, plural) means "they carry."

The following is the conjugation for **specto** in the present tense:

Person	Singular	Plural
First Person	**specto** (I look at)	**spectamus** (we look at)
Second Person	**spectas** (you look at)	**spectatis** (you all look at)
Third Person	**spectat** (he/she/it looks at)	**spectant** (they look at)

The following is the conjugation for **porto** in the present tense:

Person	Singular	Plural
First Person	**porto** (I carry)	**portamus** (we carry)
Second Person	**portas** (you carry)	**portatis** (you all carry)
Third Person	**portat** (he/she/it carries)	**portant** (they carry)

*Notice how **unus** changed to **una** to match **hora**.

Grow Your English

The Latin word **tempus** has many English derivatives. Our word *tempo* is used to describe how fast music is played or how fast tasks are performed. Something that is *temporary* is only for a short time, something that is not permanent.

From **dies** we get *diurnal*. Do you remember "nocturnal" from the previous chapter? This word is the opposite of nocturnal; it means being awake during the day and sleeping at night. What is the difference between a nocturnal and a diurnal creature? Which one are you? Can you think of other examples of both?◊◊◊ You might have guessed this, but **meridies** means the "middle of the day" or noon!

Diary, a journal in which you write every day, also comes from **dies**. Do you keep a diary or a journal?

Annus is another word that is important to the English language. We get our word *annual* from it, which means "yearly." There are other forms of the word *annual*, such as *semiannual* and *biannual*. We also get our word "anniversary" from it. Do you know what an anniversary is? **An anniversary is the annual recurrence of a date marking a significant event.**

Practice Your Latin

I. Practice writing your new Latin words by tracing the dots.

tempus hora aurora

vesper dies meridies

septimana mensis annus

◊◊◊ Some examples of nocturnal animals include moths, owls, and cats. Some examples of diurnal animals include people, dogs, horses, and cows.

II. **Fill out the Calendar!** Draw lines to match the English words to the correct Latin words on the calendar.

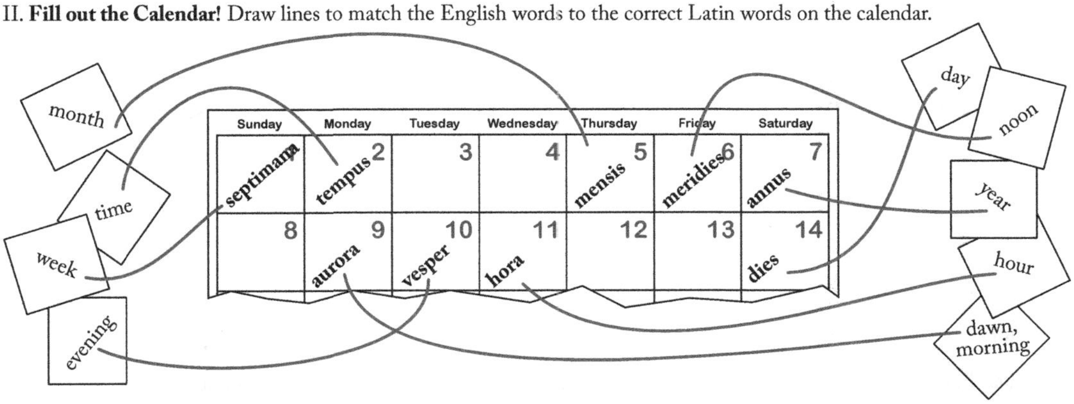

III. Circle the best word to complete each sentence.

1. Simeon is planning out his ____ (**meridies** / **dies** / **annus**), from **aurora** to **nox**.
2. It's Simeon's birthday! Since it only comes once a ____ (**septimana** / **dies** / **annus**), pick his gift carefully.
3. I like to watch the stars come out one by one in the ____ (**vesper** / **hora** / **mensis**).
4. August, the hottest ____ (**mensis** / **septimana** / **dies**) of the year in many climates, is the perfect time to go swimming.
5. It takes me one ____ (**tempus** / **meridies** / **hora**) to do my homework each afternoon.
6. I would love to learn five musical instruments, but I don't have enough ____ (**tempus** / **dies** / **meridies**)!
7. Simeon likes to take a break at ____ (**nox** / **meridies** / **vesper**) to eat his lunch.
8. I plan to finish reading my book in **septem dies**—one ____ (**nox** / **septimana** / **annus**).

IV. Using the words from the following word bank, fill in the best Latin word to complete each sentence. (Hint: Some of the words will be used more than once.)

Word Bank: hora mensis meridies dies septimana aurora vesper

1. In the Answers may vary, but should be either vesper or hora., after dinner, we like to read stories and play games.
2. A peanut butter and jelly sandwich is my favorite food to eat at meridies.
3. I got up early in the aurora and watched the sun rise.
4. Every dies during the holidays, we visit my grandparents.
5. We change classes about every hora at my school.
6. February is the shortest mensis of the year.
7. I ride my bike every dies, unless it is rainy.
8. My mom makes pancakes once a septimana, on Saturdays!
9. Simeon's favorite mensis of the year is December because he gets to celebrate Christmas with his family.

Show What You Know

I. Write the meaning, in English, of the famous saying from this chapter: **Tempus fugit!**

Time flees (flies!)

II. Draw lines to match the correct English meaning to each Latin word.

1. **dies**	hour
2. **septimana**	dawn, morning
3. **tempus**	evening
4. **aurora**	day
5. **annus**	time
6. **mensis**	noon
7. **hora**	week
8. **meridies**	month
9. **vesper**	year

III. Write out the **hora** chant.

Case	Singular	Plural
Nominative	**hora**	**horae**
Genitive	horae	horarum
Dative	horae	horis
Accusative	horam	horas
Ablative	hora	horis

IV. **Derivatives:** Write the Latin word from which each English word is derived. You may need to use a word more than once.

1. temporary tempus
2. anniversary annus
3. diary dies
4. diurnal dies
5. annual annus

Colors

Chapter 28

Words to Learn

1. **color** — color
   colores — colors
2. **ruber, rubra, rubrum*** — red
3. **caeruleus, caerulea, caeruleum** — blue
4. **flavus, flava, flavum** — yellow
5. **viridis, viride**** — green
6. **aurantius, aurantia, aurantium** — orange
7. **purpureus, purpurea, purpureum** — purple
8. **ater, atra, atrum** — black
9. **albus, alba, album** — white

Review Words

1. **mons** — mountain
2. **saxum** — rock
3. **collis** — hill
4. **structor** — builder
5. **venator** — hunter

*Some Latin adjectives will end in **-er** in the nominative singular case when you might expect **-us**.
****Viridis, viride** is a third declension adjective that has a different pattern and different endings than the second declension adjectives that you have learned. You will learn the pattern and endings for adjectives such as **viridis, viride** in your later study of Latin.

203

Chapter Song

<u>The Colores Song</u> [Track 28(C)/58(E)]

I love to paint when it's time for art,
I make each color play a part.
Ruber is the color of my go-cart.
Aurantius is the color of morning sky, morning sky, morning sky.
It's also the color of a fruit I like
And **flavus** is the color of banana pie!

My favorite animal is black and white.
It loves to kick and it just might bite,
The stripes are a style that's quite the sight.
The black stripes we'll call **atra, atra, atra**.
The snowy white stripes are **alba**, white,
But the black stripes we'll call **atra**.

Viridis, green, are the leaves in spring.
Caeruleus, blue, are the birds on wing.
Purpureus, the royal robes of a king.
Flavus, the glow of candlelight, candlelight, candlelight.
Purpureus, the royal robes of a king,
And **flavus** is color of his golden ring.

Well, I love to paint and I love art,
Yes, and every color has a part
And I think the colors all look smart.
Atra, alba, and **ruber** bright, **ruber** bright, **ruber** bright.
Atra and **alba** sure look nice,
But I'm in love with **ruber** bright.

204 Chapter 28: Colors

Famous Saying

Veritas vos liberabit. = The truth will make you free.

This saying is chiseled in stone over the entrance to the library at the University of Virginia, though it's written in Greek instead of Latin. There are many different ways in which this saying can be applied. It may be a truth that helps you understand how you should live or how to handle a specific situation. It might simply be understanding how to do something or how something works that gives you freedom.

Chapter Lesson

Your new chant is a second declension masculine noun with all of its endings. This is the new set of endings that you learned in chapter 26, only now they have been applied to a noun. The second declension endings have been italicized so that you can see them better. Chant and memorize!

Case	Singular	Plural
Nominative	**hort*us***	**hort*i***
Genitive	**hort*i***	**hort*orum***
Dative	**hort*o***	**hort*is***
Accusative	**hort*um***	**hort*os***
Ablative	**hort*o***	**hort*is***

Grow Your English

You can see that our language borrowed the word *color* directly from Latin, as well as all the "colorful" words related to it.

An *albino* is a person or creature that is lacking pigment (color), so he or she appears very **albus**. Do you see how "albino" is derived from **albus**?

Practice Your Latin

I. Practice writing your new Latin words by tracing the dots.

color colores ruber rubra

rubrum caeruleus caerulea

caeruleum flavus flava

flavum viridis viride

aurantius aurantia aurantium

purpureus purpurea

purpureum ater atra atrum

albus alba album

II. In the blank provided, write the name of an item in your classroom or your house for each color. **Answers will vary. The English translations of the Latin words have been provided for your reference.**

a. **flavus** yellow

b. **caeruleus** blue

c. **purpureus** purple

d. **albus** white

e. **ruber** red

f. **ater** black

g. **viridis** green

h. **aurantius** orange

i. **multi colores** many colors

Hint: You haven't learned the Latin word **multi**, but it should be easy for you to figure out what it means, since it means the same thing in English that it does in Latin!

III. Fill in the blanks with the correct Latin color. (Hint: Some of the blanks could have more than one answer.)

1. Name three colors that apples can be! ruber (red), viridis (green), flavus (yellow)
2. Name three colors that you may see in the sky. Answers will vary, but should probably be one of the following colors: caelum (blue), albus (white), aurantius (orange), ater (black), ruber (red), purpureus (purple), flavus (yellow)
3. Roses are ruber (red), violets are purpureus (purple) or caeruleus (blue)
4. A tiger is aurantius (orange) with ater (black) stripes.
5. My favorite sports team's colors are Answers will vary. and Answers will vary..
6. In my salad are aurantius (orange) carrots, viridis (green) lettuce, and ruber (red) tomatoes.
7. Brush your teeth to keep them nice and albus (white)!
8. Sometimes the ocean looks caeruleus (blue), and sometimes it looks viridis (green).
9. The ater (black) horse blended into the dark night.
10. When I'm sunburned, my cheeks and nose turn ruber (red).
11. The American flag is ruber (red), albus (white), and caeruleus (blue).
12. My favorite color is Answers will vary..

IV. **Color by Number!** Color each section according to the corresponding number provided in the box below. On the blank provided, write the Latin word for the picture you discovered.

corona

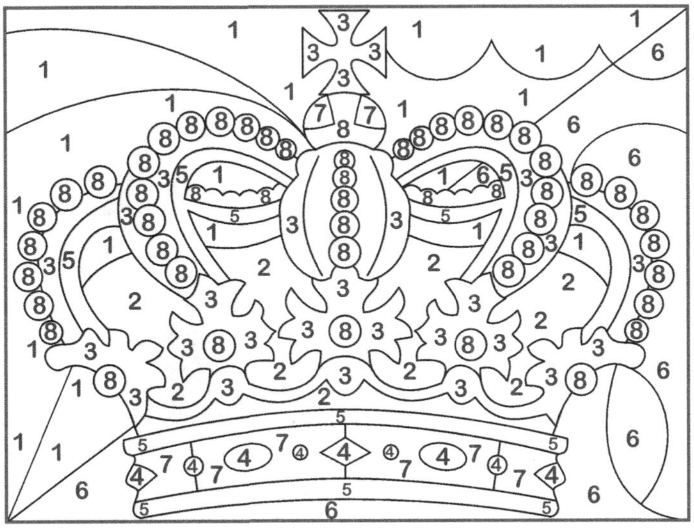

1 - **ruber** red
2 - **caeruleus** blue
3 - **flavus** yellow
4 - **viridis** green
5 - **aurantius** orange
6 - **purpureus** purple
7 - **ater** black
8 - **albus** white

Show What You Know

I. Write the meaning, in English, of the famous saying from this chapter: **Veritas vos liberabit.**

The truth will set you free.

II. Draw lines to match the correct English meaning to each Latin word.

1. **purpureus, purpurea, purpureum**	blue
2. **colores**	green
3. **viridis, viride**	red
4. **caeruleus, caerulea, caeruleum**	yellow
5. **aurantius, aurantia, aurantium**	white
6. **ruber, rubra, rubrum**	colors
7. **flavus, flava, flavum**	orange
8. **ater, atra, atrum**	purple
9. **albus, alba, album**	black

III. In the following table, write out the **hortus** chant. The first one has been filled in for you. ◊

Case	Singular	Plural
Nominative	**hortus**	horti
Genitive	horti	hortorum
Dative	horto	hortis
Accusative	hortum	hortos
Ablative	horto	hortis

◊ If students have difficulty filling out this table, you can point them to the table on p. 205 of the SE.

IV. **Derivatives:** Write the Latin word from which each English word is derived.

1. albino albus
2. colorful color

Chapter 29 Around the Palace

Words to Learn

1. **tyrannus** ruler, dictator
2. **solium** throne
3. **servus** male slave
4. **gemma** jewel
5. **aurum** gold
6. **regnum** kingdom
7. **regno** I reign

Review Words

1. **sub** under
2. **supra** above
3. **rex** king
4. **regina** queen
5. **corona** crown

Chapter Song

Mr. King Folium [Track 29(C)/59(E)]

There was an old **rex**
Named Mr. King **Folium**.
He sat on a throne
Named Mr. **Solium**
And told his **servus**

To bring him a nummy-num.
Hungry old Mr. King **Folium, Folium**.

There was a little queen
Named Mrs. Queen **Regina**.
She loved to dress up
In her gold, gold **corona**.
That **aurum** crown
Had a great big **gemma**
Always on Queen **Regina, Regina**.

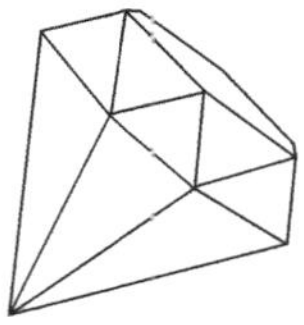

A frog one day said,
"I'll take over.
I'll make a fine **tyrannus, tyrannus**, ruler.
I'll steal the crown **gemma**
from the royal jeweler.
Regno, I rule, I'm the ruler, ruler!"

Queen **Regina** and Mr. King **Folium**
Had a powwow
And took back the **regnum**.
"Mr. Mean Frog, your time has finally come.
Leave our **solium** and our **regnum, regnum**!"

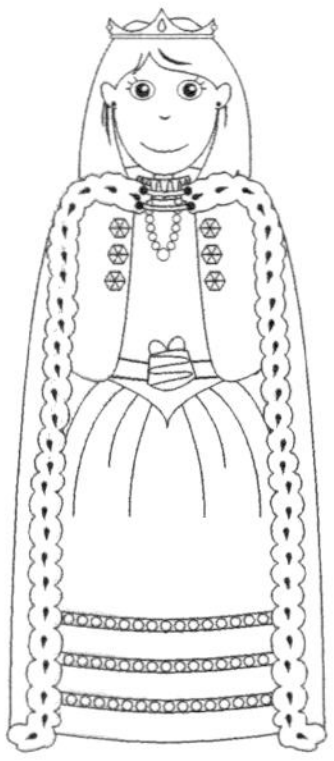

Famous Saying

Regnat populus. = The people rule.

Regnat populus was adopted as the official motto of the state of Arkansas in 1907. Note that **populus** (people) is a singular noun because it refers to "people" as one group. The plural of **populus** is **populi** (peoples). You might have noticed that you learned this saying in chapter 14!

Chapter Lesson

The new endings for this chapter are second declension *neuter* noun endings. Remember that in Latin, nouns can be masculine, feminine, or neuter. In Latin, many different kinds of places or things can be neuter! Neuter nouns in the second declension will always end in **-um** in the nominative case. This set of endings is very similar to the second declension masculine endings; in fact, you will only see three endings that are different. Find and circle them! Now practice chanting the neuter endings.

Case	Singular	Plural
Nominative	**-um**	**-a**
Genitive	**-i**	**-orum**
Dative	**-o**	**-is**
Accusative	**-um**	**-a**
Ablative	**-o**	**-is**

Now that you have learned the noun endings for second declension neuter nouns, try chanting or singing them to help you master them. Try chanting the endings slowly and quietly, then chant them loudly and quickly. Chant these ending frequently enough that you can't forget them!

Grow Your English

Do you see the letters **reg** in several of the words in this chapter's vocabulary list? Our language uses this root for words that have to do with ruling or royalty. Something that is *regal* is royal or kingly! To *regulate* means to control something. A *region* may just mean a geographical area to us, but at its root it means an area that is ruled.

Think of the Latin word **corona** and see if you can guess the meaning of the English word *coronate*, if you do not already know it. Coronate means to crown a person—to invest that person with royal power.

Where do you think the English word *gem* comes from? Do you have any in your house? You probably do, but back in Ancient Rome, they would only be found in the wealthiest homes. Gem is derived from gemma.

Practice Your Latin

I. Practice writing your new Latin words by tracing the dots.

tyrannus solium servus

gemma aurum regnum regno

II. Draw lines to match each **gemma** to its proper setting.

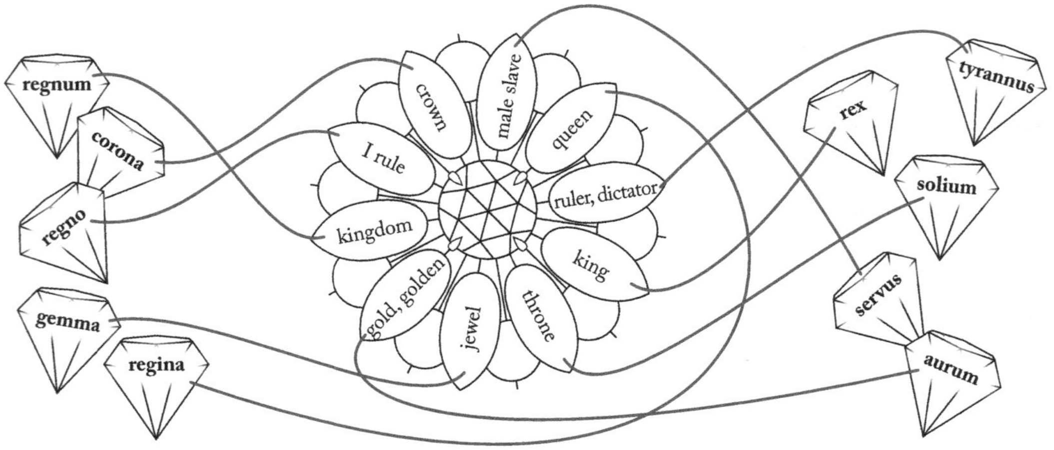

III. What is wrong with this picture? Follow the directions to fix the problems!

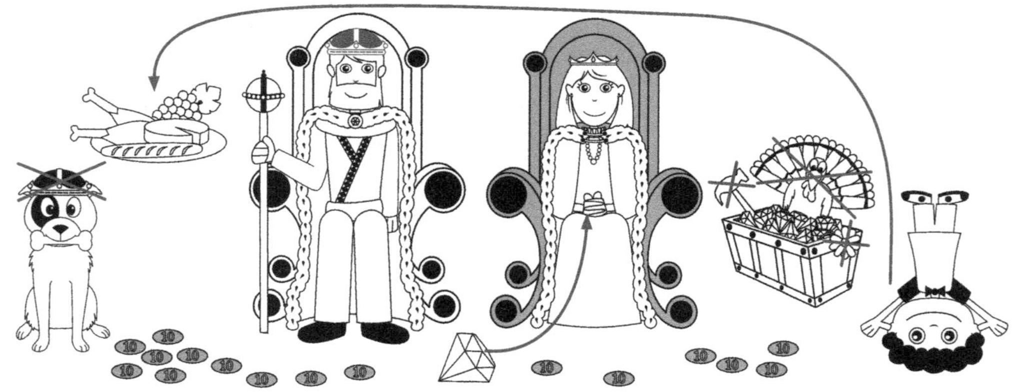

1. Cross out the **corona** on the head of the **canis**.
   Cross out the crown on the head of the dog.
2. Find the **gemma** on the floor and draw an arrow to put it on the **regina**'s finger.
   Find the jewel on the floor and draw and arrow to put it on the queen's finger
3. The **regina**'s **solium** should be **aureum**. Color it!
   The queen's throne should be gold. Color it!
4. Why is the **servus** standing on his head? Draw an arrow to point him to the platter he should be holding for the **rex**.
   Why is the male slave standing on his head? Draw an arrow to point him to the platter he should be holding for the king.
5. The **aurum** coins are scattered! Help the **rex** find them by coloring them the correct color.
   The gold coins are scattered! Help the king find them by coloring them the correct color.
6. Cross out any item in the jewelry box that is not a **gemma**.
   Cross any items in the jewerly box that is not a jewel.
7. The **rex** needs a **corona**. Give him one!
   The kind needs a crown. Give him one!

IV. Visiting a King and Queen: Imagine that you have been invited to join a king and queen in their palace for a wonderful feast in their throne room. What do you think you would you see when you visit the castle? On a separate sheet of paper, draw everything you would see on the visit and label as many items as you can with Latin words from the following word bank.

Word Bank: corona solium servus gemma rex regina cibus epulae

Show What You Know

I. Write the meaning, in English, of the famous saying from this chapter: **Regnat populus.**

The people rule.

II. Circle the correct meaning for each of the following words.

1. **regnum**	gold	kingdom	jewels	king
2. **regno**	I rule, I reign	queen	ruler	male slave
3. **gemma**	crown	gold	king	jewel
4. **solium**	kingdom	king	throne	slave
5. **regina**	king	crown	jewel	queen
6. **aurum**	crown	gold	ruler	I rule
7. **corona**	jewel	male slave	crown	throne
8. **servus**	male slave	king	kingdom	queen
9. **tyrannus**	gold	dictator	male slave	throne
10. **rex**	kingdom	crown	I rule	king

III. In the following table, fill in the second declension neuter chant.

Case	Singular	Plural
Nominative	**-um**	-a
Genitive	-i	-orum
Dative	-o	-is
Accusative	-um	-a
Ablative	-o	-is

IV. **Derivatives:** In the blank provided, write the Latin word from which each English word is derived.

1. regulate rex
2. coronate corona
3. regal rex
4. gem gemma

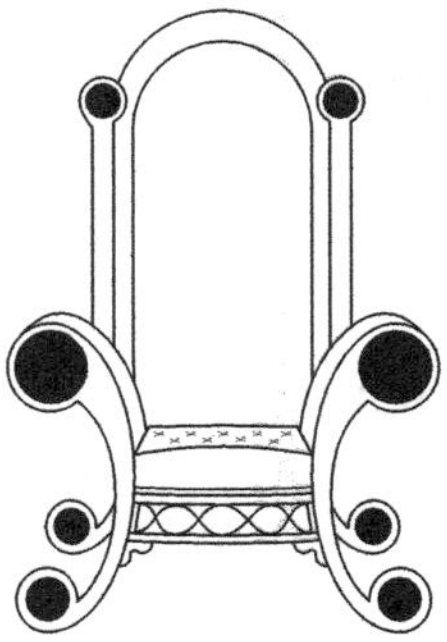

Chapter 30

Adjectives

Words to Learn

1. **magnus, magna, magnum**	great, big
2. **parvus, parva, parvum**	small
3. **pulcher, pulchra, pulchrum***	pretty, handsome
4. **altus, alta, altum**	high
5. **longus, longa, longum**	long
6. **brevis, breve**	short
7. **bonus, bona, bonum**	good
8. **malus, mala, malum**	bad
9. **rotundus, rotunda, rotundum**	round
10. **quadratus, quadrata, quadratum**	square
11. **triangulus, triangula, triangulum**	triangular

Review Words

1. **contra**	against
2. **inter**	between, among
3. **ante**	before
4. **cum**	with
5. **post**	after

*Remember, sometimes Latin adjectives will end in **-er** in the nominative singular case.

Chapter Song

Adjectives Chant [Track 30(C)/60(E)]◊

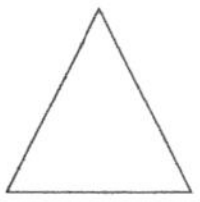

My puppy is small, he's cute and kind of **parvus**,
And most of the time he's really very **bonus**.
His tail is long; it's a tail **longus**,
His tummy is round and just a bit **rotundus**.

Is your puppy **brevis**, short and small?
Or is your puppy **altus**, high and tall?
Magnus, **parvus**, big or small?
Is it round and **rotundus**, shaped like a ball?

Maybe it's **quadratus**, shaped like a square?
Malus, bad and hairy, and mean like a bear?
Or **triangulus**, like an arrow in the air?
Or **pulchra**, **pulcher**, beautiful, and fair?

◊ This chant begs for some illustrative motions! For instance, you could have students make the following motions for the Latin words in the song:
Parvus: cup hands tightly together
Magnus: open arms wide
Longus: place hands far apart
Rotundus: shape hands into a ball
Brevis: bend down with hand low to the ground
Altus: stand up with hand at chest level
Quadratus: use hands to form a rectangle
Malus: frown and grimace with two fists raised
Triangulus: use hands to form a triangle
Pulchra: place open palms under the chin and smile

◊◊ Other examples of the magnum opus of an artist include Da Vinci's *Mona Lisa* and Monet's *Water Lilies*.

◊◊◊ Students can be prompted to recall adjectives of various kinds, such as colors and adjectives that describe size and shape. As they recall these adjectives in English, you may want to point out the Latin adjectives in this chapter that describe size and shape and the adjectives that describe color in chapter 28.

Famous Saying

Magnum opus = a great work, one's major life accomplishment

Handel's *Messiah*, a beautiful musical piece, is a **magnum opus**. Michelangelo's statue, *David*, is a **magnum opus**. Can you think of the **magnum opus** of another artist? What will your **magnum opus** be?◊◊

Chapter Lesson

All of the words in this chapter's vocabulary list have one thing in common. Do you know what it is? They can all describe or modify nouns, so they are adjectives. Can you think of other examples of adjectives in English? You probably noticed that your new words have three options for endings (except **brevis**, which only has two endings). Adjectives are flexible! That is because they have to match whatever kind of noun they are describing or modifying, whether it is masculine, feminine, or neuter.◊◊◊

In the last chapter, you learned the second declension neuter endings. Let's see what one of our new adjectives looks like with those endings.

CASE	SINGULAR	PLURAL
Nominative	**bon*um***	**bon*a***
Genitive	**bon*i***	**bon*orum***
Dative	**bon*o***	**bon*is***
Accusative	**bon*um***	**bon*a***
Ablative	**bon*o***	**bon*is***

Add this to your chanting routine!

Grow Your English

A *bonus* is always good, whatever kind it is. Any word that starts with *mal* means something bad. Examples are *malicious* (mean; evil intentions), *malpractice* (a doctor or other professional doing something wrong) and *malignant* (harmful, deadly).

Altus gives us our English word *altitude*. Can you guess where we got our words *long* and *brief*? **longus and brevis**

A *rotunda* is a circular building design. Many famous buildings, such as the United States Capitol building, have a rotunda. **Rotunda** is the feminine form of **rotundus**.

Magnify means to make something bigger. What Latin word do you think it came from? **magnus**

Practice Your Latin

I. Practice writing your new Latin words by tracing the dots.

magnus magna magnum

parvus parva parvum

pulcher pulchra pulchrum

altus alta altum longus

longa longum brevis breve

bonus bona bonum malus

mala malum rotundus

rotunda rotundum quadratus

quadrata quadratum

triangulus triangula

triangulum

II. In the blank provided, write the name of an item (or person) that could be described by each of these words. Feel free to use Latin words as answers, if you can! **Answers will vary. The English translations of the Latin words have been provided for your reference.**

1. **pulcher** pretty, handsome

2. **altus** high

3. **malus** bad

4. **brevis** short

5. **quadratus** square

6. **bonus** good

7. **longus** long

8. **rotundus** round

9. **parvus** small

10. **triangulus** triangular

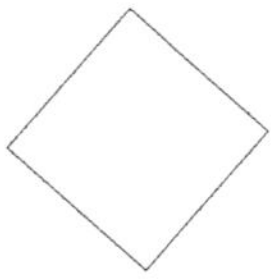

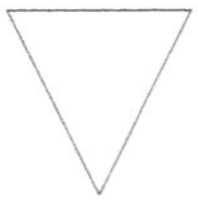

III. Draw pictures to illustrate these opposites.

Answers will vary. The English translations of the Latin words have been provided so that you can ensure that students are illustrating the correct concepts.

1. **magnus / parvus**
great, big / small

2. **altus / brevis**
high / short

3. **longus / brevis**
long / short

4. **rotundus / quadratus**
round / square

5. **malus / bonus**
bad / good

IV. Fill in each blank with the Latin adjective that fits best. (Hint: Some of the Latin adjectives you have learned will be used more than once.) **Answers may vary. Suggested answers have been provided.**

1. The ___magnus___ hippopotamus tripped over the ___parvus___ mouse.

2. A globe and a basketball both have a ___rotundus___ shape.

3. I studied hard for my test and got a ___bonus___ grade.

4. The sunset was so ___bonus, brevis, pulcher___ that we watched until it was gone.

5. Our class was cut ___brevis___ because of a fire drill!

6. I drew a ___quadratus___ pattern with chalk to play hopscotch.

7. The ladder was not ___longus___ enough to reach the third-floor window.

8. Snakes that have heads with a ___triangulus___ shape can be dangerous!

9. This is a ___malus___ apple; it has a worm in it!

10. Some planes fly so ___altus___ in the sky that you can't even see them.

V. Answer these question with Latin adjectives of your choice. **Answers will vary. Suggested answers have been provided**

1. I like to cut my sandwich into two ___triangulus___ shapes.

2. My dog has a ___rotundus, brevis, parvus, triangulus___ head.

3. The little lake house was built in a ___rotundus, quadratus, triangulus___ shape.

4. My new baby sister is very ___parvus, pulcher___.

Show What You Know

I. Write the meaning, in English, of the famous saying from this chapter: **Magnum opus**.

___a great work, one's major life accomplishment___

II. Draw lines to match the correct English meaning to each Latin word. (Hint: Be sure to pay attention to the word endings because they may provide clues.)

1. **altus**	good
2. **bonus**	pretty, handsome
3. **pulcher**	square
4. **quadratus**	short
5. **longus**	high
6. **parvus**	long
7. **triangulus**	round
8. **magnus**	bad
9. **brevis**	small
10. **rotundus**	triangular
11. **malus**	great, big

III. In the following table, fill in the **bonum** chant.

Case	Singular	Plural
Nominative	**bonum**	bona
Genitive	boni	bonorum
Dative	bono	bonis
Accusative	bonum	bona
Ablative	bono	bonis

IV. **Derivatives:** In the blank provided, write the Latin word from which each English word is derived.

1. malicious ___malus___
2. altitude ___altus___
3. magnify ___magnus___
4. bonus ___bonus___

Congratulations!

You have just learned 175 Latin words and a good bit of Latin grammar. You are now perfectly poised to start *Latin for Children Primer A* (*LFCA*). In fact, you have already learned the grammar for the first unit of *LFCA* (and part of the second unit) as well as 75 Latin words from *LFCA*—so you will start the book with review! You have learned present, imperfect (past), and future tense verb endings, the being (or linking) verb *sum*, and about a verb's person, number, and tense. As for nouns, you have learned first declension noun endings, second declension masculine and neuter noun endings, noun and adjective cases, and have begun learning the endings for adjectives. Look at all you've accomplished!

The Latin for Children series is designed very much like *Song School Latin Book 2* but focuses more on teaching you how to read and translate Latin. You will find many similar puzzles, chants, and activities that will bring delight to your continuing study of Latin. Each level of Latin for Children also includes a teaching video, reader, and activity book.

To see a sample of the first few chapters of *Latin for Children Primer A*, please visit its product page at ClassicalAcademicPress.com.

Christopher A. Perrin, Publisher

Word Review

Word Search: You have already learned many words from *Latin for Children Primer A*! Below is a list of fifty-three words you know that you will see again in *Latin for Children Primer A*. Find them in the crossword puzzle!

donum gift
caelum sky
puella girl
puer boy
malus bad
folium leaf
murus wall
narro I tell
prope near
saxum rock
cibus food
aurum gold
altus high
vir man
annus year
longus long
poeta poet
video I see

voco I call
navigo I sail
ventus wind
post after
unda wave
fabula story
bonus good
parvus small
amo I love
equus horse
aqua water
nauta sailor
familia family
casa house
laboro I work
regina queen
ante before
cena dinner

agricola farmer
clamo I shout
trans across
femina woman
contra against
fenestra window
ad to, toward
extra outside of
amicus male friend
humus ground, dirt
magister male teacher
amica female friend
magistra female teacher
inter between, among
ludus school, game, play
patria country, fatherland
supra over, above, on top of

M	U	C	X	L	U	D	U	S	P	A	R	V	U	S	C	A	S	A
C	P	L	G	V	M	J	L	O	N	G	U	S	J	L	R	M	B	F
A	C	A	M	H	U	M	U	S	E	Q	U	U	S	T	V	O	C	O
E	E	M	A	M	I	C	A	H	N	N	R	A	N	N	A	R	R	O
L	N	O	Q	A	A	G	M	E	N	E	I	O	R	E	G	I	N	A
U	A	Q	B	Z	L	S	O	A	T	L	C	M	O	F	B	M	P	V
M	S	E	B	R	T	D	T	S	I	G	U	G	A	O	A	A	O	E
P	U	X	O	L	U	Q	I	M	S	N	I	S	A	L	U	G	S	N
U	P	T	N	L	S	G	A	U	O	V	N	R	N	I	R	I	T	T
E	R	R	U	P	A	F	R	D	A	A	F	W	T	U	U	S	Q	U
R	A	A	S	M	A	U	L	N	R	V	I	E	E	M	M	T	U	S
L	M	K	F	C	M	T	A	T	F	P	L	N	N	C	E	R	N	D
A	I	B	E	V	E	Z	R	K	Y	R	T	D	T	E	P	A	D	P
B	C	V	M	K	A	G	R	I	C	O	L	A	J	E	S	W	A	A
O	U	I	I	P	O	E	T	A	A	P	N	S	V	I	R	T	V	Q
R	S	D	N	C	D	V	A	O	D	E	E	N	A	U	T	A	R	U
O	H	E	A	K	M	F	A	B	U	L	A	C	P	U	E	L	L	A
W	X	O	N	P	M	A	L	U	S	C	I	B	U	S	A	X	U	M

Master Your Words

Congratulations! You've learned more than forty new words and have reviewed twenty-five words! Let's make sure that you have mastered all of these newest words. In the blanks provided, write the correct English translation for each of the following Latin words.

Chapter 26 New Words

1. **dormio** I sleep
2. **fessus, fessa, fessum** tired
3. **lectus** bed
4. **fabula** story
5. **balneum** bath
6. **prex** prayer
7. **stratum** blanket
8. **lux** light
9. **nox** night
10. **carmen** song

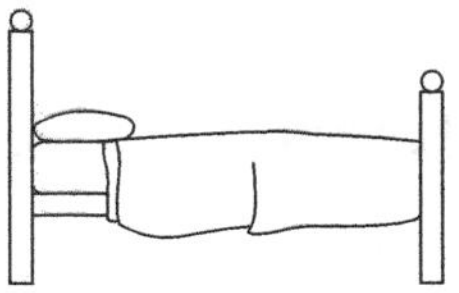

Chapter 26 Review Words

1. **unda** wave

2. **lacus** lake
3. **flumen** river
4. **diligenter** carefully
5. **forte** bravely

Chapter 27 New Words

1. **tempus** time
2. **hora** hour
3. **aurora** dawn, morning
4. **vesper** evening
5. **dies** day
6. **meridies** noon
7. **septimana** week
8. **mensis** month
9. **annus** year

Chapter 27 Review Words

1. **flos** flower
2. **hortus** garden

3. **folium** — leaf

4. **negotium** — job, occupation

5. **tabernarius** — shopkeeper

Chapter 28 New Words

1. **color** — color

   colores — colors

2. **ruber, rubra, rubrum** — red

3. **caeruleus, caerulea, caeruleum** — blue

4. **flavus, flava, flavum** — yellow

5. **viridis, viride** — green

6. **aurantius, aurantia, aurantium** — orange

7. **purpureus, purpurea, purpureum** — purple

8. **ater, atra, atrum** — black

9. **albus, alba, album** — white

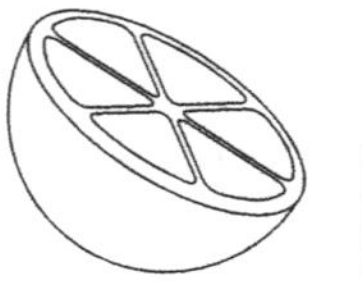

Chapter 28 Review Words

1. **mons** — mountain

2. **saxum** — rock

3. **collis** — hill

4. **structor** — builder

5. **venator** — hunter

Chapter 29 New Words

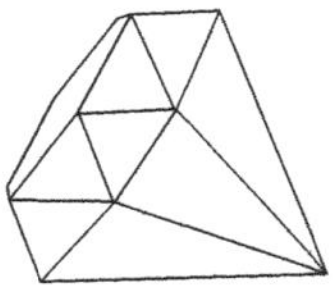

1. **tyrannus** — ruler, dictator

2. **solium** — throne

3. **servus** — male slave

4. **gemma** — jewel

5. **aurum** — gold

6. **regnum** — kingdom

7. **regno** — I reign

Chapter 29 Review Words

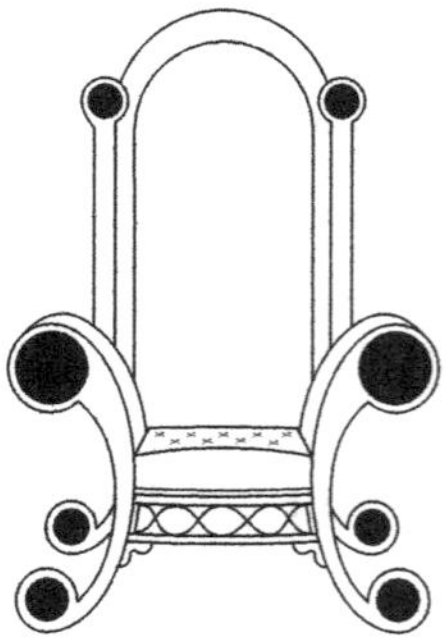

1. **sub** — under

2. **supra** — above

3. **rex** — king

4. **regina** — queen

5. **corona** — crown

Chapter 30 New Words

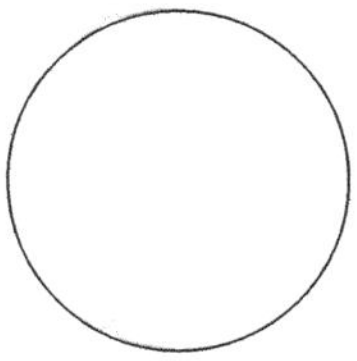

1. **magnus, magna, magnum** — great, big
2. **parvus, parva, parvum** — small
3. **pulcher, pulchra, pulchrum** — pretty, handsome
4. **altus, alta, altum** — high
5. **longus, longa, longum** — long
6. **brevis, breve** — short
7. **bonus, bona, bonum** — good
8. **malus, mala, malum** — bad
9. **rotundus, rotunda, rotundum** — round
10. **quadratus, quadrata, quadratum** — square
11. **triangulus, triangula, triangulum** — triangular

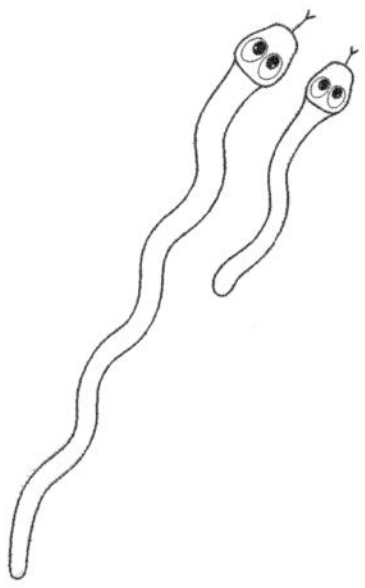

Chapter 30 Review Words

1. **contra** — against
2. **inter** — between, among
3. **ante** — before
4. **cum** — with
5. **post** — after

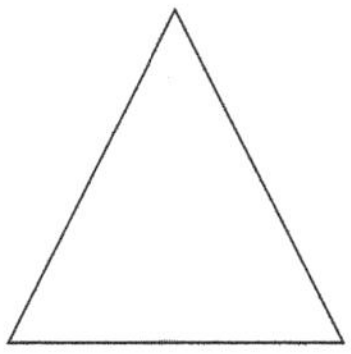

Master Your Songs

Bedtime Song [Track 26(C)/56(E)]

First a bath, **balneum**,
Then I tidy my bedroom,
Then my **pater** tucks me in,
In my fuzzy blue **stratum**.

A **fabula**,
A bedtime tale,
Makes me sleepy, without fail. *(x2)*

I say a **prex**, say a prayer,
Sing a **carmen** with my **mater**,
But she tells me that time flies
So I close my **fessus** eyes.

Nox brings rest
For a new day,
Strength for work and for play. *(x2)*

Dormio, I sleep tight
In my **lectus**, through the **nox**, night
With my **nox lux**, shining bright light,
Keeping company tonight.

Dormio, sweetly sleep
In my **lectus**, counting sheep. *(x2)*

<u>Grand Old Father Time</u> [Track 27(C)/57(E)]

The grand old Father Time,
He marches every day.
The **Pater Tempus** chimes
Every **hora**, while we play.

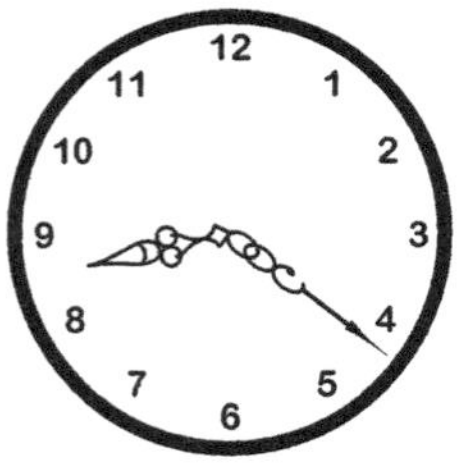

Each **dies**, day, he calls,
As **aurora** breaks the sky,
And then as evening, **vesper**, falls
He bids **dies** good-bye.

Each **septimana** is a week,
Five days for work and school,
Then two days for rest and play
But remember your lunch at **meridies**
Each day when you're at school.

Each **mensis** a new moon comes
For **nox** to light the night.
Every **annus**, every night,
Pater Tempus brings us light.

The grand old Father Time,
He marches every day.
The **Pater Tempus** chimes
Every **hora**, while we play.

<u>The Colores Song</u> [Track 28(C)/58(E)]

I love to paint when it's time for art,
I make each color play a part.
Ruber is the color of my go-cart.
Aurantius is the color of morning sky, morning sky, morning sky.
It's also the color of a fruit I like
And **flavus** is the color of banana pie!

My favorite animal is black and white.
It loves to kick and it just might bite,
The stripes are a style that's quite the sight.
The black stripes we'll call **atra, atra, atra.**
The snowy white stripes are **alba**, white,
But the black stripes we'll call **atra**.

Viridis, green, are the leaves in spring.
Caeruleus, blue, are the birds on wing.
Purpureus, the royal robes of a king.
Flavus, the glow of candlelight, candlelight, candlelight.
Purpureus, the royal robes of a king,
And **flavus** is color of his golden ring.

Well, I love to paint and I love art,
Yes, and every color has a part
And I think the colors all look smart.
Atra, alba, and **ruber** bright, **ruber** bright, **ruber** bright.
Atra and **alba** sure look nice,
But I'm in love with **ruber** bright.

Mr. King Folium [Track 29(C)/59(E)]

There was an old **rex**
Named Mr. King **Folium.**
He sat on a throne
Named Mr. **Solium**
And told his **servus**
To bring him a nummy-num.
Hungry old Mr. King **Folium, Folium.**

There was a little queen
Named Mrs. Queen **Regina.**
She loved to dress up
In her gold, gold **corona.**
That **aurum** crown
Had a great big **gemma**
Always on Queen **Regina, Regina.**

A frog one day said,
"I'll take over.
I'll make a fine **tyrannus, tyrannus,** ruler.
I'll steal the crown **gemma**
from the royal jeweler.
Regno, I rule, I'm the ruler, ruler!"

Queen **Regina** and Mr. King **Folium**
Had a powwow
And took back the **regnum.**
"Mr. Mean Frog, your time has finally come
Leave our **solium** and our **regnum, regnum!**"

Adjectives Chant [Track 30(C)/60(E)]

My puppy is small, he's cute and kind of **parvus,**
And most of the time he's really very **bonus.**
His tail is long; it's a tail **longus,**
His tummy is round and just a bit **rotundus.**

Is your puppy **brevis,** short and small?
Or is your puppy **altus,** high and tall?
Magnus, parvus, big or small?
Is it round and **rotundus,** shaped like a ball?

Maybe it's **quadratus,** shaped like a square?
Malus, bad and hairy, and mean like a bear?
Or **triangulus,** like an arrow in the air?
Or **pulchra, pulcher,** beautiful, and fair?

Word Review Activities

I. **Word Search:** Write the Latin translations of the following English words on the blanks provided and then find and circle them in the word search. Be sure to include all of the forms of each of the words.

colors colores
time tempus
noon meridies
week septimana
month mensis
purple purpureus, purpurea, purpureum
kingdom regnum
I reign regno
gold aurum
hour hora
black ater, atra, atrum
day dies
evening vesper
prayer prex
night nox

A	P	I	P	U	R	P	U	R	E	U	S	F	K	O	G	D	I	L	E	P	H
U	U	M	H	G	N	M	E	R	I	D	I	E	S	R	B	M	K	A	T	R	A
R	R	Q	E	N	S	E	P	T	I	M	A	N	A	G	I	V	E	S	P	E	R
U	P	E	T	N	O	R	A	Q	U	L	C	O	L	O	R	E	S	H	Y	C	P
M	U	V	F	G	S	X	I	N	A	D	F	M	S	G	A	T	R	U	M	L	R
W	R	E	G	N	O	I	G	E	T	K	Y	E	S	P	F	J	Z	K	R	D	E
L	E	C	J	U	N	E	S	C	E	O	I	T	E	M	P	U	S	H	B	P	X
F	A	L	H	O	R	A	X	H	R	D	J	F	P	U	R	P	U	R	E	U	M

II. Draw lines to match the Latin phrases to the correct pictures.

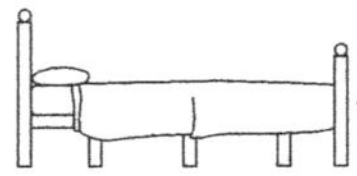
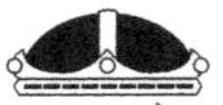

1. **tres tringula gemma**
   three triangular jewels
2. **longus lectus**
   long bed
3. **ater nox**
   black night
4. **flava lux**
   yellow light
5. **malus tyrannus**
   bad ruler/dictator
6. **pulchra aurora**
   pretty dawn/morning
7. **fessus servus**
   tired male slave
8. **rotunda corona**
   round crown

III. **Mosaic:** Color the pieces of the mosaic according to the following directions. **Hint:** The Latin word **figura** means "form, shape, or figure."

parva quadrata figura: ruber
the small square shape: red
magna quadrata figura: purpureus
the big square shape: purple
parva triangula figura: flavius
the small triangular shape: yellow
magna triangula figura: caeruleus
the big triangular shape: blue
parva rotunda figura: viridis
the small round shape: green
magna rotunda figura: aurantius
the big round shape: orange
Fill in the other spaces with **ater**.
black

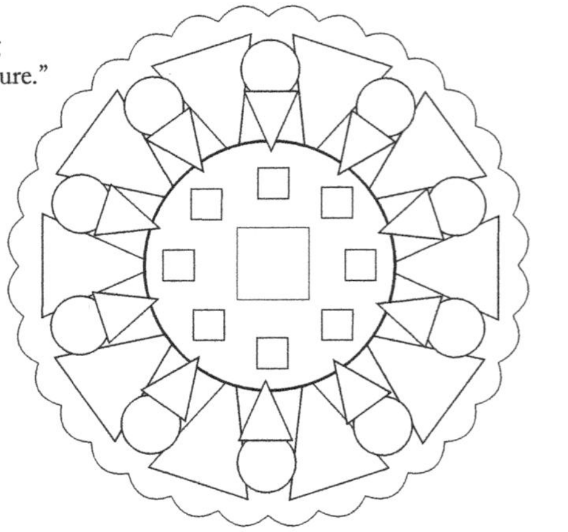

Master Your Chants

Second Declension Masculine Endings Chant

Case	Singular	Plural
Nominative	**-us**	**-i**
Genitive	**-i**	**-orum**
Dative	**-o**	**-is**
Accusative	**-um**	**-os**
Ablative	**-o**	**-is**

Mensa Chant

Case	Singular	Plural
Nominative	**mensa**	**mensae**
Genitive	**mensae**	**mesarum**
Dative	**mensae**	**mensis**
Accusative	**mensam**	**mensas**
Ablative	**mensa**	**mensis**

Hortus Chant

Case	Singular	Plural
Nominative	**hortus**	**horti**
Genitive	**horti**	**hortorum**
Dative	**horto**	**hortis**
Accusative	**hortum**	**hortos**
Ablative	**horto**	**hortis**

Second Declension Neuter Noun Endings Chant

Case	Singular	Plural
Nominative	**-um**	**-a**
Genitive	**-i**	**-orum**
Dative	**-o**	**-is**
Accusative	**-um**	**-a**
Ablative	**-o**	**-is**

Bonum Chant

Case	Singular	Plural
Nominative	**bonum**	**bona**
Genitive	**boni**	**bonorum**
Dative	**bono**	**bonis**
Accusative	**bonum**	**bona**
Ablative	**bono**	**bonis**

Now that you have reviewed your chants, you should be able to fill out the following charts without looking at the ones you just reviewed. See if you can fill them out from memory. The first one in each table has been filled in for you.

Case	Singular	Plural
Nominative	**bonum**	bona
Genitive	boni	bonorum
Dative	bono	bonis
Accusative	bonum	bona
Ablative	bono	bonis

Case	Singular	Plural
Nominative	**hortus**	horti
Genitive	horti	hortorum
Dative	horto	hortis
Accusative	hortum	hortos
Ablative	horto	hortis

Case	Singular	Plural
Nominative	**mensa**	mensae
Genitive	mensae	mesarum
Dative	mensae	mensis
Accusative	mensam	mensas
Ablative	mensa	mensis

Master Your Famous Sayings

On the lines provided, write the English translations of the famous Latin sayings.

1. **Fiat lux!** Let there be light!
2. **Tempus fugit!** Time flees (flies)!
3. **Veritas vos liberabit.** The truth will make you free.
4. **Regnat populus.** The people rule.
5. **Magnum opus** a great work, one's major life accomplishment

Master Your Derivatives

In the blanks provided, write the Latin words from which these English words are derived.

1. fable fabula
2. dormitory dormio

3. temporary tempus
4. annual annus
5. albino albus, alba, album
6. regal regnum
7. coronate corona
8. magnify magnus, magna, magnum
9. altitude altus, alta, altum

Draw!

Draw a picture of a scene that has in it at least ten of the items listed in the following word bank. Label each item in your scene with the correct Latin words from this review chapter. Use color! (If you need more room, use a separate sheet of paper.)

Word Bank:

mathematica	**lectio**
scriptio	**familia**
amicus	**amica**
rex	**regina**
miles	**gladius**
poeta	**architectus**
artifex	**medicus**
balneum	**lux**
carmen	

Chapter 32

End-of-Book Review

Fabula

Read the story to yourself. Next, take turns reading it with a partner, and as you do so, translate it completely into English. In order to help you translate the verbs in the story, study the list of verbs that follows the story. You can also look up the meaning of any of these Latin words in your glossary.◊

It is a cold **vesper** in the **mensis** of **Februarius. Milites** are marching **cito ad** the **regnum.** Their plan is to march **circum** the city, and in the **aurora pugnabunt contra** the **populus** and **vincebunt** the **regnum.**

Dum the **milites** are marching **extra** the city, almost every child is taking his or her **balneum** and getting ready to climb into **lectus.** In the **casa** of the **rex** and **regina,** a **poeta** is reciting a **longum** poem and **unus parvus musicus** is strumming a **triangulus** instrument.

Earlier that **dies,** at **meridies,** there was a **magnae epulae**◊◊ for the **celebratio** of the birthday of the **regina.** The **servi** made a **bonus cena, amici** played **ludi,** and **familae canebant carmen** for the **regina.** The **rex** gave the **regina** a **pulchra rubra flos.**

Nunc, post the celebration, all the **populus**◊◊◊ in the **regnum est fessus,** and they do **non** know about the **milites ambulant cito ad regnum.**

While standing on the **altus murus,** a **vigil** hears someone **clamat** far away. He **vocat ad** another **vigil** and says, "**Tace! Audi diligenter!**" They both hear faint noises. "**Equitabo nunc ex** the city and **spectabo** those who are shouting," **dicit** the **vigil.** "**Portabo** my **gladius!**" The **vigil** takes his **equus ex** the stable and **equitat forte ad** the noises. When **erat prope, videbat** many **mali milites** in the **atra nox.** He had never seen so many **milites dum vivebat!** He **lente** moved away, and then **currebat cum equus** to the city. By this **tempus,** the **rex, regina, senatores,** and most of the **viri dormiebant.** He wakes them and **dicit,** "A **bellum** is about to start!"◊◊◊◊

◊ Modify these instructions as needed to suit your students' comprehension level. The following is an alternative option to what is provided in the student text: First, read aloud to the class the story as it is written. Then, go through it again, pausing at the Latin words and calling on students to supply the English translations of the Latin words. Then, if students are at an appropriate reading level, allow them to read through the story again, all in English, out loud to partners. Another option is to assign one sentence each to individual students ahead of time to read and translate. Then, after students have worked independently translating their assigned sentences, you could have the class read through the story, having students read aloud their assigned sentences.

Note that the Latin nouns in this story are all in the nominative case, even though in actual Latin prose nouns that are the object of a verb would be in the accusative case. In their later Latin study, students will learn the use of the accusative and other Latin noun cases.

Teacher's Notes are continued on the following pages.

List of Verbs

- **pugnabunt:** from **pugno**; **-bunt** is a future tense ending (see chapter 22)
- **vincebunt:** from **vinco**; **-bunt** is a future tense ending (see chapter 22)
- **canebant:** from **cano** (see *SSL1* chapter 17 and *SSL2* chapter 16); **-bant** is an imperfect tense ending (see chapter 21)
- **est:** a present form of **sum** (see chapter 15)
- **ambulant:** from **ambulo**; **-nt** is a future tense ending (see chapter 20)
- **clamat:** from **clamo**; **-t** is a present tense ending (see chapter 4)
- **vocat:** from **voco**; **-t** is a present tense ending (see chapter 4)
- **tace:** imperative (command) (see *SSL1* chapter 11; *SSL2* chapter 10)
- **audi:** imperative (command) (see *SSL1* chapter 11; *SSL2* chapter 10)
- **equitabo:** from **equito**; **-bo** is a future tense ending (see chapter 22)
- **spectabo:** from **specto**; **-bo** is a future tense ending (see chapter 22)
- **dicit:** from **dico**; **-t** is a present tense ending (see chapter 4)
- **portabo:** from **porto**; **-bo** is a future tense ending (see chapter 22)
- **equitat:** from **equito**; **-t** is a present tense ending (see chapter 4)
- **erat:** an imperfect form of **sum** (see chapter 18)
- **videbat:** from **video**; **-bat** is an imperfect tense ending (see chapter 21)
- **vivebat:** from **vivo**; **-bat** is an imperfect tense ending (see chapter 21)
- **currebat:** from **curro**; **-bat** is an imperfect tense ending (see chapter 21)
- **dormiebant:** from **dormio**; **-bant** is an imperfect tense ending (see chapter 21)

◊◊ In the Latin, epulae is plural referring to the "dishes" at a feast or banquet. We therefore modify the plural epulae with the plural form of the adjective magnae. Some students may note the use of the plural here and want to know why.

◊◊◊ In Latin, populus is a singular noun that considers people as a group. We have kept populus in the singular, thus we have used the singular noun est in the phrase populus est fessus, meaning "the people/population is tired." It is fine to render this in English as "the people are tired."

What happens next? You write the end of the story, using at least one Latin word in each sentence.

◊◊◊◊ The following is a translation of the entire story. The translated words have been bolded.

It is a cold **evening in the month of February. The soldiers are marching quickly to the kingdom.** Their plan is to march **around** the city, and in the **morning they will fight against** the **people** and **they will conquer** the **kingdom.**

While the **soldiers** are marching **outside of** the city, almost every child is taking his or her **bath** and getting ready to climb into **bed.** In the **house** of the **king** and **queen,** a **poet** is reciting a **long** poem and **one small musician (male)** is strumming a **triangular** instrument.

Earlier that **day,** at **noon,** there was a **great feast** for the **celebration** of the birthday of the **queen.** The **slaves** made a **good dinner, friends** played **games,** and **families sang a song** for the **queen.** The **king** gave the **queen** a **pretty red flower.**

(continued on next page)

Now, after the celebration, all the people in the kingdom are tired, and they do not know about the **soldiers walking quickly to the kingdom.**

While standing on the **high wall,** a **guard** hears someone **shout** far away. He **calls** to another **guard** and says, **"Be quiet! Listen carefully!"** They both hear faint noises. **"I will ride (ride a horse) now** out of the city and **I will look at** those who are shouting," **says the guard. "I will carry my sword!"** The **guard** takes his **horse** out of the stable and **rides bravely** toward the noises. When **he was near, he was seeing** many **bad soldiers** in the **black night.** He had never seen so many **soldiers while he was living (i.e., in his life)!** He slowly moved away, and then **was running** with **his horse** to the city. By this **time,** the **king, queen, senators,** and most of the **men were sleeping.** He wakes them and says, "A **war** is about to start!"

Note: You and your students may note that both the original diglot version and the English translation of the story switch tenses in ways that would be awkward in fluent English prose. We have done this to give students practice reading and decoding verbs from all three tenses they have learned—present, future, and imperfect (past).

Verax or Non Verax? (Truthful or Not Truthful?)

Read these sentences and in the blank provided, write *T* for true and *F* for false.

1. F Apples are usually a light shade of **caeruleum**.
   blue
2. T Sometimes shoes hide **sub** my **lectus**.
   under bed
3. F Most **discipuli** have to go to **ludus** on **Dies Saturni** and **Dies Solis**.
   students school Saturday Sunday
4. T My **pater vehor in vehiculo** to his **negotium** every work **dies**.
   father rides in a car job day

5. F An **architectus** usually works on tearing down houses.
   architect
6. T Fire engines are **rubra**!
   red
7. F I have **octo** fingers on each **manus**.
   eight hand
8. T My **mater** is very **benefica**.
   mother kind/generous
9. F In **autumnus**, the **foilia (folium)** turn **viridis**.
   fall leaves green
10. T At **aurora**, the **caelum** can be many different **colores**, even **purpureus**.
    dawn sky colors purple
11. T **Rex** Solomon was known for being **sapiens**.
    king wise
12. F A **corona** is useful for staying warm in the **hiems**.
    crown winter
13. F You should **coqueo** your hands before eating.
    cook
14. F Lazy **populi** usually **laborant** from **aurora ad vesper**.
    people work dawn to evening
15. T A good **miles** must be **fortis**.
    soldier brave/strong
16. F **Venators** are known for making beautiful music.
    hunters
17. F A **diligens** and **fidelis** student will usually fail tests.
    careful/attentive faithful
18. F Only a **puella** can **purgat**.
    girl clean
19. F There are **septem menses** (from **mensis**) in an **annus**.
    seven months years
20. F It's very **malus** to **susurro** in a library.
    bad whisper

Matching

Translate each Latin phrase and then draw a line to the picture that matches it.

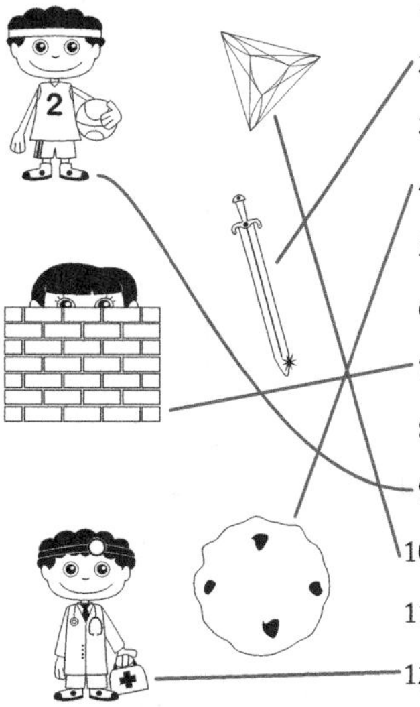

1. **parva feles** small cat
2. **longus gladius** long sword
3. **unus flos** one flower
4. **rotundum crustulum** round cookie
5. **pulchra puella** pretty girl
6. **magna casa** big house
7. **altus murus** high wall
8. **quadratum stratum** square blanket
9. **fortis athleta** strong athlete
10. **triangula gemma** triangular jewel
11. **sapiens venator** wise hunter
12. **beneficus medicus** kind doctor

Colores!

Color the items in the preceding matching exercise according to the following instructions.

parva feles: atra black
longus gladius: caeruleus blue
unus flos: ruber red
rotundum crustulum: flavum yellow
pulchra puella: purpurea purple
magna casa: viridis green
altus murus: albus white
quadratum stratum: aurantium orange
fortis athleta: flava yellow
triangula gemma: rubra red
sapiens venator: viridis green
beneficus medicus: purpureus purple

Crossword Puzzle

Use the following clues to complete the crossword puzzle.

Across

1. There are septem (seven) days in a **septimana** (week).
4. When I go to the zoo, specto (I look at) all of the different animals.
5. My birthday comes once an annus (year).
10. The venator (hunter) killed the bear.
11. This poem was written by a famous poeta (poet).
12. It's meridies (noon), time for lunch!
13. Amo (I love) my **mater** (mother) very much!
16. Dies Mercurii (Wednesday) is right in the middle of the **septimana** (week).
18. A patriot loves his patria (country/fatherland).
19. Say a prex (prayer) before bedtime.
20. The third month of the year is Martius (March).
22. I wrapped my little sister in a stratum (blanket).
23. An architectus (architect) draws plans for buildings.

Down

2. There are **quattuor septimana** (four weeks) in a mensis (month).
3. This **cibus** (food) tastes so bonus (good)!

5. The ______ agricola ______ is planting his fields.
farmer

6. The **nauta** sailed ______ trans ______ the ocean.
sailor — across

7. You may feel very ______ fessus ______ after running a long race.
tired

8. Babies have to eat very ______ saepe ______.
often

9. Pumpkins are ______ aurantius ______.
orange

14. The ______ medicus ______ can help when you are sick!
doctor

15. Candles give ______ lux ______.
light

17. The picture is hanging ______ supra ______ the fireplace.
above

21. I walked ______ sub ______ the bridge.
under

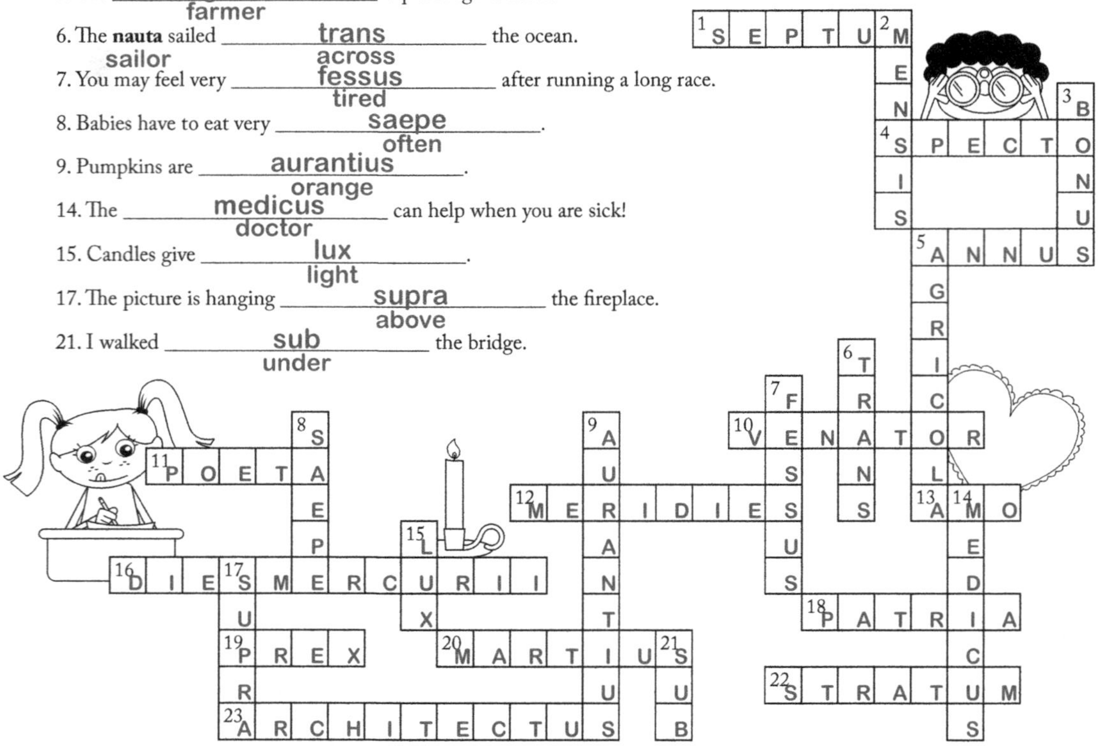

Review Games!

It's time to play some vocabulary review games!

◊◊◊◊◊ For variation, you may also call out English words that must be translated correctly into Latin.

Quick Draw

Your teacher will divide your class into two teams. Each team will send one player up to the whiteboard to compete with a player from the other team. Players face the teacher with their backs to the whiteboard, holding a dry-erase marker behind their backs. The teacher then calls out a vocabulary word in Latin. As soon as the Latin word is called out, the students turn around and write out the English translation of the word on the whiteboard. The first player to correctly translate the Latin word wins a point for his or her team. After a round or two (in which every student competes at the whiteboard), the team with the most points wins.◊◊◊◊◊

Team Tag with Flash Cards

Using Latin vocabulary flash cards that contain only Latin words (no English translation), your teacher will place two equal stacks of flash cards on a desk or table in the front of the room. Your teacher will divide your class into two groups and then will direct you to form two single-file lines facing the desk.

When the game starts, the first person in line for each team races to the desk, takes the first card in the team's pile, shows the card to the team, announces the English translation of the word or phrase, places the card in a discard pile, and then races to tag the next person in line. One student from each team will be assigned as the translation checker. The translation checker will pronounce the translation correct or incorrect after hearing a student translate out loud. If a student doing the translating does not know the English translation or gives an incorrect translation, he or she puts the card on the bottom of the pile and selects the next card. The student who is translating keeps selecting cards until he or she provides the correct translation of a word or phrase or until five cards have been selected. If the student goes through five cards without having given a correct translation, that student goes to the back of the line and the next student in line takes a turn. The two teams play at the same time, and the first team to correctly translate all the Latin vocabulary cards in its pile wins the game.

Famous Sayings Review

This game can be played in two ways:

1. For a larger class, each student will write down his or her favorite famous Latin saying from this book on a piece of paper and put it into a basket. Then your teacher will mix up all the pieces of paper and have each student take a piece of paper from the basket. Each student must translate out loud the Latin saying on the paper he or she takes. This game will not have a winner.
2. For a smaller class, your teacher will ask each student to write down several of the famous Latin sayings from the book on cards or separate pieces of paper. Once all of the Latin sayings from the book have been written down, your teacher will fold them up and put them in a basket. Students will then take turns taking a card (or piece of paper) from the basket and translating out loud the famous saying found on it. The student who translates the most famous sayings correctly is the winner.

Appendix A

Chapter-by-Chapter Glossary: New Vocabulary

Chapter 1: What Day Is It?

1. **Qui dies est?** — What day is it?
2. **Hodie est ______.** — Today is ______.

Chapter 2: Days of the Week

1. **Dies Solis** — Sunday
2. **Dies Lunae** — Monday
3. **Dies Martis** — Tuesday
4. **Dies Mercurii** — Wednesday
5. **Dies Iovis** — Thursday
6. **Dies Veneris** — Friday
7. **Dies Saturni** — Saturday

Chapter 3: Months of the Year

1. **Qui mensis est?** — What month is it?
2. **Hic mensis est . . .** — This month is . . .
3. **Ianuarius** — January
4. **Februarius** — February
5. **Martius** — March
6. **Aprilis** — April

Chapter 4: More Months of the Year

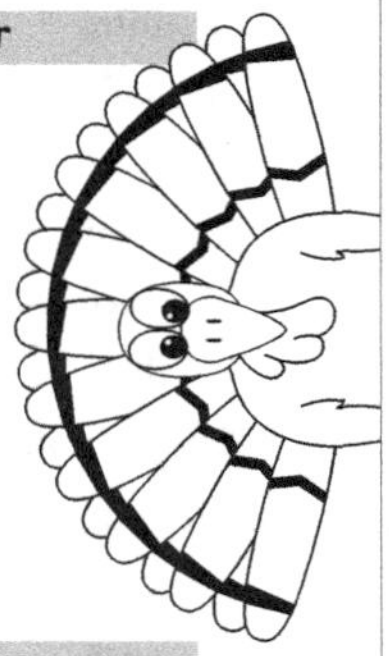

1. **Maius** — May
2. **Iunius** — June
3. **Iulius** — July
4. **Augustus** — August
5. **September** — September
6. **October** — October
7. **November** — November
8. **December** — December

Chapter 5: Numbers

1. **unus** — one
2. **duo** — two
3. **tres** — three
4. **quattuor** — four
5. **quinque** — five

Chapter 6: More Numbers

1. **sex** — six
2. **septem** — seven
3. **octo** — eight
4. **novem** — nine
5. **decem** — ten

Chapter 8: Helping at Home

1. **laboro** — I work
2. **lavo** — I wash
3. **coquo** — I cook
4. **pasco** — I feed
5. **purgo** — I clean

Chapter 9: Communicating with Others

1. **dico** — I speak, say
2. **clamo** — I shout
3. **susurro** — I whisper
4. **scribo** — I write
5. **oro** — I pray

Chapter 10: Ways to Travel

1. **ambulo** — I walk
2. **curro** — I run
3. **equito** — I ride a horse
4. **volo** — I fly
5. **navigo** — I sail
6. **vehor in vehiculo** — I ride in a car

Chapter 11: Things to Learn in School

1. **mathematica** — math
2. **grammatica** — grammar, language arts
3. **lectio** — reading
4. **scriptio** — writing
5. **physica** — science
6. **historia** — history

Chapter 12: Celebration

1. **epulae** — feast
2. **familia** — family
3. **celebratio** — celebration
4. **ludus** — game, school, play
5. **musica** — music
6. **amicus** — male friend
   amica — female friend

Chapter 14: Royalty

1. **rex** — king
2. **regina** — queen
3. **corona** — crown
4. **patria** — country, fatherland
5. **populus** — people
6. **rego** — I rule, direct

Chapter 15: Military Matters

1. **miles**	soldier
2. **gladius**	sword
3. **bellum**	war
4. **pugno**	I fight
5. **vinco**	I conquer
6. **video**	I see

Chapter 16: Everyday Actions

1. **porto**	I carry
2. **specto**	I look at
3. **narro**	I tell
4. **vivo**	I live
5. **amo**	I love
6. **voco**	I call

Chapter 17: Adverbs: How We Do Things

1. **nunc**	now
2. **numquam**	never
3. **saepe**	often
4. **cito**	fast, quickly
5. **lente**	slowly
6. **semper**	always

Chapter 18: More Adverbs

1. **non**	not
2. **forte**	bravely
3. **pessime**	badly, terrible
4. **diligenter**	carefully
5. **bene**	well, fine
6. **optime**	best

Chapter 20: When I Grow Up, Part I

1. **negotium**	job, occupation
2. **poeta**	poet
3. **vigil**	guard, policeman, fireman
4. **tabernarius**	shopkeeper
5. **architectus**	architect
6. **artifex**	artist
7. **medicus**	doctor

Chapter 21: When I Grow Up, Part II

1. **agricola**	farmer
2. **structor**	builder
3. **nauta**	sailor
4. **venator**	hunter
5. **athleta**	athlete
6. **musicus** **musica**	male musician female musician
7. **scriptor**	writer
8. **senator**	senator, politician

Chapter 22: Where Things Are, Part I

1. **sub**	under
2. **supra**	over, above, on top of
3. **prope**	near
4. **trans**	across
5. **ex**	out of
6. **ad**	to, toward
7. **circum**	around
8. **pone**	behind

Chapter 23: Where Things Are, Part II

1. **contra**	against
2. **dum**	while
3. **extra**	outside of
4. **inter**	between, among
5. **ante**	before
6. **post**	after
7. **cum**	with
8. **sursum**	up
9. **de**	down from, concerning, about

Chapter 24: Growing Virtues

1. **fortis, forte**	brave, strong
2. **fidelis, fidele**	faithful
3. **humilis, humile**	humble
4. **diligens, diligentis**	careful, attentive
5. **sapiens, sapientis**	wise
6. **oboediens, oboedientis**	obedient
7. **verax, veracis**	truthful, honest
8. **beneficus, benefica, beneficum**	kind, generous
9. **studiosus, studiosa, studiosum**	eager to learn
10. **virtus**	virtue, courage, excellence

Chapter 26: Time for Bed!

1. **dormio**	I sleep
2. **fessus, fessa, fessum**	tired
3. **lectus**	bed
4. **fabula**	story
5. **balneum**	bath
6. **prex**	prayer
7. **stratum**	blanket
8. **lux**	light
9. **nox**	night
10. **carmen**	song

Chapter 27: A Time for Everything

1. **tempus**	time
2. **hora**	hour
3. **aurora**	dawn, morning
4. **vesper**	evening
5. **dies**	day
6. **meridies**	noon
7. **septimana**	week
8. **mensis**	month
9. **annus**	year

Chapter 28: Colors

1. **color** **colores**	color colors
2. **ruber, rubra, rubrum**	red
3. **caeruleus, caerulea, caeruleum**	blue
4. **flavus, flava, flavum**	yellow
5. **viridis, viride**	green
6. **aurantius, aurantia, aurantium**	orange
7. **purpureus, purpurea, purpureum**	purple
8. **ater, atra, atrum**	black
9. **albus, alba, album**	white

Chapter 29: Around the Palace

1. **tyrannus**	ruler, dictator
2. **solium**	throne
3. **servus**	male slave
4. **gemma**	jewel
5. **aurum**	gold
6. **regnum**	kingdom
7. **regno**	I reign

Chapter 30: Adjectives

1. **magnus, magna, magnum**	great, big
2. **parvus, parva, parvum**	small
3. **pulcher, pulchra, pulchrum**	pretty, handsome
4. **altus, alta, altum**	high
5. **longus, longa, longum**	long
6. **brevis, breve**	short
7. **bonus, bona, bonum**	good
8. **malus, mala, malum**	bad
9. **rotundus, rotunda, rotundum**	round
10. **quadratus, quadrata, quadratum**	square
11. **triangulus, triangula, triangulum**	triangular

Appendix B
Chapter-by-Chapter Glossary: Review Vocabulary

Chapter 1

Latin	English	Book	Chapter
1. **salve**	hello	1	1
2. **vale**	good-bye	1	1
3. **discipuli**	students	1	1
4. **magister**	male teacher	1	1
magistra	female teacher	1	1

Chapter 2

Latin	English	Book	Chapter
1. **Quid est tuum praenomen?**	What is your name?	1	2
2. **Meum praenomen est . . .**	My name is . . .	1	2

Chapter 3

Latin	English	Book	Chapter
1. **hiems**	winter	1	25
2. **ver**	spring	1	25
3. **autumnus**	fall	1	25
4. **aestas**	summer	1	25

Chapter 4

Latin	English	Book	Chapter
1. **Quid agis?**	How are you?	1	3
2. **bene**	well, fine	1	3
3. **optime**	best	1	3
4. **pessime**	badly, terrible	1	3
5. **pater**	father	1	5
6. **mater**	mother	1	5

Chapter 5

Latin	English	Book	Chapter
1. **soror**	sister	1	5
2. **frater**	brother	1	5
3. **puella**	girl	1	6
4. **puer**	boy	1	6
5. **vir**	man	1	6
6. **femina**	woman	1	6

Chapter 6

Latin	English	Book	Chapter
1. **mensa**	table	1	7
2. **sella**	chair	1	7
3. **stylus**	pencil	1	7
4. **liber**	book	1	7

Chapter 8

Latin	English	Book	Chapter
1. **casa**	house	1	8
2. **porta**	door, gate	1	8
3. **murus**	wall	1	8
4. **fenestra**	window	1	8
5. **Qui dies est?**	What day is it?	2	1
6. **Hodie est ______.**	Today is______.	2	1

Chapter 9

Latin	English	Book	Chapter
1. **sede**	sit	1	10
sedete	sit (to more than one person)		
2. **surge**	rise, stand up	1	10
surgite	rise, stand up (to more than one person)		
3. **scribe**	write	1	10
scribite	write (to more than one person)		
4. **repete**	repeat	1	10
repetite	repeat (to more than one person)		

Chapter 10

Latin	English	Book	Chapter
1. **audi**	listen	1	11
audite	listen (to more than one person)		
2. **tace**	be quiet	1	11
tacete	be quiet (to more than one person)		
3. **attolle manum**	raise your hand	1	11
attollite manus	raise your hands (to more than one person)		
4. **Qui mensis est?**	What month is it?	2	3
5. **Martius**	March	2	3

Chapter 11

Latin	English	Book	Chapter
1. **amabo te**	please	1	12
2. **tibi gratias ago**	thank you	1	12
3. **ignosce mihi**	excuse me	1	12
4. **Maius**	May	2	4
5. **Iunius**	June	2	4

Chapter 12

Latin	English	Book	Chapter
1. **canis**	dog	1	14
2. **feles**	cat	1	14
3. **pisces**	fish	1	14
4. **quattuor**	four	2	5
5. **quinque**	five	2	5

Chapter 14

Latin	English	Book	Chapter
1. **leo**	lion	1	15
2. **avis**	bird	1	15
3. **ursa**	bear	1	15
4. **septem**	seven	2	6
5. **decem**	ten	2	6

Chapter 15

Latin	English	Book	Chapter
1. **agnus**	lamb	1	16
2. **infans**	baby	1	16
3. **lavo**	I wash	2	8
4. **coquo**	I cook	2	8
5. **pasco**	I feed	2	8

Chapter 16

Latin	English	Book	Chapter
1. **cano**	I sing	1	17
2. **laudo**	I praise	1	17
3. **do**	I give	1	17
4. **dico**	I say, speak	2	9
5. **scribo**	I write	2	9

Chapter 17

Latin	English	Book	Chapter
1. **manus**	hand	1	19
2. **pes**	foot	1	19
3. **caput**	head	1	19
4. **corpus**	body	1	19
5. **ambulo**	I walk	2	10

Chapter 18

Latin	English	Book	Chapter
1. **auris**	ear	1	20
2. **oculus**	eye	1	20
3. **os**	mouth	1	20
4. **grammatica**	grammar, language arts	2	11
5. **physica**	science	2	11

Chapter 20

Latin	English	Book	Chapter
1. **cibus**	food	1	21
2. **cena**	dinner	1	21
3. **edo**	I eat	1	21
4. **familia**	family	2	12
5. **ludus**	game, school, play	2	12

Chapter 21

Latin	English	Book	Chapter
1. **panis**	bread	1	22
2. **crustulum**	cookie	1	22
3. **lac**	milk	1	22
4. **patria**	country, fatherland	2	14
5. **populus**	people	2	14

Chapter 22

Latin	English	Book	Chapter
1. **nix**	snow	1	24
2. **imber**	rain	1	24
3. **nimbus**	cloud	1	24
4. **arcus**	rainbow	1	24
5. **vinco**	I conquer	2	15

Chapter 23

Latin	English	Book	Chapter
1. **hiems**	winter	1	25
2. **ver**	spring	1	25
3. **autumnus**	fall	1	25
4. **aestas**	summer	1	25

Chapter 24

Latin	English	Book	Chapter
1. **caelum**	sky	1	26
2. **stella**	star	1	26
3. **sol**	sun	1	26
4. **saepe**	often	2	17
5. **cito**	fast, quickly	2	17

Chapter 26

Latin	English	Book	Chapter
1. **unda**	wave	1	28
2. **lacus**	lake	1	28
3. **flumen**	river	1	28
4. **diligenter**	carefully	2	18
5. **forte**	bravely	2	18

Chapter 27

Latin	English	Book	Chapter
1. **flos**	flower	1	29
2. **hortus**	garden	1	29
3. **folium**	leaf	1	29
4. **negotium**	job, occupation	2	20
5. **tabernarius**	shopkeeper	2	20

Chapter 28

Latin	English	Book	Chapter
1. **mons**	mountain	1	30
2. **saxum**	rock	1	30
3. **collis**	hill	1	30
4. **structor**	builder	2	21
5. **venator**	hunter	2	21

Chapter 29

Latin	English	Book	Chapter
1. **sub**	under	2	22
2. **supra**	over, above, on top of	2	22
3. **rex**	king	2	14
4. **regina**	queen	2	14
5. **corona**	crown	2	14

Chapter 30

Latin	English	Book	Chapter
1. **contra**	against	2	23
2. **inter**	between, among	2	23
3. **ante**	before	2	23
4. **cum**	with	2	23
5. **post**	after	2	23

Appendix C

Alphabetical Glossary

Latin	English	Book:Chapter
ad	to, toward	2:22*
aestas	summer	1:25/2:3,23
agnus	lamb	1:16/2:15
agricola	farmer	2:21
albus, alba, album	white	2:28
altus, alta, altum	high	2:30
amabo te	please	1:12/2:11
ambulo	I walk	2:10,17
amica	female friend	2:12
amicus	male friend	2:12
amo	I love	2:16
angelus	angel	1:16
annus	year	2:27
ante	before	2:23,30
aperi librum	open the book	1:11
aperite libros	open the books (to more than one person)	1:11
Aprilis	April	2:3
aqua	water	1:21
arbor	tree	1:30
architectus	architect	2:20
arcus	rainbow	1:24/2:22
artifex	artist	2:20
ater, atra, atrum	black	2:28
athleta	athlete	2:21
attolle manum	raise your hand	1:11/2:10
attollite manus	raise your hands (to more than one person)	1:11/2:10
audi	listen	1:11/2:10
audite	listen (to more than one person)	1:11/2:10
Augustus	August	2:4
aurantius, aurantia, aurantium	orange	2:28

*The numbers in this column indicate in what book and chapter the word appears. For example, "2:22" means *Song School Latin Book 2*, Chapter 22.

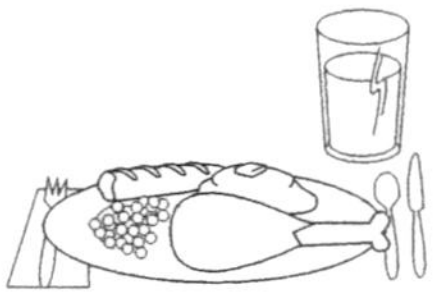

Latin	English	Book:Chapter
auris	ear	1:20/2:18
aurora	dawn, morning	2:27
aurum	gold	2:29
autumnus	fall	1:25/2:3,23
avis	bird	1:15/2:14
balneum	bath	2:26
bellum	war	2:15
bene	well, fine	1:3/2:4,18
beneficus, benefica, beneficum	kind, generous	2:24
bibo	I drink	1:21
bonus, bona, bonum	good	2:30
brevis, breve	short	2:30
caelum	sky	1:26/2:24
caeruleus, caerulea, caeruleum	blue	2:28
canis	dog	1:14/2:12
cano	I sing	1:17/2:16
caput	head	1:19/2:17
carmen	song	2:26
casa	house	1:8/2:8
celebratio	celebration	2:12
cena	dinner	1:21/2:20
cibus	food	1:21/2:20
circum	around	2:22
cito	fast, quickly	2:17,24
clamo	I shout	2:9
collis	hill	1:30/2:28
color	color	2:28
colores	colors	2:28
contra	against	2:23,30
coquo	I cook	2:8,15
corona	crown	2:14,29
corpus	body	1:19/2:17
crustulum	cookie	1:22/2:21

cum	with	2:23,30
curro	I run	2:10
de	down from, concerning, about	2:23
decem	ten	2:6,14
December	December	2:4
dico	I speak, say	2:9,16
Dies Iovis	Thursday	2:2
Dies Lunae	Monday	2:2
Dies Martis	Tuesday	2:2
Dies Mercurii	Wednesday	2:2
Dies Saturni	Saturday	2:2
Dies Solis	Sunday	2:2
Dies Veneris	Friday	2:2
dies	day	2:27
diligens, diligentis	careful, attentive	2:24
diligenter	carefully	2:18,26
discipuli	students	1:1/2:1
do	I give	1:17/2:16
donum	gift	1:17
dormio	I sleep	2:26
dum	while	2:23
duo	two	2:5
edo	I eat	1:21/2:20

elephantus	elephant	1:15
epulae	feast	2:12
equito	I ride a horse	2:10
equus	horse	1:14
ex	out of	2:22
extra	outside of	2:23
fabula	story	2:26
familia	family	2:12,20
Februarius	February	2:3
feles	cat	1:14/2:12
femina	woman	1:6/2:5
fenestra	window	1:8/2:8
fessus, fessa, fessum	tired	2:26

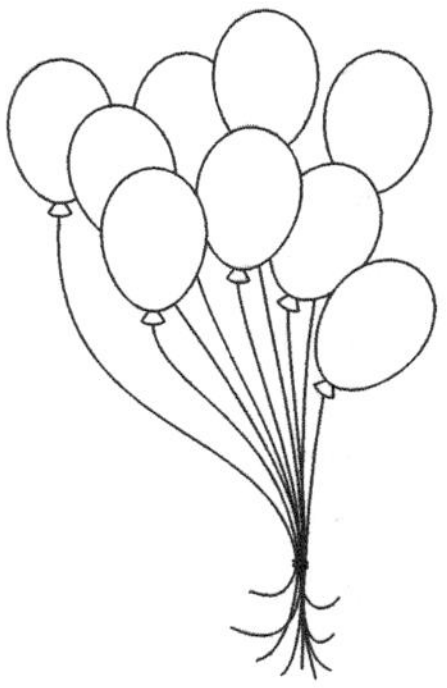

fidelis, fidele	faithful	2:24
flavus, flava, flavum	yellow	2:28
flos	flower	1:29/2:27
flumen	river	1:28/2:26
folium	leaf	1:29/2:27
forte	bravely	2:18,26
fortis, forte	brave, strong	2:24
frater	brother	1:5/2:5
fructus	fruit	1:22
gemma	jewel	2:29
gladius	sword	2:15
grammatica	grammar, language arts	2:11,18
herba	plant	1:29
Hic mensis est ...	This month is	2:3
hiems	winter	1:25/2:3,23
historia	history	2:11
Hodie est ______.	Today is ______.	2:1,8
hora	hour	2:27
hortus	garden	1:29/2:27
humilis, humile	humble	2:24
humus	ground, dirt	1:29
Ianuarius	January	2:3
ignosce mihi	excuse me	1:12/2:11

imber	rain	1:24/2:22
infans	baby	1:16/2:15
inter	between, among	2:23,30
Iulius	July	2:4
Iunius	June	2:4,11
laboro	I work	2:8
lac	milk	1:22/2:21
lacus	lake	1:28/2:26
laudo	I praise	1:17/2:16
lavo	I wash	2:8,15
lectio	reading	2:11
lectus	bed	2:26
lente	slowly	2:17
leo	lion	1:15/2:14
liber	book	1:7/2:6
longus, longa, longum	long	2:30

ludus	game, school, play	2:12,20
luna	moon	1:26
lux	light	2:26
magister	male teacher	1:1/2:1
magistra	female teacher	1:1/2:1
magnus, magna, magnum	great, big	2:30
Maius	May	2:4,11
malus, mala, malum	bad	2:30
manus	hand	1:19/2:17
mare	sea	1:28
Martius	March	2:3,10
mater	mother	1:5/2:4
mathematica	math	2:11
medicus	doctor	2:20
mensa	table	1:7/2:6
mensis	month	2:27
meridies	noon	2:27
Meum praenomen est	My name is . . .	1:2/2:2
miles	soldier	2:15
mons	mountain	1:30/2:28
murus	wall	1:8/2:8
musica	female musician	2:21

musica	music	2:12
musicus	male musician	2:21
nares	nose	1:20
narro	I tell	2:16
nauta	sailor	2:21
navigo	I sail	2:10
navis	ship, boat	1:28
negotium	job, occupation	2:20,27
nimbus	cloud	1:24/2:22
nix	snow	1:24/2:22
non	not	2:18
novem	nine	2:6
November	November	2:4
nox	night	2:26
numquam	never	2:17
nunc	now	2:17
oboediens, oboedientis	obedient	2:24
octo	eight	2:6

October	October	2:4
oculus	eye	1:20/2:18
optime	best	1:3/2:4,18
oro	I pray	2:9
os	mouth	1:20/2:18
panis	bread	1:22/2:21
parvus, parva, parvum	small	2:30
pasco	I feed	2:8,15
pastor	shepherd	1:16
pater	father	1:5/2:4
patria	country, fatherland	2:14,21
pes	foot	1:19/2:17
pessime	badly, terrible	1:3/2:4,18
physica	science	2:11,18
pisces	fish	1:14/2:12
poeta	poet	2:20
pone	behind	2:22
populus	people	2:14,21
porta	door, gate	1:8/2:8
porto	I carry	2:16
post	after	2:23,30
prex	prayer	2:26
prope	near	2:22
puella	girl	1:6/2:5
puer	boy	1:6/2:5
pugno	I fight	2:15
pulcher, pulchra, pulchrum	pretty, handsome	2:30
pullus	chicken	1:22
purgo	I clean	2:8
purpureus, purpurea, purpureum	purple	2:28
quadratus, quadrata, quadratum	square	2:30
quattuor	four	2:5,12
Qui dies est?	What day is it?	2:1,8
Qui mensis est?	What month is it?	2:3,10
Quid agis?	How are you?	1:3/2:4

Quid est tuum praenomen?	What is your name?	1:2/2:2
quinque	five	2:5,12
regina	queen	2:14,29
regno	I reign	2:29
regnum	kingdom	2:29
rego	I rule, direct	2:14
repete	repeat	1:10/2:9
repetite	repeat (to more than one person)	1:10/2:9
rex	king	2:14,29
rotundus, rotunda, rotundum	round	2:30
ruber, rubra, rubrum	red	2:28
saepe	often	2:17,24

salve	hello	1:1/2:1
sapiens, sapientis	wise	2:24
saxum	rock	1:30/2:28
scribe	write	1:10/2:9
scribite	write (to more than one person)	1:10/2:9
scribo	I write	2:9,16
scriptio	writing	2:11
scriptor	writer	2:21
sede	sit	1:10/2:9
sedete	sit (to more than one person)	1:10/2:9
sella	chair	1:7/2:6
semper	always	2:17
senator	senator, politician	2:21
septem	seven	2:6,14
September	September	2:4
septimana	week	2:27
servus	male slave	2:29
sex	six	2:6
silva	forest	1:30
sol	sun	1:26/2:24
solium	throne	2:29
soror	sister	1:5/2:5

specto	I look at	2:16
stella	star	1:16,26/2:24
stratum	blanket	2:26
structor	builder	2:21,28
studiosus, studiosa, studiosum	eager to learn	2:24
stylus	pencil	1:7/2:6
sub	under	2:22,29
sum	I am	1:3
supra	over, above, on top of	2:22,29
surge	rise, stand up	1:10/2:9
surgite	rise, stand up (to more than one person)	1:10/2:9
sursum	up	2:23
susurro	I whisper	2:9
tabernarius	shopkeeper	2:20,27
tace	be quiet	1:11/2:10
tacete	be quiet (to more than one person)	1:11/2:10
tempus	time	2:27
tibi gratias ago	thank you	1:12/2:11
trans	across	2:22
tres	three	2:5
triangulus, triangula, triangulum	triangular	2:30
tyrannus	ruler, dictator	2:29
unda	wave	1:28/2:26
unus	one	2:5
ursa	bear	1:15/2:14
vale	good-bye	1:1/2:1
vehor in vehiculo	I ride in a car	2:10
venator	hunter	2:21,28
ventus	wind	1:24
ver	spring	1:25/2:3,23
verax, veracis	truthful, honest	2:24
vesper	evening	2:27
video	I see	2:15
vigil	guard, policeman, fireman	2:20
vinco	I conquer	2:15,22
vir	man	1:6/2:5
viridis, viride	green	2:28
virtus	virtue, courage, excellence	2:24
vivo	I live	2:16
voco	I call	2:16
volo	I fly	2:10

Appendix D

Summary of Grammar

This appendix contains a concise review of the grammar covered in *Song School Latin Book 2*. Scattered throughout this summary, you'll see numbers, preceded by the letter *c*, in parentheses. Those numbers indicate the chapter of this book in which a concept was first introduced.◊

◊ There are some things covered in this summary that are not specifically addressed in the book. The information is included here to provide a fuller overview of the Latin grammar presented in *Song School Latin, Book 2*.

Verbs

Verbs are words that show action, such as "walk" and "carry" (c1). Here are some examples:

***Ambulo* cito.** I *walk* quickly.
***Porto* coronam.** I *carry* the crown.

A *linking verb* is a kind of verb that links or connects one thing to another (c14). A linking verb is also called a *being verb* because it shows what something is—its state of being. In the present tense, English linking verbs are:

I *am*
you *are*
he/she/it *is*
we *are*
you *are*
they *are*

The following are some example sentences in which being verbs in both English and Latin are used.

Marcus *est* puer. Mark *is* a boy.
Julia *est* puella. Julia *is* a girl.
Amici *sunt* pueri. The friends *are* boys.
Amicae *sunt* puellae. The friends *are* girls.

Here are the Latin linking verbs in the present tense (c15):

sum (I am)
es (you are)
est (he/she/it is)
sumus (we are)

estis (you all are)
sunt (they are)

Verbs have three features or traits: *person*, *number*, and *tense*. Let's take a look at each of these features.

Tense

Tense is the verb trait that tells you what the action of the verb is and when, or at what time, the action of the verb takes place (c18). The following three sentences show Mark carrying a crown in the past, present (now), and future.

Marcus portabat coronam. Mark *was carrying* the crown. (past tense)
Marcus portat coronam. Mark *carries* the crown. (present tense)
Marcus portabo coronam. Mark *will carry* the crown. (future tense)

In Latin, verb endings tell you the tense of the verb. The following are the Latin past, present, and future tense endings:

Past (Imperfect) Tense Endings (c21)	
SINGULAR	PLURAL
-bam	**-bamus**
-bas	**-batis**
-bat	**-bant**

Present Tense Endings (c2)	
SINGULAR	PLURAL
-o	**-mus**
-s	**-tis**
-t	**-nt**

Future Tense Endings (c22)	
SINGULAR	PLURAL
-bo	**-bimus**
-bis	**-bitis**
-bit	**-bunt**

Number

Number is the verb feature that tells you *what number* of people are doing the action of the verb (c23). If only one person is doing the action of the verb, we call the verb *singular*. If two or more people are doing the action of the verb, we call the verb *plural*. The following are three example sentences that show that the verb is singular because only one person is doing the action.

Porto coronam. *I* carry the crown.
Marcus portat coronam. *Mark* carries the crown.
Portas coronam. *You* carry the crown.

The following are three sentences that show two or more people doing the action.

Portamus coronam. *We* carry the crown.
Portatis coronam. *You all* carry the crown.
Marcus et Julia portant coronam. *Mark and Julia* carry the crown.

Latin verb endings tell you if the verb is singular or plural:

Porto: Present Tense (c27)			
SINGULAR		PLURAL	
VERB	MEANING	VERB	MEANING
port*o*	I carry	**porta*mus***	we carry
porta*s*	you carry	**porta*tis***	you all carry
porta*t*	he/she/it carries	**porta*nt***	they carry

As you can see from the preceding table, the present tense *singular* Latin endings are **-o, -s, -t.** The present tense *plural* endings are **-mus, -tis, -nt.**

<u>Person</u>

Person is the verb trait that tells you *who* is doing the action of the verb (c11). Person can be either singular (one person) or plural (two or more people). There are three kinds of "person" who may be doing the action of a verb:

Singular			
PERSON	EXPLANATION	LATIN	ENGLISH
First Person	This is when you, yourself, are doing the action.	**Porto.**	*I* carry.
Second Person	This is when the person to whom you are speaking or to whom you are close physically is doing the action.	**Portas.**	*You* carry.
Third Person	This is when the person about whom you are talking (who is not close to you and can't hear you) is doing the action.	**Portat.**	*He* carries.

Plural			
PERSON	EXPLANATION	LATIN	ENGLISH
First Person	This is when another person or a group of people are right with you, joining you in the action.	**Portamus.**	*We* carry.
Second Person	This is when you are talking to two or more other people who are doing the action.	**Portatis.**	*You all* carry.
Third Person	This is when you are talking about two or more other people who are doing the action.	**Portant.**	*They* carry.

Now study the following charts and note that the three traits of verbs—person, number, and tense—are all included.

Present *Tense* (Endings: -o, -s, -t, -mus, -tis, -nt)

PERSON	NUMBER: Singular		PERSON	NUMBER: Plural	
First Person	**porto**	I carry	First Person	**portamus**	we carry
Second Person	**portas**	you carry	Second Person	**portatis**	you all carry
Third Person	**portat**	he/she/it carries	Third Person	**portant**	they carry

Imperfect (Past) *Tense* (Endings: -bam, -bas, -bat, -bamus, -batis, -bant)

PERSON	NUMBER: Singular		PERSON	NUMBER: Plural	
First Person	**portabam**	I was carrying	First Person	**portabamus**	we were carrying
Second Person	**portabas**	you were carrying	Second Person	**portabatis**	you all were carrying
Third Person	**portabat**	he/she/it was carrying	Third Person	**portabant**	They were carrying

Future *Tense* (Endings: -bo, -bis, -bit, -bimus, -bitis, -bunt)

PERSON	NUMBER: Singular		PERSON	NUMBER: Plural	
First Person	**portabo**	I will carry	First Person	**portabimus**	we will carry
Second Person	**portabis**	you will carry	Second Person	**portabitis**	you all will carry
Third Person	**portabit**	he/she/it will carry	Third Person	**portabunt**	they will carry

We can note the three traits (person, number, and tense) of any verb like this:

Porto: first person, singular, present tense
Portamus: first person, plural, present tense
Portabas: second person, singular, imperfect tense
Portabamus: first person, plural, imperfect tense
Portabo: first person, singular, future tense
Portat: third person, singular, present tense

The listing of these three traits is called *parsing* a verb. It means that we are listing all the *parts* of the verb.

Nouns

Nouns are words that name a person, place, or thing (c1). *Marcus* is a noun because he's a person and *Rome* is a noun because it is a place. A *crown* is a noun because it is a thing. The following sentences show nouns being used.

***Marcus* portat *coronam*.**	*Mark* carries the *crown*.
***Julia* ambulat in *Roma*.**	*Julia* walks in *Rome*.

In Latin, nouns have three traits: *gender*, *number*, and *case*. Let's take a look at these three noun traits.

Number

Number is the noun trait that tells you if you have one noun (such as one crown) or two or more nouns (such as two crowns) (c23). When you have just one of a person, place, or thing, the noun is *singular*. When you have two or more of a person, place, or thing, the noun is *plural*. In Latin, there are both singular and plural endings for nouns. For example:

Singular: **corona** (crown)
Plural: **coronae** (crowns)

Gender

Gender is the noun trait that tells you whether the noun is *masculine, feminine*, or *neuter* (c24). In Latin, most nouns are either masculine or feminine, but there are a good many that are neuter, too. Each of the noun genders—masculine, feminine, and neuter—has its own set of endings. Look at the following examples of **puella, amicus**, and **regnum**:

Puella (Girl): Feminine		**Amicus** (Friend): Masculine		**Regnum** (Kingdom): Neuter	
puell*a*	**puell*ae***	**amic*us***	**amic*i***	**regn*um***	**regn*a***
puell*ae*	**puell*arum***	**amic*i***	**amic*orum***	**regn*i***	**regn*orum***
puell*ae*	**puell*is***	**amic*o***	**amic*is***	**regn*o***	**regn*is***
puell*am*	**puell*as***	**amic*um***	**amic*os***	**regn*um***	**regn*a***
puell*a*	**puell*is***	**amic*o***	**amic*is***	**regn*o***	**regn*is***
Declension: First		Declension: Second, Masculine		Declension: Second, Neuter	

Noun Families or Declensions (c24)

The three nouns **puella, amicus**, and **regnum** each belong to their own family of nouns. **Puella** belongs to a family of nouns that are feminine and have the same endings. We call that family the *first declension*. **Amicus** belongs to a family of nouns that are masculine and have the same endings. We call that family the *second declension—masculine* (c28). **Regnum** belongs to a family of nouns that are neuter and have the same endings. We call that family the *second declension—neuter* (c29).

Case

Case is the noun trait that tells you what *job* a noun is doing in a sentence (c23). There are five normal case endings for nouns. Once you note what case a noun has, you will know the job it does in a sentence! The first case is the *nominative* case. This case tells you that the noun is doing the job of a *subject noun* (*SN*), and that means that it is the subject of the sentence and is doing the action of the verb. Take a look at the following sentences:

SN V DO
Mark carries the crown.

SN V DO
Marcus portat coronam.

You can see that Mark (or **Marcus**) is the subject noun (SN) in the sentence—Mark is doing the action of carrying. The *V* stands for verb. The verb in the sentence is "carries" (**portat**). The *DO* stands for direct object. The direct object in a sentence does not do the action of the verb but instead receives the action of the verb. Crown (**coronam**) is the direct object because it is receiving the action of carrying. In Latin, the direct object is put in another case called the *accusative* case. Here is how we would say "Marcus carries the girl" in Latin.

SN V DO
Marcus portat puellam.

Here are all five cases for Latin nouns with brief descriptions of the noun jobs they perform within a sentence.

Case	Noun Job
Nominative	Subject Noun (SN)
Genitive	Shows Possession: Possessive Noun Adjective (PNA)
Dative	Indirect Object (IO)
Accusative	Direct Object (DO); Object of Preposition (OP)
Ablative	Object of Preposition (OP)

In this book, the case endings are introduced (c23). You will study the various noun jobs in your later study of Latin.

Now let's study the words **puella** and **amicus** and look at their gender, number, and case.

Puella (girl) GENDER: Feminine		
	NUMBER	
CASE	Singular	Plural
Nominative	**puell*a***	**puell*ae***
Genitive	**puell*ae***	**puell*arum***
Dative	**puell*ae***	**puell*is***
Accusative	**puell*am***	**puell*as***
Ablative	**puell*a***	**puell*is***
	DECLENSION: FIRST	

Amicus (friend) GENDER: Masculine		
	NUMBER	
CASE	Singular	Plural
Nominative	**amic*us***	**amic*i***
Genitive	**amic*i***	**amic*orum***
Dative	**amico**	**amic*is***
Accusative	**amic*um***	**amic*os***
Ablative	**amico**	**amic*is***
	DECLENSION: SECOND, MASCULINE	

In the preceding chart, you can see the three noun traits of *gender*, *number*, and *case*. Let's study the noun chart for the forms of **puella**.

- The gender of **puella** is feminine.
- The case of **puella** is nominative. It can also be ablative.
- The number of **puella** is singular.
- We can note three noun traits of **puella** as: feminine, nominative, and singular.

Let's look at some other forms of **puella** and **amicus** (from the preceding chart) and list their noun traits.

- **puellam:** feminine, accusative, singular
- **puellarum:** feminine, genitive, plural
- **amicus:** masculine, nominative, singular
- **amici:** masculine, genitive, singular *or* masculine, nominative, plural

Noun and Adjective Agreement

If nouns can be a person, place, or thing, *adjectives* are a part of speech that describe or tell us something about a person, place, or thing (c24). In other words, adjectives describe nouns.

Since Latin nouns have gender, number, and case, the adjectives that describe those nouns must match them and have the same gender, number, and case. Check out the following examples:

A SN
Magna corona. The big crown.

A SN
Parva corona. The small crown.

Both **magna** and **parva** are adjectives (labeled with *A* to indicate that they are adjectives) that describe "crown." Notice that **magna** has the same ending as **corona**—they both end in **a**. Both **magna** and **corona** are feminine, nominative, and singular—they match in gender, case, and number. Now take a look at the following sentence:

Marcus portat magnam coronam. Marcus carries the big crown.

Again, notice that **magnam** and **coronam** have the same ending, **-am**. Both the adjective **magnam** and the noun **coronam** are feminine, accusative, and singular. They match or "agree" in gender, case, and number.

Noun and Verb Agreement

As you know, nouns can be singular or plural, and so can verbs. So, when nouns and verbs are used in a sentence, they need to match in number. This simply means that when we have a singular subject, such as **Marcus**, we must use a singular form of a verb, such as **portat** (which can mean "*he* carries," but not "*they* carry"). See the following examples:

Correct: **Marcus portat** (he/she/it carries) **coronam.** Mark carries the crown.
Incorrect: **Marcus portant** (they carry) **coronam.**

Correct: **Marcus et Julia portant** (they carry) **coronam.** Mark and Julia carry the crown.
Incorrect: **Marcus et Julia portat** (he carries) **coronam.**

Correct: **Amicae portant** (they carry) **coronam.** The friends carry the crown.
Incorrect: **Amicae portat** (he carries) **coronam.**

Parts of Speech

Language has eight parts of speech. Each part of speech is a class of words that performs a particular function in language. The following is a list of the eight parts of speech along with brief explanations and examples:

1. **Noun:** A word used for a person, place, or thing (c1). *English examples:* Mark, Rome, crown. ***Mark*** carries the ***crown***. *Latin examples:* **Marcus, Roma, corona. *Marcus* portat *coronam*.**
2. **Pronoun:** A word used to replace a noun (c11). *Example:* "He" is a pronoun that can replace "Mark." *English example:* ***Mark*** carries the crown. ***He*** carries the crown. *Latin example:* ***Marcus*** **portat coronam. *Ille*** (he) **portat coronam.**
3. **Verb:** A word used to express action (c1). *English example:* Mark ***carries*** the crown. *Latin example:* **Marcus *portat* coronam.**
4. **Adverb:** A word used to describe verbs, adjectives, and other adverbs (c17,18). *English example:* Mark walks ***bravely***. *Latin example:* **Marcus ambulat *forte*.**
5. **Adjective:** A word used to describe nouns (c24). *English example:* Mark carries the ***big*** crown. *Latin example:* **Marcus portat coronam *magnam*.**
6. **Preposition:** A word placed before a noun to express a relationship of space, time, or other relations (c22). *English example:* Mark walks ***around*** the crown. *Latin example:* **Marcus ambulat *circum* coronam.**
7. **Conjunction:** A word used to connect words, phrases, or sentences. *English example:* Mark ***and*** Julia carried the crown. *Latin example:* **Marcus *et* Julia portant coronam.**
8. **Interjection:** A word used to express emotion and often used in isolation. *English example:* ***Oh!*** The crown is big. *Latin example:* ***Heu!*** **Corona est magna.**

Latin Roots to Grammatical Words

Almost all the words we use to study grammar come from Latin words. Here are the Latin roots to many of the new grammatical words you have learned:

1. **Grammar:** This word came into Latin from the Greek word **gramma**, which means "letter." You could say that grammar is the study of how letters work!
2. **Noun:** This word comes from the Latin word **nomen**, which means "name."
3. **Pronoun:** This word means "for or on behalf of the noun." **Pro** in Latin can mean "for" and "on behalf of."

4. **Verb:** This word comes from the Latin word **verbum**, which means "word."
5. **Adverb:** This word means "to the verb." In Latin, **ad** can mean "to" or "toward."
6. **Adjective:** This word comes from the Latin **adicere**, which means "to throw to or to cast to." The adjective, you might say, is thrown to the noun.
7. **Preposition:** This word is from the Latin words **pre** and **positio** and means "a placing before." Prepositions are usually placed before nouns.
8. **Conjunction:** This word is from the Latin word **conjunctio** and means "a joining together." Conjunctions join words together.
9. **Interjection:** This word is from the Latin words **inter** (among) and **iacere** (to throw). An interjection is something "thrown into" a conversation.
10. **Conjugation:** This word is from the Latin words **cum** (with) and **iungere** (to join). A conjugation is a joining of a verb's stem with all its endings.
11. **Declension:** This word is from the Latin words **de** (of) and **clinatus** (inclined, bent). Think of a noun declension as having the endings "bent" on the end.
12. **Nominative:** This word is from the Latin word **nominare**, which means "to name."
13. **Genitive:** This word is related to the Latin word **gignere** (to beget). The genitive often shows possession.
14. **Dative:** This word is from the Latin word **dativus** (to do with giving). Related to **do** (I give) and **dare** (to give).
15. **Accusative:** This word is from the Latin word **accussativus** (which means "accusative") and is related to **accusatio** (accusation), which contains a root meaning of pointing to the cause of something.
16. **Ablative:** This word is related to the Latin word **aufere** (the participle is **ablatum**), which means "to carry away." The ablative case is often used with prepositions that express movement away from a place.
17. **Parsing:** This word is from the Latin word **pars** (part). To parse a verb or noun is to name or show all of its parts (such as person, number, and tense or gender, case, and number).

Reference Charts Appendix E

For easy review, study, and reference, the charts in this appendix are presented in the order in which they appear in the book.

Verb Charts for the Present Tense

O-S-T Chant (Present Tense Verb Endings)

(Ch. 2)

O-S-T Chant	
-o	**-mus**
-s	**-tis**
-t	**-nt**

(Ch. 3)

O-S-T Chant: Singular		
First Person	**-o**	I
Second Person	**-s**	you
Third Person	**-t**	he/she/it

(Ch. 4)

O-S-T Chant				
Person	Singular		Plural	
First Person	**-o**	I	**-mus**	we
Second Person	**-s**	you	**-tis**	you all
Third Person	**-t**	he/she/it	**-nt**	they

Laudo

(Ch. 4)

Laudo with Endings	
laud*o*	***I*** praise
lauda*s*	***you*** praise
lauda*t*	***he/she/it*** praises
lauda*mus*	***we*** praise
lauda*tis*	***you all*** praise
lauda*nt*	***they*** praise

(Ch. 6)

Laudo with Endings				
	Singular		Plural	
Person	Ending	Meaning	Ending	Meaning
First Person	**laud*o***	I praise	**lauda*mus***	we praise
Second Person	**lauda*s***	you praise	**lauda*tis***	you all praise
Third Person	**lauda*t***	he/she/it praises	**lauda*nt***	they praise

Do

(Ch. 5)

Do with Endings	
d*o*	***I*** give
da*s*	***you*** give
da*t*	***he/she/it*** gives
da*mus*	***we*** give
da*tis*	***you all*** give
da*nt*	***they*** give

Lavo

(Ch. 8)

Lavo Chant			
SINGULAR		PLURAL	
lav*o*	I wash	**lava*mus***	we wash
lava*s*	you wash	**lava*tis***	you all wash
lava*t*	he/she/it washes	**lava*nt***	they wash

Clamo

(Ch. 9)

Clamo Chant			
SINGULAR		PLURAL	
clam*o*	I shout	**clama*mus***	we shout
clama*s*	you shout	**clama*tis***	you all shout
clama*t*	he/she/it shouts	**clama*nt***	they shout

Noun and Pronoun Charts

Comparison of Singular and Plural Nouns

(Ch. 12)

SINGULAR		PLURAL	
amicus	friend (male)	**amici**	friends (male)
amica	friend (female)	**amicae**	friends (female)
discipulus	student (male)	**discipuli**	students (male)
discipula	student (female)	**discipulae**	students (female)
ludus	game	**ludi**	games
familia	family	**familiae**	families

Pronouns

(Ch. 12)

	PERSON	EXPLANATION	PRONOUN(S)
SINGULAR (when one person does the action)	First Person	When I am the one doing the action	**I**
	Second Person	When the person you are talking *to* is doing the action	**you**
	Third Person	When the person you are talking *about* is doing the action	**he/she/it**
PLURAL (when two or more people do the same action)	First Person	When the people you are *with* are doing the action	**we**
	Second Person	When the people who you are talking *to* are doing the action	**you all**
	Third Person	When the people you are talking *about* are doing the action	**they**

Linking Verb Charts

Sum

Present Tense (Ch. 15)

Person	Singular	Plural
First Person	**sum** (I am)	**sumus** (we are)
Second Person	**es** (you are)	**estis** (you all are)
Third Person	**est** (he/she/it is)	**sunt** (they are)

Past Tense (Ch. 18)

Person	Singular	Plural
First Person	**era*m*** (I was)	**era*mus*** (we were)
Second Person	**era*s*** (you were)	**era*tis*** (you all were)
Third Person	**era*t*** (he/she/it was)	**era*nt*** (they were)

Future Tense (Ch. 20)

Person	Singular	Plural
First Person	**ero** (I will be)	**erimus** (we will be)
Second Person	**eris** (you will be)	**eritis** (you all will be)
Third Person	**erit** (he/she/it will be)	**erunt** (they will be)

Verb Ending Charts for the Imperfect (Past) and Future Tenses

Past Tense (Ch. 21)

Person	Singular	Plural
First Person	**-bam**	**-bamus**
Second Person	**-bas**	**-batis**
Third Person	**-bat**	**-bant**

Future Tense (Ch. 22)

Person	Singular	Plural
First Person	**-bo**	**-bimus**
Second Person	**-bis**	**-bitis**
Third Person	**-bit**	**-bunt**

Noun Ending Charts of the First and Second Declensions

First Declension Endings (Ch. 24)

Case	Singular	Plural
Nominative	**-a**	**-ae**
Genitive	**-ae**	**-arum**
Dative	**-ae**	**-is**
Accusative	**-am**	**-as**
Ablative	**-a**	**-is**

Second Declension Masculine Endings (Ch. 26)

Case	Singular	Plural
Nominative	**-us**	**-i**
Genitive	**-i**	**-orum**
Dative	**-o**	**-is**
Accusative	**-um**	**-os**
Ablative	**-o**	**-is**

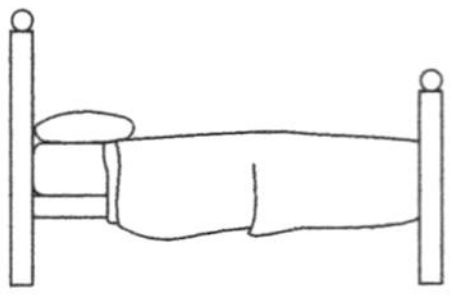

Lectus **with Endings (Ch. 26)**

Case	Singular	Plural
Nominative	**lect-us**	**lect-i**
Genitive	**lect-i**	**lect-orum**
Dative	**lect-o**	**lect-is**
Accusative	**lect-um**	**lect-os**
Ablative	**lect-o**	**lect-is**

Hora **with Endings (Ch. 27)**

Case	Singular	Plural
Nominative	**hora**	**horae**
Genitive	**horae**	**horarum**
Dative	**horae**	**horis**
Accusative	**horam**	**horas**
Ablative	**hora**	**horis**

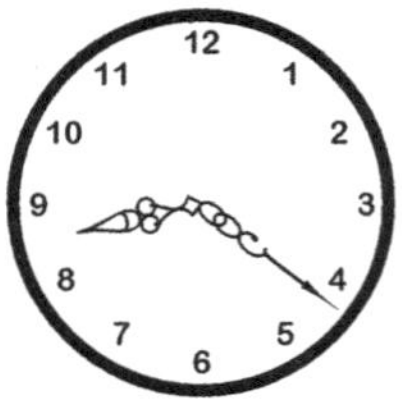

More Verb Conjugation Charts in the Present Tense

Specto: **Present Tense (Ch. 27)**

Person	Singular	Plural
First Person	**specto** (I look at)	**spectamus** (we look at)
Second Person	**spectas** (you look at)	**spectatis** (you all look at)
Third Person	**spectat** (he/she/it looks at)	**spectant** (they look at)

Porto: **Present Tense (Ch. 27)**

Person	Singular	Plural
First Person	**porto** (I carry)	**portamus** (we carry)
Second Person	**portas** (you carry)	**portatis** (you all carry)
Third Person	**portat** (he/she/it carries)	**portant** (they carry)

Masculine and Neuter Noun Endings of the Second Declension

Hortus **with Second Declension Masculine Endings (Ch. 28)**

Case	Singular	Plural
Nominative	**hort*us***	**hort*i***
Genitive	**hort*i***	**hort*orum***
Dative	**hort*o***	**hort*is***
Accusative	**hort*um***	**hort*os***
Ablative	**hort*o***	**hort*is***

Second Declension Neuter Endings (Ch. 29)

Case	Singular	Plural
Nominative	**-um**	**-a**
Genitive	**-i**	**-orum**
Dative	**-o**	**-is**
Accusative	**-um**	**-a**
Ablative	**-o**	**-is**

Adjective Endings Chart

Second Declension Neuter Endings (Ch. 30)

Case	Singular	Plural
Nominative	**bon*um***	**bon*a***
Genitive	**bon*i***	**bon*orum***
Dative	**bon*o***	**bon*is***
Accusative	**bon*um***	**bon*a***
Ablative	**bon*o***	**bon*is***

Appendix F Classroom Commands

The following are some commands that teachers and parents (and occasionally students) may use while teaching and reviewing Latin. These commands are taken from *Song School Latin Book 1* (*SSL1*).

SSL1, Chapter 10

1. **sede** — sit
   sedete — sit (to more than one person)
2. **surge** — rise, stand up
   surgite — rise, stand up (to more than one person)
3. **scribe** — write
   scribite — write (to more than one person)
4. **repete** — repeat
   repetite — repeat (to more than one person)

SSL1, Chapter 11

1. **audi** — listen
   audite — listen (to more than one person)
2. **tace** — be quiet
   tacete — be quiet (to more than one person)
3. **aperi librum** — open the book
   aperite libros — open the books (to more than one person)
4. **attolle manum** — raise your hand
   attollite manus — raise your hands (to more than one person)

Looking for more practice?

Look no further! Pages 153–199 contain activities for each chapter in *Song School Latin Book 2*. These are great resources for students who need more practice, have extra time, learn better through games and activities, or simply enjoy Latin. There is one activity page for each chapter, three pages for the review chapters, and a six-page end-of-book review. You can find the answers to each activity in the answer section that starts on page 200.

If you purchased the *SSL2* streaming video from CAP, be sure to check out the free My Library bonus content for more practice activities for your students!

A	H	O	D	I	E	M	Q	B	F
D	Q	U	P	L	I	A	U	S	D
H	U	F	M	S	D	G	I	K	I
E	O	V	A	A	O	I	D	C	S
M	A	D	G	L	D	S	I	J	C
V	B	H	I	V	A	T	E	R	I
R	A	U	S	E	L	R	S	A	P
C	P	L	T	I	E	A	E	G	U
O	E	M	E	C	N	S	S	S	L
L	S	T	R	T	B	U	T	D	I

Translate the English words below into Latin and then find the Latin words in the word search!

a. What day is it? ______________________________

b. Today is ______. ______________________________

c. hello ______________________________

d. good-bye ______________________________

Double Points if you can find the Latin word for students, male teacher, and female teacher!

1. The days of the week were erased from the calendar! Translate the English days of the week below into Latin. Then draw a line to the question mark where the day should go on the calendar.

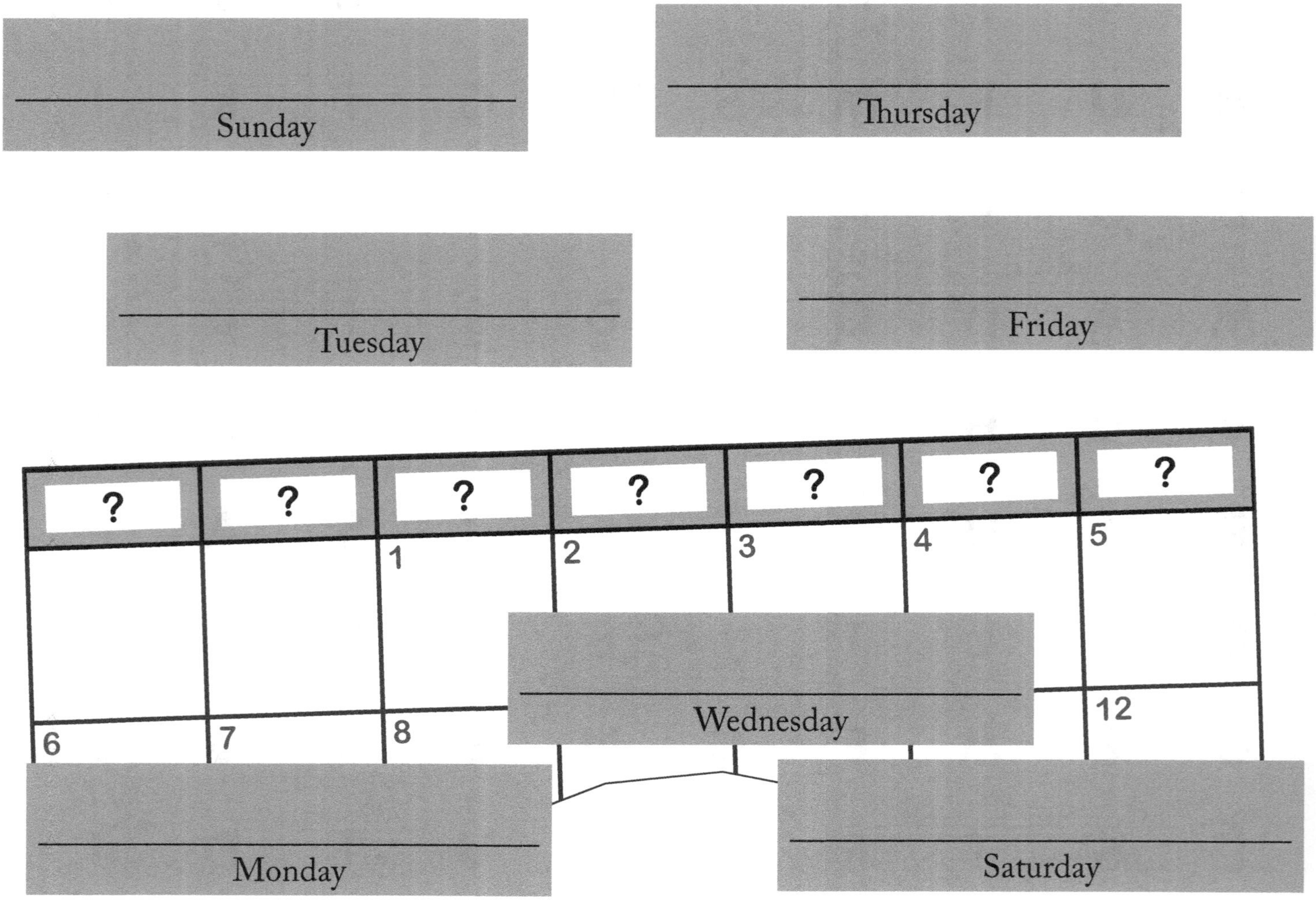

2. Do you remember how to say the following phrases in Latin? Write the the Latin translation on the line and then say them to your teacher in Latin!

a. What is your name? ______________________________

b. My name is . . . ______________________________

3. What does *carpe diem* mean? Write the translation below, then write how you plan to do what it says today.

____

____

1. Do you know *qui mensis est*? Below, translate the name of the month, and then draw a picture of what you like to do during that month.

Hic mensis est

______________________________.

(January)

Hic mensis est

______________________________.

(February)

Hic mensis est

______________________________.

(March)

Hic mensis est

______________________________.

(April)

2. January and February are both part of what season? (Write the season in Latin.)

____

On the left, translate each month into Latin. Then sing the "Months of the Year, Parts I & II" song and draw lines to match each activity (on the right) to the correct month!

____
(January)

____
(February)

____
(March)

____
(April)

____
(May)

____
(June)

____
(July)

____
(August)

____
(September)

____
(October)

____
(November)

____
(December)

marches into town,

loves the bright red cherries.

blooms in flowers and berries,

comes first in the year,

brings us coats to wear.

brings the showers down.

—off to Grandma's we go,

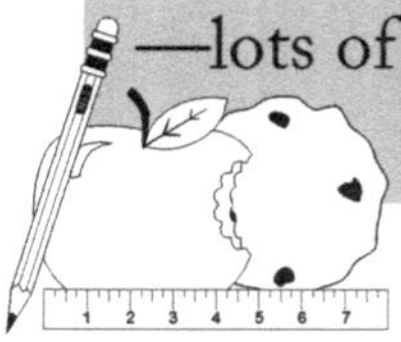
—lots of cookies to bake,

scatters leaves to rake,

starts with a bang and a flash,

—off to the beach we dash.

shovels white, white snow.

1. Using your Latin, count out loud the number of birds in each cage and then write that number, in Latin, on the line provided. Finally, color the birds.

2. What does *auxilio ab alto* mean? ____________________

3. From what Latin word is "unify" derived? ____________________

4. From what Latin word is "dual" derived? ____________________

5. From what Latin word is "quarter" derived? ____________________

1. Count up the stairs! Write the Latin word for each number on the line provided. When you get to the top, count down from ten in Latin. Then color the stairs and draw yourself walking up them.

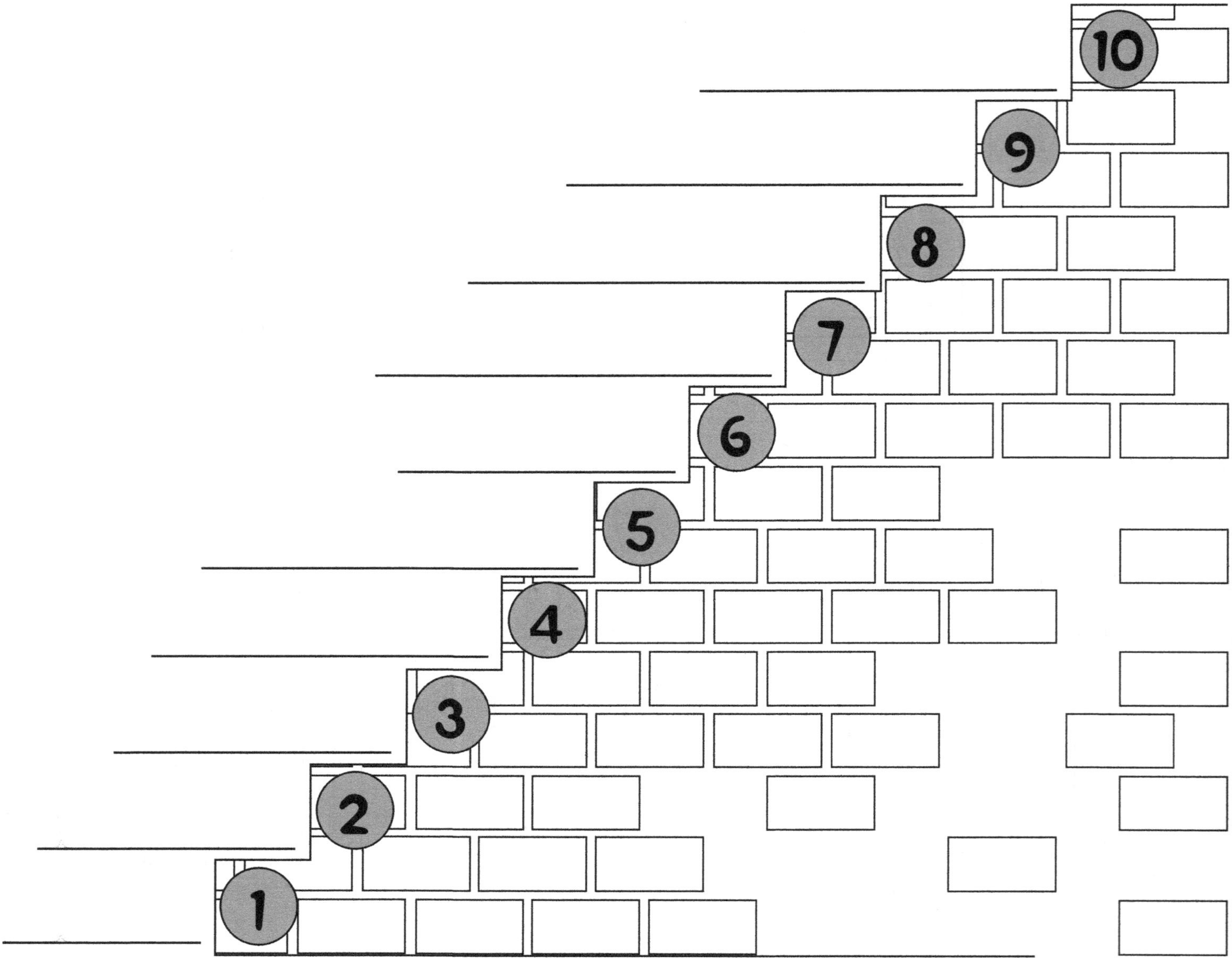

2. What does *pater familias* mean? ______________________

3. From what Latin word is "octopus" derived? ______________________

4. From what Latin word is "decimal" derived? ______________________

5. From what Latin word is "decade" derived? ______________________

1. Translate the English words into Latin and fill in the crossword puzzle!

Across

1. May ____________________
7. February ____________________
9. July ____________________
11. June ____________________
13. two ____________________
14. eight ____________________
15. five ____________________
16. March ____________________
17. three ____________________

Down

2. April ____________________
3. one ____________________
4. four ____________________
5. six ____________________
6. January ____________________
8. August ____________________
10. seven ____________________
12. nine ____________________
13. ten ____________________

2. The chapter 1 phrases got mixed up with the days of the week! Using the word bank below, see if you can put the chapter 1 phrases back together and put the days of the week in order.

Dies | Hodie | Dies | Qui | Dies | Saturni | Mercurii | est | est | Martis | Veneris | Solis | Dies | Dies | Dies | Iovis | dies | Dies | Lunae

Chapter 1 Phrases:

__________ __________ __________?
(What) (day) (is it)

__________ __________ . . .
(Today) (is)

Days of the Week:

Sunday: __________ __________

Monday: __________ __________

Tuesday: __________ __________

Wednesday: __________ __________

Thursday: __________ __________

Friday: __________ __________

Saturday: __________ __________

3. Chant the o-s-t chant as you write out the verb endings below.

4. Do you remember the famous sayings from chapters 1 through 6? Draw lines to match the Latin saying to the correct English translation.

Acta non verba	monthly, every month, or by the month
Carpe diem	Actions, not words!
Per mensem	father of the family
Ad idem	of the same mind
Auxilio ab alto	by help from on high
Pater familias	Seize the day!

5. Many English words come from Latin words. Draw lines to match the English words to the correct Latin words from which they are derived.

November	octo	diurnal
universe	sex + mensis	octagon
duel	dies	semester
unicycle	November	octopus
octave	unus	unity
diary	September	dual
unify	duo	uniform
September		

6. Color in the correct answer for each of the following statements.

a. _______________ is the term for an action word.

letter | plural | noun | verb | singular

b. _______________ means "only one."

chant | plural | noun | verb | singular

c. _______________ means "more than one."

chant | plural | noun | verb | singular

Translate each Latin word/phrase into English and then draw yourself doing each action!

laboro

____

lavo

____

purgo

____

pasco

____

coquo

____

1. Translate each Latin word into English and then draw a line to match the Latin word to the correct picture!

dico

____

clamo

____

susurro

____

scribo

____

oro

____

2. Draw a line from each Latin word to its correct place in the chart. Then fill in the chart with the correct English meaning for each of the Latin words.

Singular		Plural	

clamo　clamat　clamas　clamamus　clamatis　clamant

1. Answer the questions with the correct Latin word by writing one Latin letter in each box. Look at the drawings for hints!

a. To cross a pond what do you do?

	2				

b. If you are in a soccer game, what do you do?

1				

c. To travel a long distance very fast, what do you do?

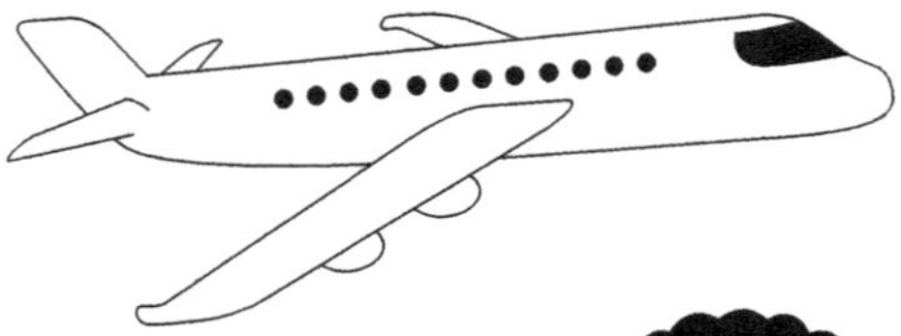

d. To go down the hallway slowly, what do you do?

	7				

e. If you have a saddle, reins, and a horse, what do you do?

4					

f. If you are driving with your mom to the store, what do you do?

				3				6		5				

2. Discover how well you did! In the activity above, find the numbers and write the letter in the corresponding blank below. Two letters are already there for you.

___	___	___	P	___	D	___	___	___	!
1	2	3		4		5	6	7	

D	Q	H	I	Y	M	R	D	S	L
H	A	T	U	C	A	K	F	C	S
I	B	G	W	E	T	P	Y	T	C
S	T	O	R	L	H	X	H	L	R
T	P	P	H	A	E	K	O	Y	I
O	F	H	I	Z	M	C	I	U	P
R	O	Y	K	B	A	P	T	G	T
I	L	S	M	A	T	R	H	I	I
A	J	I	H	D	I	C	M	Y	O
T	E	C	G	V	C	F	A	J	N
G	R	A	M	M	A	T	I	C	A

Translate the English words below into Latin and then find the Latin words in the word search!

a. math ______________________________

b. grammar, language arts ______________________________

c. reading ______________________________

d. writing ______________________________

e. science ______________________________

f. history ______________________________

1. Translate the English into Latin.

feast ____________________ celebration ____________________

family ____________________ music ____________________

game, school, play ____________________ male friend ____________________

female friend ____________________

2. Label each image with the correct Latin word from the above exercise. Then color the images!

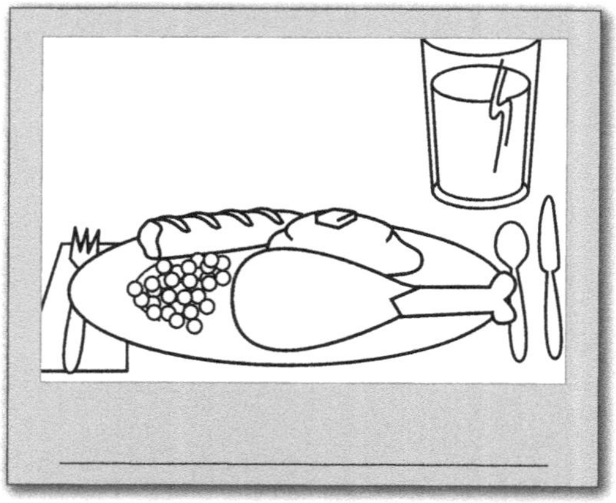

1. Translate the English words into Latin and fill in the crossword puzzle. Try translating the words directly into the crossword puzzle!

Across

1. I work
8. I speak, say
10. I cook
11. I sail
12. I clean
13. I run
14. I walk
17. family
19. I write
20. reading
22. feast
23. female friend

Down

2. male friend
3. I pray
4. history
5. science
6. I feed
7. I ride a horse
9. I whisper
13. I shout
15. music
16. I fly
18. game
21. I wash

2. Can you put together the phrases from the past few chapters? Using the word bank below, translate each English phrase into Latin.

Ora volant potentia est labora

initio Scientia Verba manet et

cogitare est littera Scribere Ab

Pray and work: ______________ ______________ ______________

To write is to think: ______________ ______________ ______________

Knowledge is power: ______________ ______________ ______________

Words fly away, the letter remains: ______________ ______________,

______________ ______________

From the beginning: ______________ ______________

3. Translate the English into Latin.

Person	Singular	Plural
First	I praise:	we praise:
Second	you praise:	you all praise:
Third	he/she/it praises:	they praise:

4. Many English words come from Latin words. Draw lines to match the English words to the correct Latin root words.

	laboro	
scribble	scribo	physician
history	physica	laborious
physical	historia	scribe
lab	grammatica	historian
math	mathematica	grammatical
inscription	ambulo	labor
grammar	curro	mathematical
current	navigo	amble
clamor	ludus	navigate
ludicrous	amicus	elude
ambulance	clamo	amicable
		navy

5. Color in the circle(s) that contain(s) the correct answer to the question.

a. Is the word *laudas* first, second, or third person? (Hint: Use the chart in question 3!)

first | second | third

b. Is the word *laudant* singular or plural? (Hint: Use the chart in question 3!)

singular | plural | neither

c. *Laudamus* is both __________ person and __________. (Be sure to color two words!)

first | second | third | plural | singular

d. Is *amicus* masculine or feminine?

masculine | feminine | neither

1. In the box below, draw a picture of a *rex* and a *regina* each sitting on a *solium*. Make sure to draw a *corona* on both the *rex* and *regina*! Then label the *rex*, *regina*, *corona*, and *solium*.

2. In the shaded box, translate the English into Latin. (Hint: It was one of your vocab words!) For bonus points, use your -o, -s, -t, -mus, -tis, -nt endings to fill in the other boxes.

Person	Singular	Plural
First	I work: ________	we work: labora________
Second	you work: labora________	you all work: labora________
Third	he/she/it works: labora______	they work: labora________

3. Translate the following Latin word into English.

populus: ________________________________

1. **Do you remember what a verb is? A verb describes things, or actions, you can do. Translate the three Latin verbs below into English.**

pugno: ______________________________

vinco: ______________________________

video: ______________________________

2. **Draw a line to match the Latin sentence on the left to the correct English translation on the right.**

Infans videt.	The king conquers.
Miles pugnat.	The baby sees.
Rex vincit.	The soldier fights.

3. **Draw a line from each Latin word to its correct place in the chart. Then fill in the chart with the correct English meaning for each of the Latin words.**

Person	Singular	Plural
First		
Second		
Third		

est   sum   estis   sumus   es   sunt

4. **Draw a picture of a fancy *gladius* in the box below.**

1. **Draw a line from each Latin word to the image it describes. Color each image and then write the English translation of the Latin word on the line below each image.**

porto **specto** **narro** **voco** **amo**

____________ ____________ ____________ ____________ ____________

2. **Draw an image that comes to your mind when you hear the word *vivo*. Write the English translation of the word *vivo* on the line below the image.**

vivo: ________________________

A	C	S	E	M	Z	N	U	N	C
W	I	V	P	O	R	P	N	U	N
P	T	K	T	E	B	X	A	M	F
V	O	C	O	M	C	I	R	Q	U
X	Q	U	L	V	J	T	R	U	P
S	A	E	P	E	A	U	O	A	O
T	M	R	D	W	N	C	W	M	R
C	O	H	T	L	E	T	Q	G	T
I	N	Y	S	E	M	P	E	R	O

Translate the English words below into Latin and then find the Latin words in the word search!

a. now ________________________________

b. never ________________________________

c. often ________________________________

d. fast, quickly ________________________________

e. slowly ________________________________

f. always ________________________________

Double Points if you can find the Latin words for I carry, I look at, I tell, I love, and I call!

1. **Translate each of the English words on the right into Latin. Then complete each of the sentences on the left by drawing a line from the sentence to the correct Latin word.**

a. If an object is green, you might say it is _____ blue.

b. Someone who fights a giant acts _____.

c. Someone who didn't do well on a test did _____ .

d. Someone who handles fragile items holds the items _____.

e. Someone who washes the dishes correctly does the job _____ .

f. Someone who wins first place does the _____.

_______________ (bravely)

_______________ (not)

_______________ (carefully)

_______________ (best)

_______________ (badly, terrible)

_______________ (well, fine)

2. **Draw a line from each Latin word to its correct place in the chart. Then fill in the chart with the correct English meaning for each of the Latin words.**

Person	Singular	Plural
First		
Second		
Third		

eras   eram   erant   eramus   erat   eratis

1. Translate the English words into Latin and fill in the crossword puzzle. Try translating the words directly into the crossword puzzle!

Across

2. I conquer
3. I look at
6. carefully
8. I live
10. queen
12. always
15. I fight
17. crown
18. I tell
21. I call
23. soldier
25. slowly
26. sword
27. I love
28. well, properly

Down

1. badly, terrible
2. I see
4. country, fatherland
5. bravely
7. never
9. I rule, direct
11. now
13. king
14. not
15. I carry
16. people
19. war
20. best
22. fast, quickly
24. often

2. **Can you put together the phrases from the past few chapters? Using the word bank below, translate each English phrase into Latin.**

Labor | Semper | vici | omnia | Regnat | vincit | fidelis | populus | vidi | Nunc | aut | Veni | numquam

Work conquers all: ________________ ________________ ____________________

The people rule: ____________________ ____________________

I came, I saw, I conquered:

____________________, ____________________, ____________________

Now or never: ____________________ ______________ ____________________

Always faithful: ________________________ ________________________

3. **Do you remember the difference between action verbs and being verbs? Circle the verbs in the sentences below. Then write what type of verb it is on the line below the sentence.**

The *rex* is kind.
____

Canis currit outside.
____

Lavo the dishes.
____

Narro the story.
____

Sunt here.
____

Es the winner.
____

Pater erat magister.
____

She speaks softly.
____

Remember:

Action Verb: describes something you can do.

Being Verb: describes something that is.

4. Look at all those Latin roots and English derivatives! Draw lines to match the English words to the correct Latin root words.

populate	reg- (regina, rego)	coronation
invincible	populus	region
regular	corona	population
survive	vinco	direct
popular	pugno	vivacious
regal	bellum	vanquish
pugnacious	video	evoke
rebel	vivo	video
portable	porto	narrative
belligerent	voco	export
nonfiction	specto	presence
spectacles	narro	none
essence	es (from sum)	vocation
vocal	pessime	optimist
spectator	optime	pessimist
narrator	non	nonsense
suspect		

5. Create your own Latin sentences! Write one sentence that uses a form of the verb *sum*, and one that uses an action verb. Look back in your book and use your vocabulary words.

Sentence with *sum* form:

____

Sentence with action verb:

____

1. Label the people below with their correct *negotium*. Then color the people!

____________________ (doctor)

____________________ (artist)

____________________ (fireman)

2. Complete each sentence by drawing a line to the correct word.

a. A(n) _____ makes rhymes and likes words.	**architectus**
b. A(n) _____ owns a store and sells items.	**medicus**
c. Someone who creates a building could be a(n) . . .	**vigil**
d. A person who puts out fires is a(n) . . .	**poeta**
e. The person who heals you when you're sick is a(n) . . .	**tabernarius**
f. A person who paints murals is a(n) . . .	**negotium**
g. When you are older, what _____ would you like?	**artifex**

3. Draw an image of someone doing one of the jobs from this chapter, and label the image with that job.

Job: ____________________

1. Label the people below with their correct *negotium*. Then color the people!

______	______	______	______
(athlete)	(builder)	(farmer)	(sailor)

______	______	______	______
(female musician)	(hunter)	(senator, politician)	(writer)

2. Draw a scene that contains three of the people above doing their jobs. Label the job that each person is doing.

Translate each underlined word into Latin, then draw someone or something doing the action of each phrase.

above the tree
____

behind the tree
____

across the hill
____

to/toward the hill
____

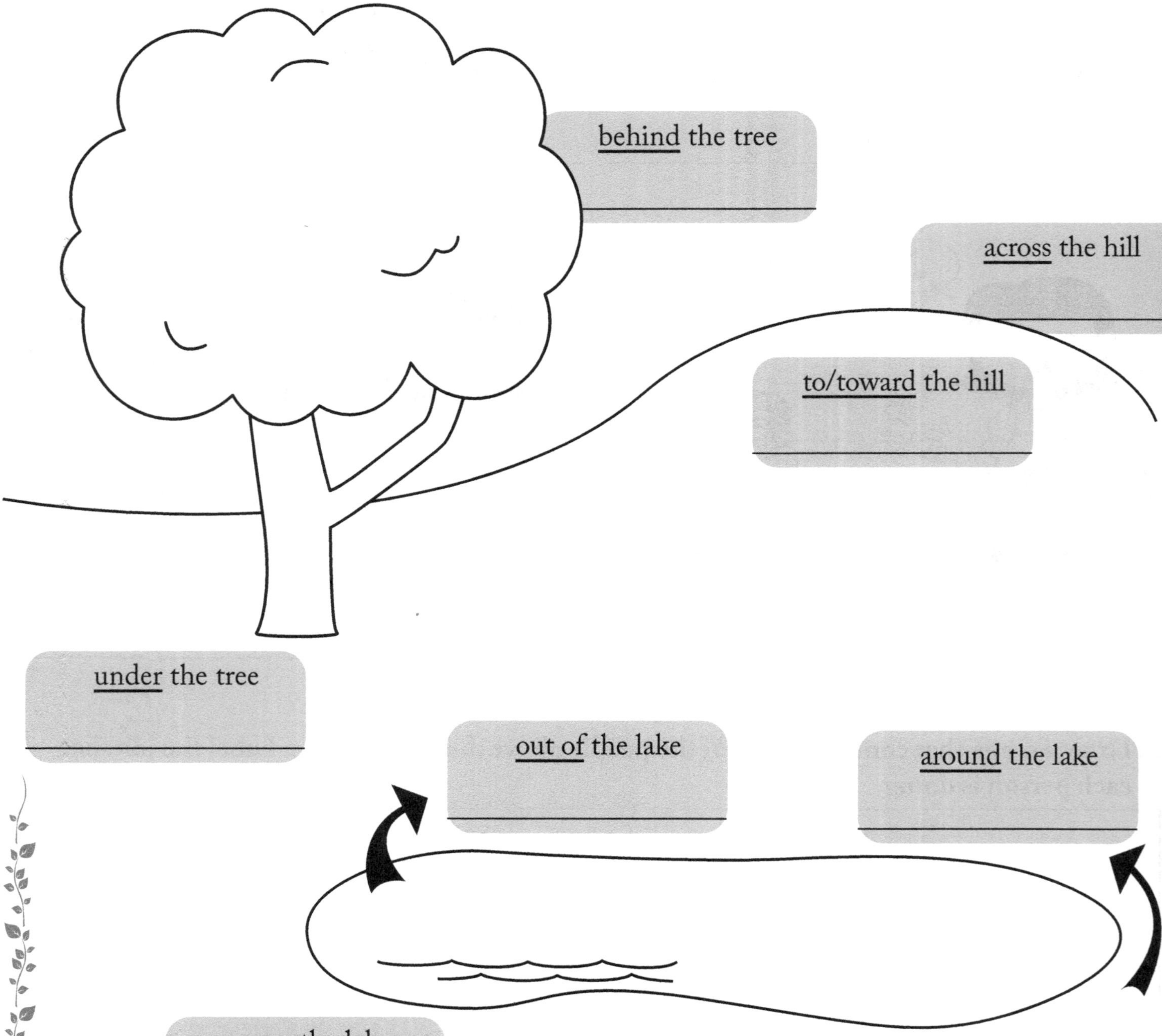

under the tree
____

out of the lake
____

around the lake
____

near the lake
____

A squirrel is darting around the yard! Starting at the top of the picture, translate each underlined word or phrase into Latin and then draw the squirrel at each spot.

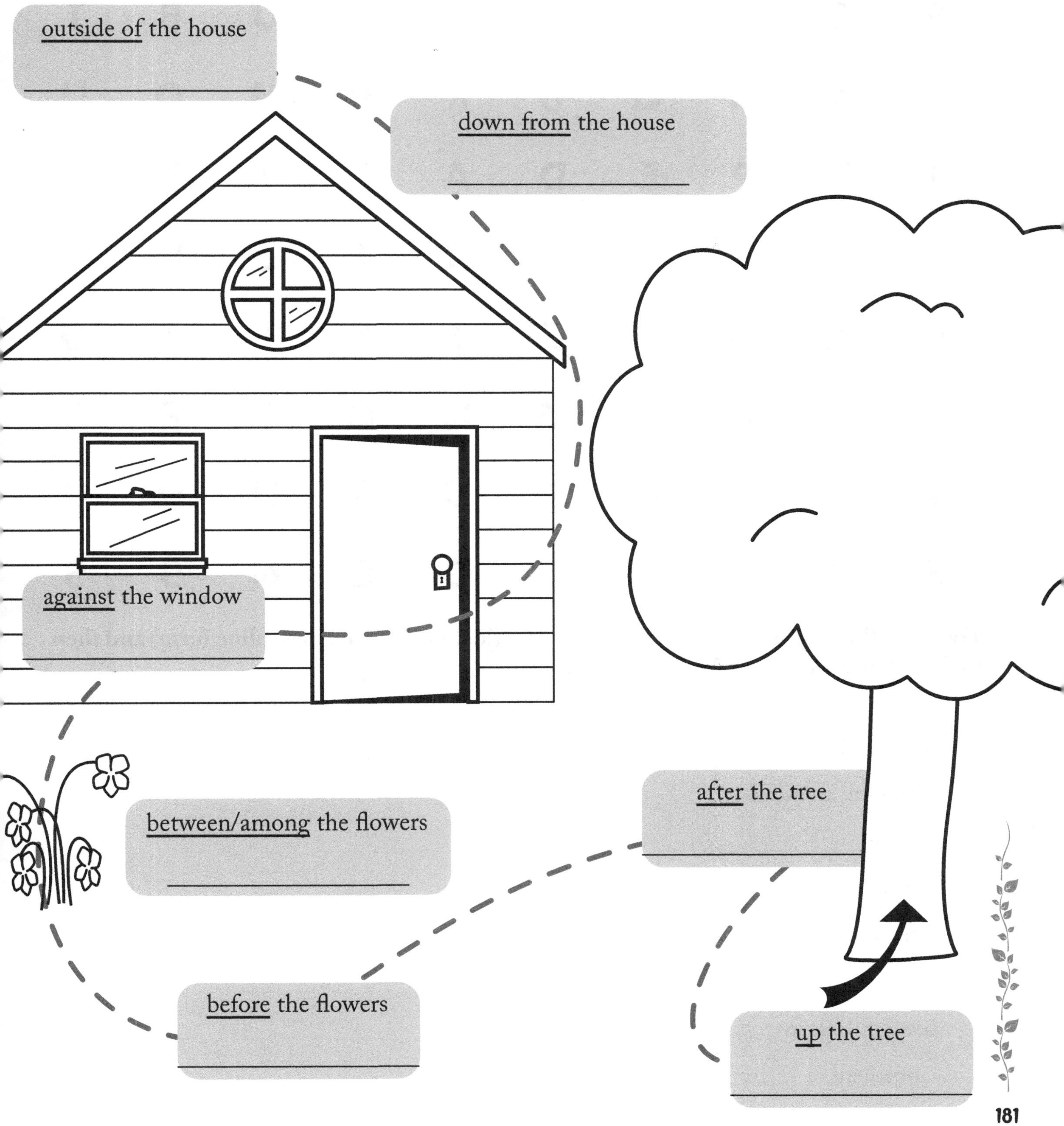

B	C	V	O	E	V	F	H	O	S
S	E	I	L	I	E	O	U	B	T
F	A	N	G	B	R	R	M	O	U
I	T	P	E	D	A	T	I	E	D
D	F	H	I	F	X	I	L	D	I
E	A	O	U	E	I	S	I	I	O
L	X	E	T	M	N	C	S	E	S
I	V	I	R	T	U	S	U	N	U
S	D	I	L	I	G	E	N	S	S

Translate the English words below into Latin (just provide the masculine form) and then find the Latin words in the word search!

a. brave, strong ____________________

b. faithful ____________________

c. careful, attentive ____________________

d. wise ____________________

e. humble ____________________

f. truthful, honest ____________________

g. kind, generous ____________________

h. eager to learn ____________________

i. obedient ____________________

j. virtue, courage, excellence ____________________

1. Translate the English words into Latin and fill in the crossword puzzle. Try translating the words directly into the crossword puzzle!

Across

1. poet
5. near
9. against
10. after
12. sailor
13. eager to learn (m)
14. brave, strong (m)
17. guard, policeman, fireman
18. wise (m)
19. outside of
22. careful, attentive (m)
23. truthful, honest (m)

Down

2. out of
3. athlete
4. virtue, courage, excellence
6. obedient (m)
7. between, among
8. across
9. with
11. humble (m)
14. faithful (m)
15. senator, politician
16. above
20. to, toward
21. down from

Note: The (m) indicates that you only need to supply the masculine form of the word.

2. **Do you know your Latin roots and English derivatives? Draw lines to match the English words to the correct Latin root words.**

veracity	fortis	medicine
fortify	diligens	vigilant
medical	verax	translucent
transmit	medicus	diligent
construction	vigil	fortitude
descend	trans	nautical
destruct	agricola	structure
agriculture	nauta	transport
translate	structor	instruct
circumstances	circum	depend
	de	

3. **Can you put together the phrases from the past few chapters? Using the word bank below, translate each English phrase into Latin.**

brevis spero Ars per Fortes astra longa aspera
fortuna diem Ad vita Dum Carpe iuvat spiro

Fortune favors the brave: __________ __________ __________

While I breathe, I hope: __________ __________, __________

Art is long, life is brief: __________ __________,

__________ __________

Seize the day: __________ __________

To the stars through difficulties: __________ __________

__________ __________

4. **Do you remember the being verbs in the present, imperfect, and future tenses? Below, circle the present verbs, underline the past verbs, and color the future verbs green.**

sumus eratis erunt sum eritis eris eras eramus

ero erant estis es erit est erat

eram sunt erimus

5. **Fill in the three charts below with the correct endings.**

Present Tense	Singular	Plural
First Person		
Second Person		
Third Person		

Imperfect Tense	Singular	Plural
First Person		
Second Person		
Third Person		

Future Tense	Singular	Plural
First Person		
Second Person		
Third Person		

1. Label each image with the correct Latin word. Then color the images!

____
(I sleep)

____
(night)

____
(bed)

____
(bath)

2. Answer the question or complete the sentence by drawing a line to the correct word.

a. At night the *luna* gives ______.	fessus
b. If a *puer* yawns, how do you think he feels?	fabula
c. Before bed, your mom might read you a ______.	lux
d. When you close your eyes and bow your head, you say a ______.	stratum
e. Let's all sing a ______.	prex
f. What do you use to keep warm?	carmen

C	S	E	P	T	I	M	A	N	A
H	E	B	R	I	S	H	O	R	A
A	N	N	U	S	J	R	K	E	N
M	I	D	E	T	E	M	P	U	S
E	S	I	U	P	N	T	A	R	E
N	D	W	S	H	M	Y	B	O	O
S	M	E	R	I	D	I	E	S	Z
I	V	A	U	R	O	R	A	F	P
S	U	X	G	V	R	N	L	Q	I

Translate the English words below into Latin and then find the Latin words in the word search!

a. time ______________________

b. hour ______________________

c. dawn, morning ______________________

d. evening ______________________

e. day ______________________

f. noon ______________________

g. week ______________________

h. month ______________________

i. year ______________________

Chapter 28: Colors

Write the English translation of each Latin word in the color the Latin word describes. Then color the image using that same color!

ruber

caeruleus

flavus

viridis

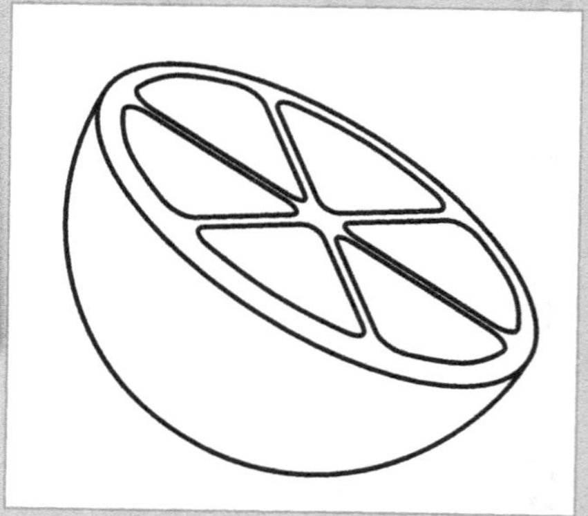

aurantius

purpureus

ater

albus

Using the picture and instructions below, draw a palace scene! Check off the boxes after you do each step.

☐ 1. Draw a **solium** at the top of the stairs.

☐ 2. Draw a **gemma** on both sides of the door frame.

☐ 3. Draw a **tyrannus** on the **solium**.

☐ 4. Behind the **solium**, color the curtain the color of **aurum**.

☐ 5. Draw a **servus** bringing the **tyrannus** a glass of water.

☐ 6. Draw **populus** from the **regnum** outside the door.

☐ 7. Draw a speech bubble from the **tyrannus** that says, "**Regno**!"

1. Complete each sentence by drawing a line to the correct Latin word.

a. Compared to a mouse, an elephant is a ______ animal.	**bonus**
b. A tall cliff is very ______.	**magnus**
c. An A on a test is a ______ grade.	**altus**
d. A ball is ______.	**rotundus**
e. Compared to ten minutes, one second is a very ______time.	**pulcher**
f. Compared to an elephant, a mouse is very ______.	**brevis**
g. A flower could be called very ______.	**quadratus**
h. To rob someone is a ______ action.	**parvus**
i. A box, or a four-sided figure, is ______.	**malus**
j. When you're waiting, ten minutes seems like a ______ time.	**triangulus**
k. A triangle, or any three-sided figure, is ______.	**longus**

2. Draw a *parva rotunda avis, a *longus flavus canis*, and an *aurantia feles** that is *brevis* and *triangula*.**

*__Avis__ and __feles__ are feminine nouns and so the adjectives that describe them have feminine endings, in this case *a*.

1. Translate the English words into Latin and fill in the crossword puzzle. Try translating the words directly into the crossword puzzle!

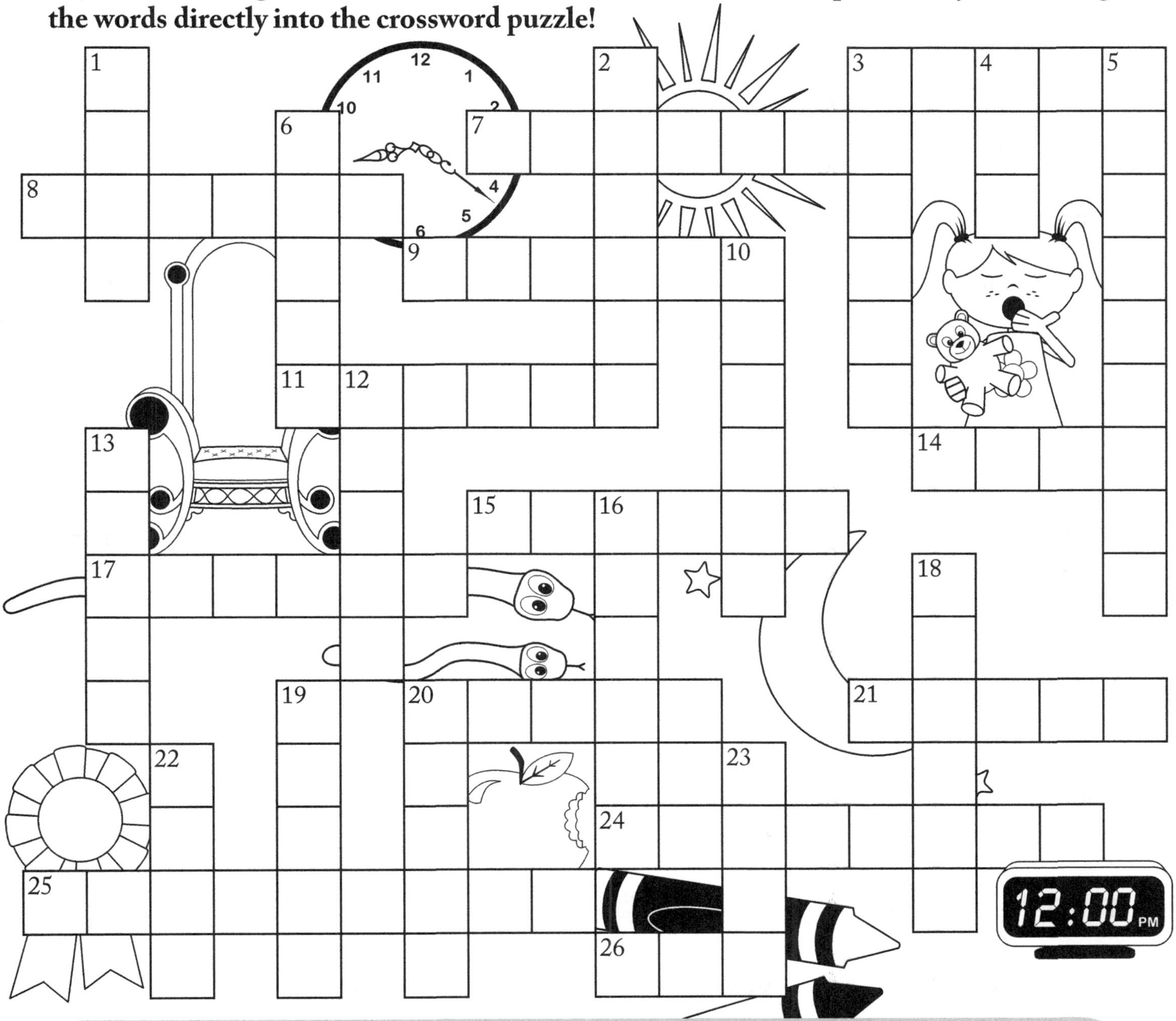

Across

3. good (m)
7. pretty, handsome (m)
8. time
9. small, young (m)
11. great, big (m)
14. hour
15. male slave
17. long (m)
20. I reign
21. year
24. noon
25. blue (m)
26. light

Down

1. day
2. yellow (m)
3. short (m)
4. night
5. week
6. gold
10. throne
12. high (m)
13. bad (m)
16. kingdom
18. month
19. white (m)
20. red (m)
22. black (m)
23. prayer

Note: The (m) indicates that you only need to supply the masculine form of the word.

2. **Do you know your Latin roots and English derivatives? Draw lines to match the English words to the correct Latin root words.**

	fabula	
nocturnal	dormio	lucid
fable	lux	dormitory
translucent	nox	fabulous
dormant	tempus	tempo
diurnal	dies	annual
temporary	annus	albino
brief	albus	diary
gem	gemma	malignant
malicious	malus	altitude
	altus	
	brevis	

3. **Can you put together the phrases from the past few chapters? Using the word bank below, translate each English phrase into Latin.**

Tempus | liberabit | fugit | Fiat | opus | Regnat

Magnum | vos | lux | populus | Veritas

Let there be light: ____________________ ____________________

Time flees (flies): ____________________ ____________________

The truth will make you free: ________________ ____________ ____________________

The people rule: ____________________ ____________________

A great work: ____________________ ____________________

4. Chant your charts as you use the words and endings on the right to fill in the charts below.

First Declension Noun Endings	Singular	Plural
Nominative		
Genitive		
Dative		
Accusative		
Ablative		

Hora Chant (First Declension)	Singular	Plural
Nominative		
Genitive		
Dative		
Accusative		
Ablative		

-a · hora · horis · -am · -arum · -a · horas · -ae · -is · horae · horarum · -ae · -ae · horae · horam · -is · hora · horae · horis · -as

5. Adjectives are words that describe or modify what?

verbs · nouns · actions · nothing

6. Color verbs *caeruleus*, nouns *ruber*, prepositions *viridis*, and adjectives *flavus*.

regno · rotundus · vesper · lectus · pone · gemma · supra · circum · bonus · ex · brevis · mensis · dies · dormio · coqueo · solium · laboro · parvus

1. Verb Chart Chant Challenge! Chant your charts as you use the words and endings on the right to fill in the charts below.

Present Tense	Singular	Plural
First Person		
Second Person		
Third Person		

Laudo Present Tense	Singular	Plural
First Person		
Second Person		
Third Person		

Imperfect Tense	Singular	Plural
First Person		
Second Person		
Third Person		

Future Tense	Singular	Plural
First Person		
Second Person		
Third Person		

laudant, -o, -bam, -bo, -bas, -nt, -bat, laudo, -bis, -bunt, -t, -bamus, laudas, -s, -batis, -tis, -bant, -bimus, laudat, -mus, -bit, laudamus, -bitis, laudatis

2. What is the ending for a verb in the future tense, first-person singular? ____________

3. Fill in the boxes below with the stem and ending of the present tense, third-person plural form of *laboro* (one letter is done for you).

					A		

4. How do you say "they work" in Latin? ____________________

5. **Noun Chart Chant Challenge! Chant your charts as you use the words and endings on the right to fill in the charts below.**

First Declension Noun Endings	Singular	Plural
Nominative		
Genitive		
Dative		
Accusative		
Ablative		

Hora Chant (First Declension)	Singular	Plural
Nominative		
Genitive		
Dative		
Accusative		
Ablative		

-ae
-a
hora
-arum
-ae
horae
hora
-ae
-am
horae
horae
-a
horam
horis
-as
-is
horarum
horas
-is
horis

6. **What is the ending for a first declension noun in the genitive singular form?**

____

7. **What is the ending for a first declension noun in the ablative plural form?**

____

8. **What is the genitive singular form of *regina*?** ____________________

9. **What is the ablative plural form of *aqua*?** ____________________

10. **What is the accusative singular form of *patria*?** ____________________

11. **What is the dative plural form of *fabula*?** ____________________

12. Noun Chart Chant Challenge Two! Chant your charts as you use the words and endings on the right to fill in the charts below.

Second Declension Masculine Endings	Singular	Plural
Nominative		
Genitive		
Dative		
Accusative		
Ablative		

Hortus Chant (Second Declension Masculine Endings)	Singular	Plural
Nominative		
Genitive		
Dative		
Accusative		
Ablative		

-um
hortus
horti
horto
-o
-orum
-i
-is
-os
hortum
-us
horti
horto
hortis
-o
-i
hortis
hortos
-is
hortorum

13. What is the ending for a second declension masculine noun in the dative singular form?

____

14. What is the ending for a second declension masculine noun in the ablative plural form?

____

15. What is the genitive plural form of *gladius*? ____________________

16. What is the nominative plural form of *ludus*? ____________________

17. What is the accusative singular form of *lectus*? ____________________

18. What is the dative plural form of *populus*? ____________________

19. Noun Chart Chant Challenge Three! Chant your charts as you use the words and endings on the right to fill in the charts below.

Second Declension Neuter Endings

	Singular	Plural
Nominative		
Genitive		
Dative		
Accusative		
Ablative		

Bonum Chant (Second Declension Neuter Endings)

	Singular	Plural
Nominative		
Genitive		
Dative		
Accusative		
Ablative		

bonum
bona
-um
-is
boni
-um
-o
bona
bonis
-orum
bonum
-a
-i
bonis
bono
-a
-o
bono
-is
bonorum

20. What is the ending for a second declension neuter noun in the accusative singular form?

____

21. What is the ending for a second declension neuter noun in the nominative plural form?

____

22. What is the accusative singular form of *bellum*? ____________________

23. What is the nominative plural form of *balneum*? ____________________

24. What is the genitive singular form of *regnum*? ____________________

25. What is the ablative singular form of *stratum*? ____________________

26. Color the pictures according to the instructions below. Check off each box after you do each step.

- ☐ Color the **rex ruber**.
- ☐ Color the **solium flavum**.
- ☐ Color the **epulae virides**.
- ☐ Color the **venator viridis**.
- ☐ Color the **ludus ruber**.
- ☐ Color the **gladius ater**.
- ☐ Color the **regina aurantia**.
- ☐ Color the **musica aurantia** and her **carmen atrum**.
- ☐ Color **duo coronae flavae**.
- ☐ Color the **artifex purpureus**.
- ☐ Color the **magnus albus canis** and the **parva caerulea avis**.
- ☐ Color the **quattuor gemmae purpureus**.
- ☐ Color the **nauta alba** and **caerulea**.

27. Read the sentences out loud. Then follow the instructions below and check off each box after you do each step.

- ☐ Translate each italicized word on the line below it.
- ☐ Circle all the nouns.
- ☐ Underline all the verbs.
- ☐ Draw triangles around all the adjectives.
- ☐ Draw small stars on either side of all the prepositions.
- ☐ Draw small hearts on either side of all the adverbs.

a. The *vigil* *clamat.*

______ ______

b. The *amicus* is *cum* the *familia.*

______ ______ ______

c. The *puer* is not *fortis* at *nox.*

______ ______ ______

d. *Porto* the *gemmam* *inter* the *rotundus* bushes.

______ ______ ______ ______

e. *Cano* my *carmen* *cito.*

______ ______ ______

f. *Scribo* a *fabula.*

______ ______

g. The *optime* *mensis* *est* *Iulius.*

______ ______ ______ ______

h. The *senator* *dicabo* *diligenter.*

______ ______ ______

Song School Latin Book 2 Activity Answers

Pages 200-223 contain the answers for the previous activities. These are most easily viewed if you turn the book 90 degrees clockwise (as if it were a calendar.)

Chapter 1: What Day Is It?

A	H	O	D	I	E	M	Q	B	E
D	Q	U	P	L	I	A	U	S	D
H	U	F	M	S	D	G	I	K	I
E	O	V	A	A	O	I	D	C	S
M	A	D	G	L	D	S	I	J	C
V	B	H	I	V	A	T	E	R	I
R	A	U	S	E	L	R	S	A	P
C	P	L	T	I	E	A	E	G	U
O	E	M	E	C	N	S	S	S	L
L	S	T	R	T	B	U	T	D	I

Translate the English words below into Latin and then find the Latin words in the word search!

a. What day is it? Qui dies est?

b. Today is ______. Hodie est ______.

c. hello salve

d. good-bye vale

Double Points if you can find the Latin word for students, male teacher, and female teacher!
discipuli, magister, magistra

153

Chapter 2: Days of the Week

1. The days of the week were erased from the calendar! Translate the English days of the week below into Latin. Then draw a line to the question mark where the day should go on the calendar.

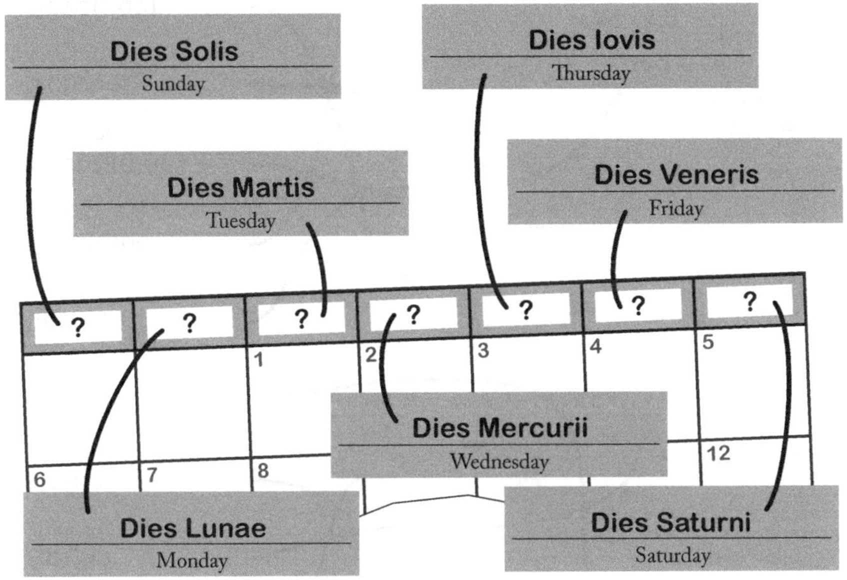

2. Do you remember how to say the following phrases in Latin? Write the the Latin translation on the line and then say them to your teacher in Latin!

a. What is your name? **Quid est tuum praenomen?**

b. My name is . . . **Meum praenomen est . . .**

3. What does *carpe diem* mean? Write the translation below, then write how you plan to do what it says today.

Seize the day!

Answers will vary.

Chapter 3: Months of the Year

1. Do you know *qui mensis est*? Below, translate the name of the month, and then draw a picture of what you like to do during that month.

2. January and February are both part of what season? (Write the season in Latin.)

hiems (winter) or aestas (summer)

This answer will depend on the hemisphere in which you live.

Chapter 4: More Months of the Year

On the left, translate each month into Latin. Then sing the "Months of the Year, Parts I & II" song and draw lines to match each activity (on the right) to the correct month!

Ianuarius
(January)

Februarius
(February)

Martius
(March)

Aprilis
(April)

Maius
(May)

Iunius
(June)

Iulius
(July)

Augustus
(August)

September
(September)

October
(October)

November
(November)

December
(December)

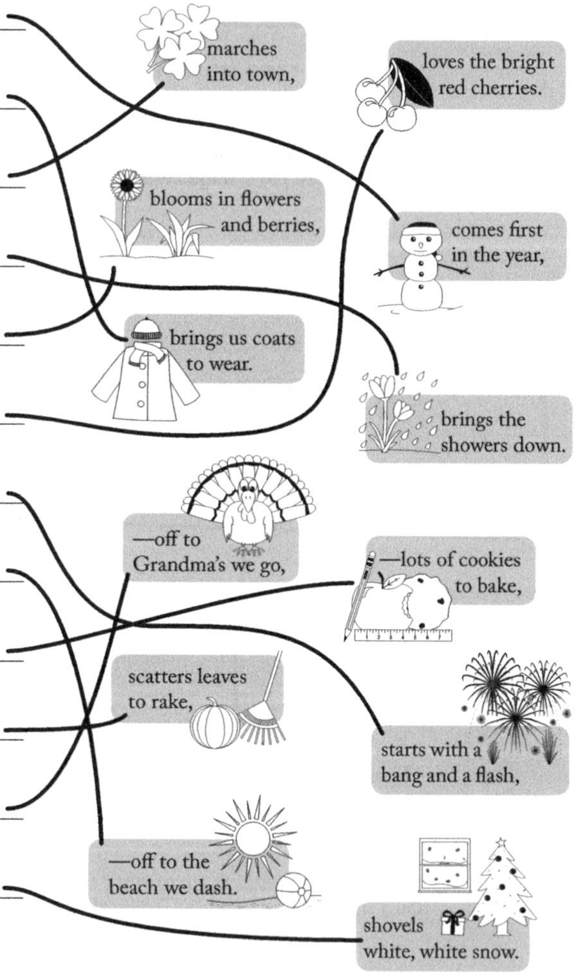

Chapter 5: Numbers

1. Using your Latin, count out loud the number of birds in each cage and then write that number, in Latin, on the line provided. Finally, color the birds.

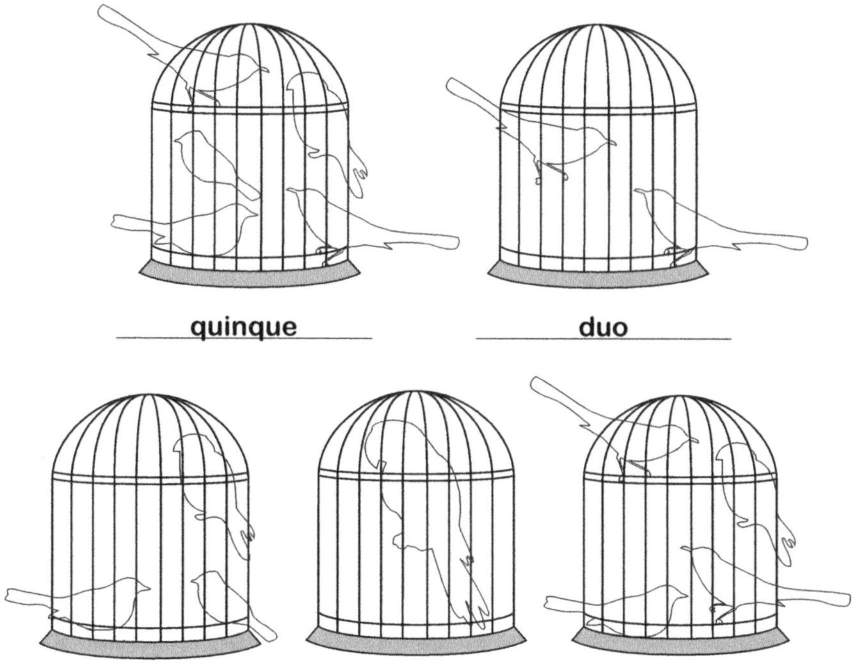

quinque   duo

tres   unus   quattuor

2. What does *auxilio ab alto* mean? It means "by help from on high."

3. From what Latin word is "unify" derived? unus

4. From what Latin word is "dual" derived? duo

5. From what Latin word is "quarter" derived? quattuor

Chapter 6: More Numbers

1. Count up the stairs! Write the Latin word for each number on the line provided. When you get to the top, count down from ten in Latin. Then color the stairs and draw yourself walking up them.

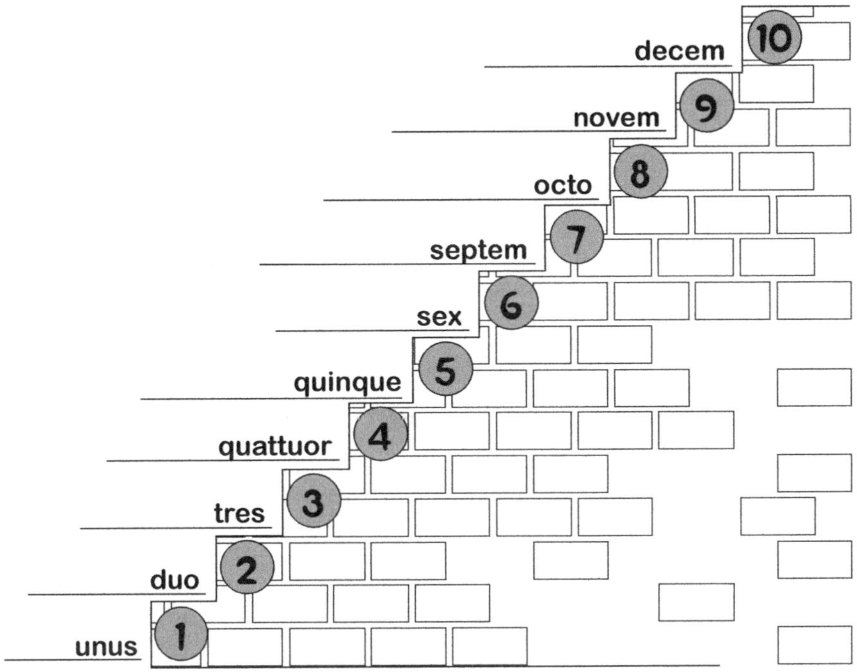

2. What does *pater familias* mean? It means "father of the family."

3. From what Latin word is "octopus" derived? octo

4. From what Latin word is "decimal" derived? decem

5. From what Latin word is "decade" derived? decem

158

Chapter 7: Review

1. Translate the English words into Latin and fill in the crossword puzzle!

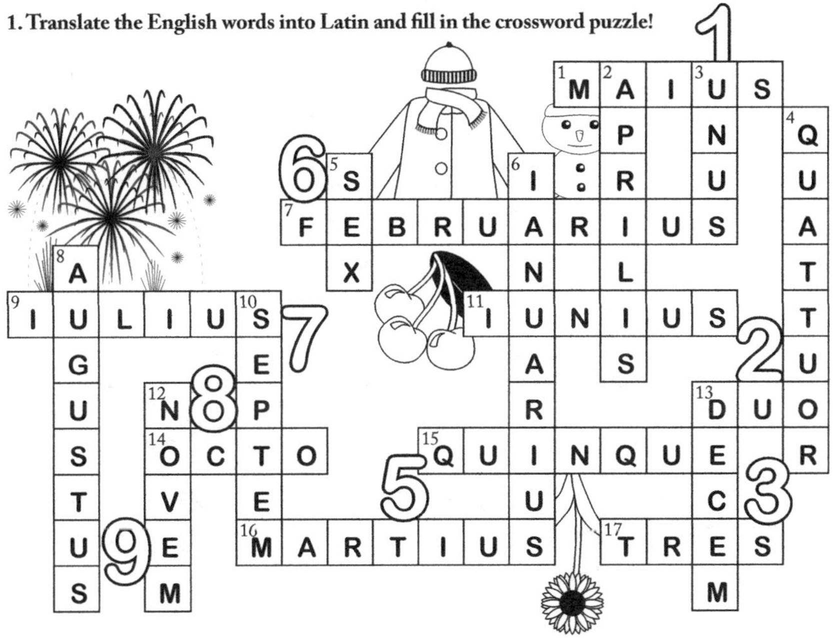

Across

1. May Maius
7. February Februarius
9. July Iulius
11. June Iunius
13. two duo
14. eight octo
15. five quinque
16. March Martius
17. three tres

Down

2. April Aprilis
3. one unus
4. four quattuor
5. six sex
6. January Ianuarius
8. August Augustus
10. seven septem
12. nine novem
13. ten decem

159

Chapter 7: Review

2. The chapter 1 phrases got mixed up with the days of the week! Using the word bank below, see if you can put the chapter 1 phrases back together and put the days of the week in order.

Dies · Hodie · Dies · Qui · Dies · Saturni · Mercurii · est · Solis · Dies · est · Martis · Veneris · Dies · Dies · Lunae · Iovis · dies · Dies

Chapter 1 Phrases:

Qui (What) dies (day) est (is it)?

Hodie (Today) est (is) . . .

Days of the Week:

Sunday: Dies Solis

Monday: Dies Lunae

Tuesday: Dies Martis

Wednesday: Dies Mercurii

Thursday: Dies Iovis

Friday: Dies Veneris

Saturday: Dies Saturni

3. Chant the o-s-t chant as you write out the verb endings below.

-o	-mus
-s	-tis
-t	-nt

Chapter 7: Review

4. Do you remember the famous sayings from chapters 1 through 6? Draw lines to match the Latin saying to the correct English translation.

Acta non verba	Actions, not words!
Carpe diem	Seize the day!
Per mensem	monthly, every month, or by the month
Ad idem	of the same mind
Auxilio ab alto	by help from on high
Pater familias	father of the family

5. Many English words come from Latin words. Draw lines to match the English words to the correct Latin words from which they are derived.

November, universe, duel, unicycle, octave, diary, unify, September	octo, sex + mensis, dies, November, unus, September, duo	diurnal, octagon, semester, octopus, unity, dual, uniform
November	November	
universe	unus	
duel	duo	dual
unicycle	unus	
octave	octo	octagon, octopus
diary	dies	diurnal
unify	unus	unity, uniform
September	September	
	sex + mensis	semester

6. Color in the correct answer for each of the following statements.

a. ______ is the term for an action word.

letter · plural · noun · **verb** (colored) · singular

b. ______ means "only one."

chant · plural · noun · verb · **singular** (colored)

c. ______ means "more than one."

chant · **plural** (colored) · noun · verb · singular

Chapter 8: Helping at Home

Translate each Latin word/phrase into English and then draw yourself doing each action!

laboro
I work

lavo
I wash

Drawings will vary.

purgo
I clean

pasco
I feed

coquo
I cook

Chapter 9: Communicating with Others

1. Translate each Latin word into English and then draw a line to match the Latin word to the correct picture!

dico
I speak, say

clamo
I shout

susurro
I whisper

scribo
I write

oro
I pray

2. Draw a line from each Latin word to its correct place in the chart. Then fill in the chart with the correct English meaning for each of the Latin words.

Singular		Plural	
clamo	I shout	clamamus	we shout
clamas	you shout	clamatis	you all shout
clamat	he/she/it shouts	clamant	they shout

clamo clamat clamas clamamus clamatis clamant

Chapter 10: Ways to Travel

1. Answer the questions with the correct Latin word by writing one Latin letter in each box. Look at the drawings for hints!

a. To cross a pond what do you do?

N	A	V	I	G	O
	2				

b. If you are in a soccer game, what do you do?

C	U	R	R	O
1				

c. To travel a long distance very fast, what do you do?

V	O	L	O

d. To go down the hallway slowly, what do you do?

A	M	B	U	L	O
	7				

e. If you have a saddle, reins, and a horse, what do you do?

E	Q	U	I	T	O
4					

f. If you are driving with your mom to the store, what do you do?

V	E	H	O	R	I	N	V	E	H	I	C	U	L	O
				3				6		5				

2. Discover how well you did! In the activity above, find the numbers and write the letter in the corresponding blank below. Two letters are already there for you.

C A R P E D I E M!
1 2 3   4   5 6 7

Chapter 11: Things to Learn in School

D	Q	H	I	Y	M	R	D	S	L
H	A	T	U	C	A	K	F	C	S
I	B	G	W	E	T	P	Y	T	C
S	T	O	R	L	H	X	H	L	R
T	P	P	H	A	E	K	O	Y	I
O	F	H	I	Z	M	C	I	U	P
R	O	Y	K	B	A	P	T	G	T
I	L	S	M	A	T	R	H	I	I
A	J	I	H	D	I	C	M	Y	O
T	E	C	G	V	C	F	A	J	N
G	R	A	M	M	A	T	I	C	A

Translate the English words below into Latin and then find the Latin words in the word search!

a. math mathematica

b. grammar, language arts grammatica

c. reading lectio

d. writing scriptio

e. science physica

f. history historia

Chapter 12: Celebration

1. Translate the English into Latin.

feast **epulae**

celebration **celebratio**

family **familia**

music **musica**

game, school, play **ludus**

male friend **amicus**

female friend **amica**

2. Label each image with the correct Latin word from the above exercise. Then color the images!

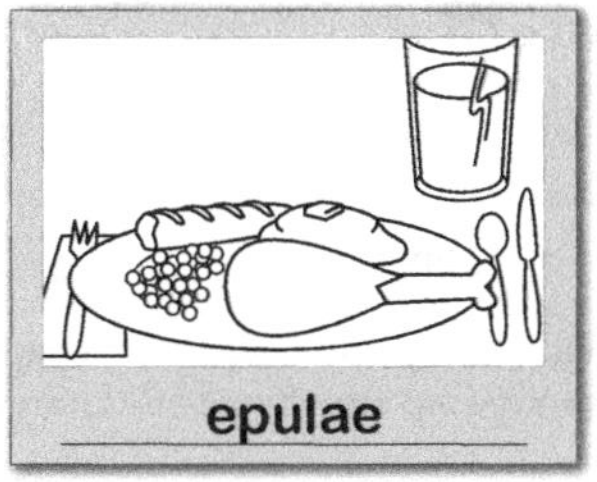

Chapter 13: Review

1. Translate the English words into Latin and fill in the crossword puzzle. Try translating the words directly into the crossword puzzle!

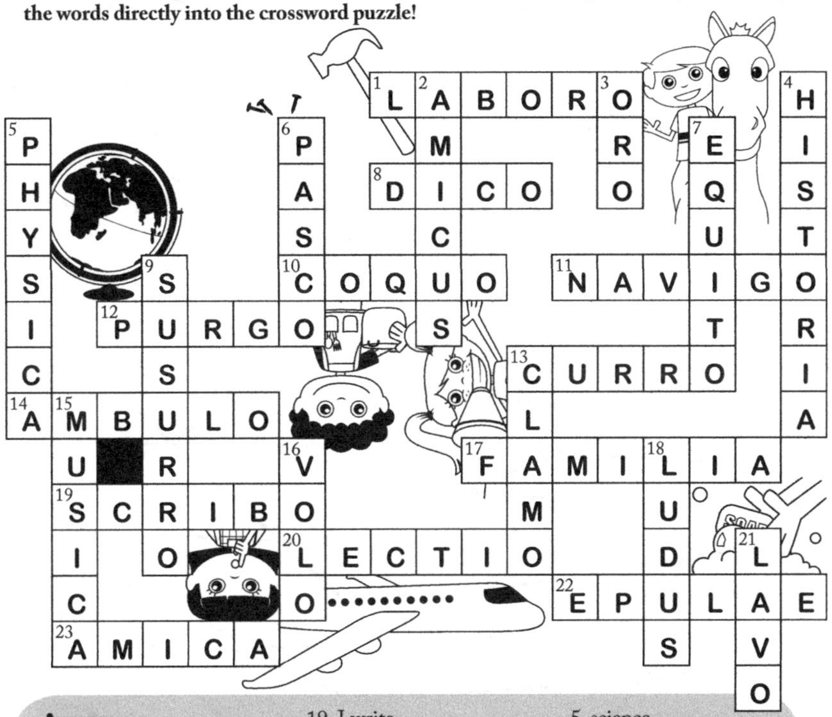

Across

1. I work
8. I speak, say
10. I cook
11. I sail
12. I clean
13. I run
14. I walk
17. family
19. I write
20. reading
22. feast
23. female friend

Down

2. male friend
3. I pray
4. history
5. science
6. I feed
7. I ride a horse
9. I whisper
13. I shout
15. music
16. I fly
18. game
21. I wash

Chapter 13: Review

2. Can you put together the phrases from the past few chapters? Using the word bank below, translate each English phrase into Latin.

Ora | volant | potentia | est | labora | initio | Scientia | Verba | manet | et | cogitare | est | littera | Scribere | Ab

Pray and work: Ora et labora

To write is to think: Scribere est cogitare

Knowledge is power: Scientia potentia est

Words fly away, the letter remains: Verba volant, littera manet

From the beginning: Ab initio

3. Translate the English into Latin.

Person	Singular	Plural
First	I praise: laudo	we praise: laudamus
Second	you praise: laudas	you all praise: laudatis
Third	he/she/it praises: laudat	they praise: laudant

Chapter 13: Review

4. Many English words come from Latin words. Draw lines to match the English words to the correct Latin root words.

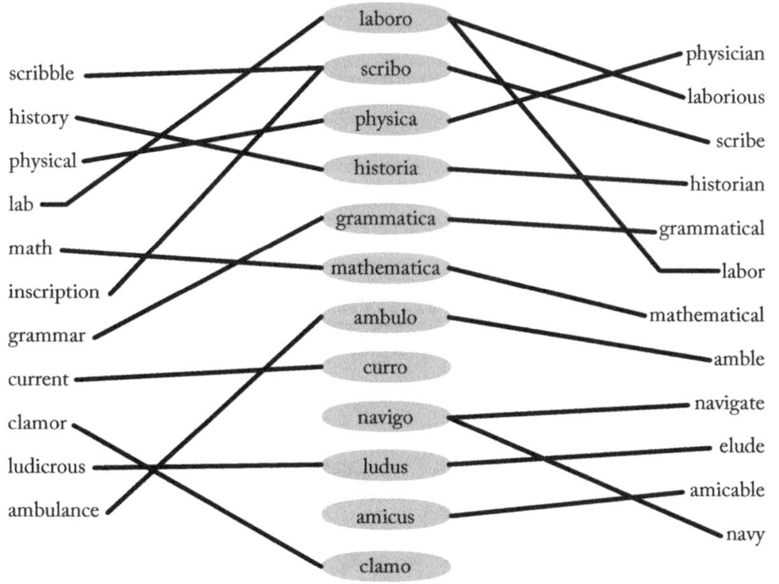

5. Color in the circle(s) that contain(s) the correct answer to the question.

a. Is the word *laudas* first, second, or third person? (Hint: Use the chart in question 3!)

first | second (colored) | third

b. Is the word *laudant* singular or plural? (Hint: Use the chart in question 3!)

singular | plural (colored) | neither

c. *Laudamus* is both __________ person and __________. (Be sure to color two words!)

first (colored) | second | third | plural (colored) | singular

d. Is *amicus* masculine or feminine?

masculine (colored) | feminine | neither

Chapter 14: Royalty

1. In the box below, draw a picture of a *rex* and a *regina* each sitting on a *solium*. Make sure to draw a *corona* on both the *rex* and *regina*! Then label the *rex*, *regina*, *corona*, and *solium*.

Drawings will vary, but should contain a king (*rex*) and a queen (*regina*), each standing next to a throne (*solium*). The king and queen should each be wearing a crown (*corona*).

2. In the shaded box, translate the English into Latin. (Hint: It was one of your vocab words!) For bonus points, use your -o, -s, -t, -mus, -tis, -nt endings to fill in the other boxes.

Person	Singular		Plural	
First	I work:	laboro	we work:	labora**mus**
Second	you work:	labora**s**	you all work:	labora**tis**
Third	he/she/it works:	labora**t**	they work:	labora**nt**

3. Translate the following Latin word into English.

populus: **people**

Chapter 15: Military Matters

1. Do you remember what a verb is? A verb describes things, or actions, you can do. Translate the three Latin verbs below into English.

pugno: **I fight**

vinco: **I conquer**

video: **I see**

2. Draw a line to match the Latin sentence on the left to the correct English translation on the right.

Infans videt.	The king conquers.
Miles pugnat.	The baby sees.
Rex vincit.	The soldier fights.

3. Draw a line from each Latin word to its correct place in the chart. Then fill in the chart with the correct English meaning for each of the Latin words.

Person	Singular	Plural
First	I am	we are
Second	you are	you all are
Third	he/she/it is	they are

est sum estis sumus es sunt

4. Draw a picture of a fancy *gladius* in the box below.

Drawings will vary, but should portray some sort of sword.

Chapter 16: Everyday Actions

1. Draw a line from each Latin word to the image it describes. Color each image and then write the English translation of the Latin word on the line below each image.

I love — I carry — I tell — I look at — I call

2. Draw an image that comes to your mind when you hear the word *vivo*. Write the English translation of the word *vivo* on the line below the image.

Drawings will vary. If students have difficulty coming up with ideas of what to draw, you could suggest that they use the word *vivo* in a sentence, such as "*Vivo* in a tall, red house," or "*Vivo* in Kentucky," and then have them draw a picture of that.

vivo: I live

Chapter 17: Adverbs: How We Do Things

A	C	S	E	M	Z	N	U	N	C
W	I	V	P	O	R	P	N	U	N
P	T	K	T	E	B	X	A	M	F
V	O	C	O	M	C	I	R	Q	U
X	Q	U	L	V	J	T	R	U	P
S	A	E	P	E	A	U	O	A	O
T	M	R	D	W	N	C	W	M	R
C	O	H	T	L	E	T	Q	G	T
I	N	Y	S	E	M	P	E	R	O

Translate the English words below into Latin and then find the Latin words in the word search!

a. now nunc

b. never numquam

c. often saepe

d. fast, quickly cito

e. slowly lente

f. always semper

Double Points if you can find the Latin words for I carry, I look at, I tell, I love, and I call!
porto, specto, narro, amo, voco

Chapter 18: More Adverbs

1. Translate each of the English words on the right into Latin. Then complete each of the sentences on the left by drawing a line from the sentence to the correct Latin word.

a. If an object is green, you might say it is ____ blue.

b. Someone who fights a giant acts ____.

c. Someone who didn't do well on a test did ____.

d. Someone who handles fragile items holds the items ____.

e. Someone who washes the dishes correctly does the job ____.

f. Someone who wins first place does the ____.

forte (bravely)

non (not)

diligenter (carefully)

optime (best)

pessime (badly, terrible)

bene (well, fine)

2. Draw a line from each Latin word to its correct place in the chart. Then fill in the chart with the correct English meaning for each of the Latin words.

Person	Singular	Plural
First	I was	we were
Second	you were	you all were
Third	he/she/it was	they were

eras eram erant eramus erat eratis

Chapter 19: Review

1. Translate the English words into Latin and fill in the crossword puzzle. Try translating the words directly into the crossword puzzle!

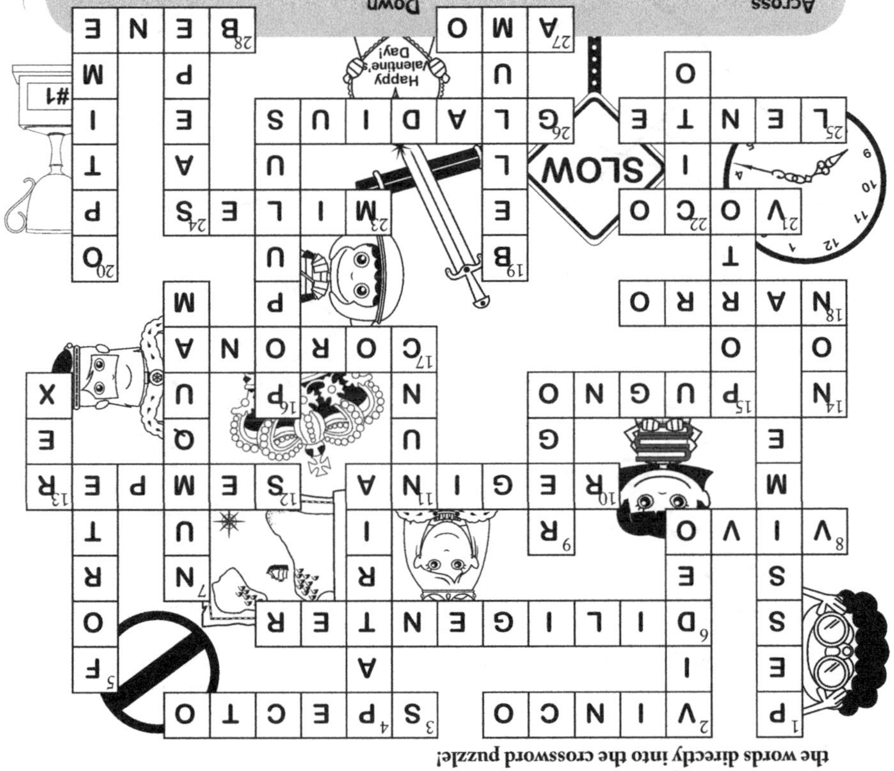

Across

2. I conquer
3. I look at
6. carefully
8. I live
10. queen
12. always
15. I fight
17. crown
18. I tell
21. I call
23. soldier
25. slowly
26. sword
27. I love
28. well, properly

Down

1. badly, terrible
2. I see
4. country, fatherland
5. bravely
7. never
9. I rule, direct
11. now
13. king
14. not
15. I carry
16. people
19. war
20. best
22. fast, quickly
24. often

2. Can you put together the phrases from the past few chapters? Using the word bank below, translate each English phrase into Latin.

Labor, Semper, vici, omnia, Regnat, vincit, populus, vidi, Nunc, aut, Veni, numquam, fidelis

Work conquers all: Labor omnia vincit

The people rule: Regnat populus

I came, I saw, I conquered:

Veni, vidi, vici

Now or never: Nunc aut numquam

Always faithful: Semper fidelis

3. Do you remember the difference between action verbs and being verbs? Circle the verbs in the sentences below. Then write what type of verb it is on the line below the sentence.

The *rex* (is) kind. — being

Canis (*currit*) outside. — action

(*Lavo*) the dishes. — action

(*Narro*) the story. — action

(*Sunt*) here. — being

(*Es*) the winner. — being

Pater (*erat*) *magister.* — being

She (speaks) softly. — action

Remember:

Action Verb: describes something you can do.

Being Verb: describes something that is.

4. Look at all those Latin roots and English derivatives! Draw lines to match the English words to the correct Latin root words.

English words (left): populate, invincible, regular, survive, popular, regal, pugnacious, rebel, portable, belligerent, nonfiction, spectacles, essence, vocal, spectator, narrator, suspect

Latin roots: reg- (regina, rego), populus, corona, vinco, pugno, bellum, video, vivo, porto, voco, specto, narro, es (from sum), pessime, optime, non

English words (right): coronation, region, population, direct, vivacious, vanquish, evoke, video, narrative, export, presence, none, vocation, optimist, pessimist, nonsense

5. Create your own Latin sentences! Write one sentence that uses a form of the verb *sum*, and one that uses an action verb. Look back in your book and use your vocabulary words.

Sentence with *sum* form:

Sentences will vary.

Sentence with action verb:

Sentences will vary.

Chapter 20: When I Grow Up, Part I

1. Label the people below with their correct *negotium*. Then color the people!

medicus	artifex	vigil
(doctor)	(artist)	(fireman)

2. Complete each sentence by drawing a line to the correct word.

a. A(n) _____ makes rhymes and likes words. → poeta

b. A(n) _____ owns a store and sells items. → tabernarius

c. Someone who creates a building could be a(n) . . . → architectus

d. A person who puts out fires is a(n) . . . → vigil

e. The person who heals you when you're sick is a(n) . . . → medicus

f. A person who paints murals is a(n) . . . → artifex

g. When you are older, what _____ would you like? → negotium

3. Draw an image of someone doing one of the jobs from this chapter, and label the image with that job.

Drawings and labels will vary.

Job: ____________________

Chapter 21: When I Grow Up, Part II

1. Label the people below with their correct *negotium*. Then color the people!

athleta	structor	agricola	nauta
(athlete)	(builder)	(farmer)	(sailor)

musica	venator	senator	scriptor
(female musician)	(hunter)	(senator, politician)	(writer)

2. Draw a scene that contains three of the people above doing their jobs. Label the job that each person is doing.

Drawings will vary.

Chapter 22: Where Things Are, Part I

Translate each underlined word into Latin, then draw someone or something doing the action of each phrase. Drawings will vary.

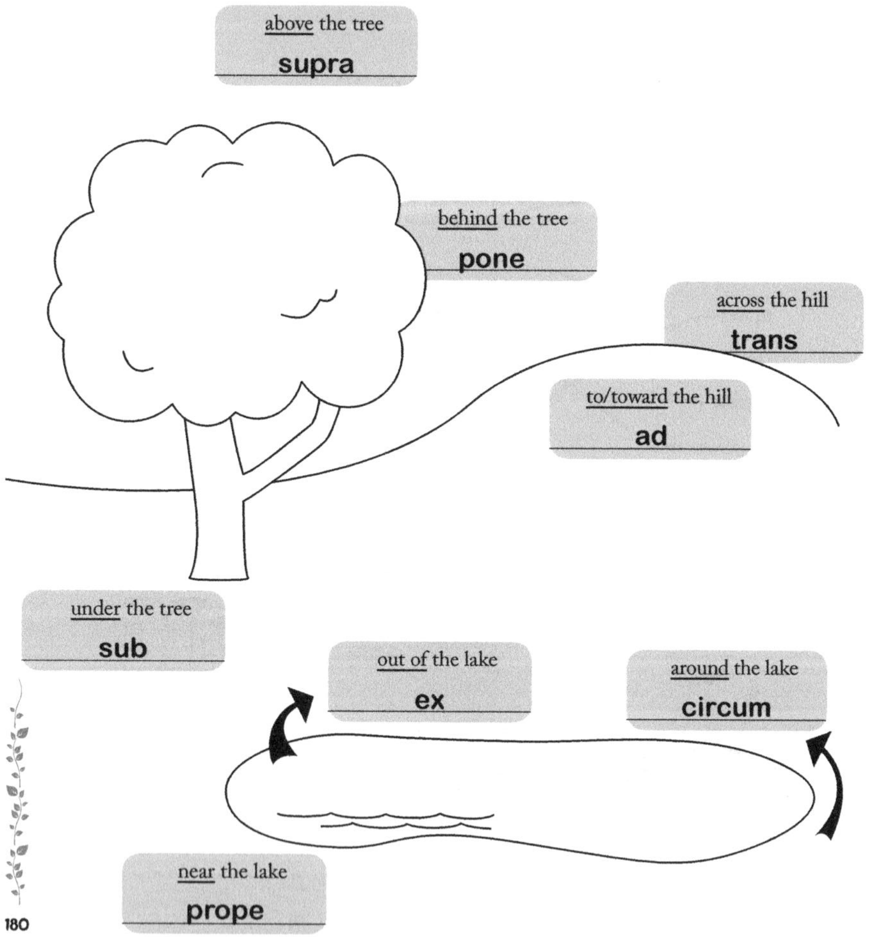

Chapter 23: Where Things Are, Part II

A squirrel is darting around the yard! Starting at the top of the picture, translate each underlined word or phrase into Latin and then draw the squirrel at each spot.

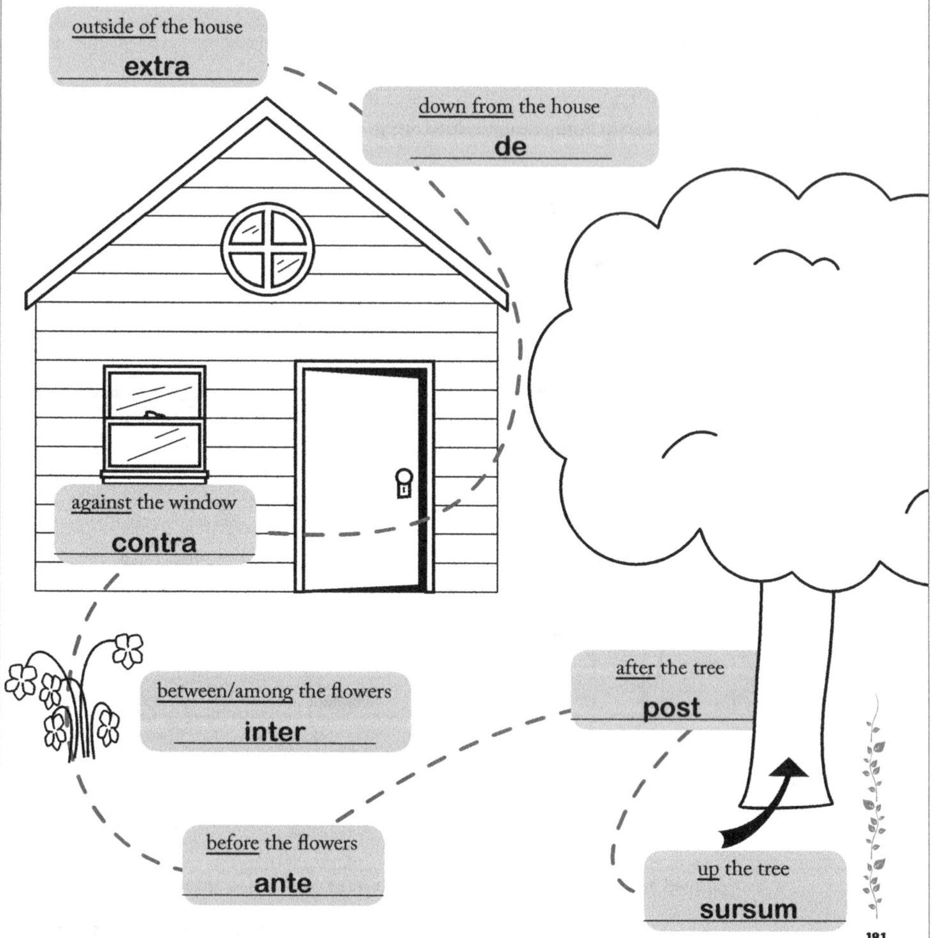

Chapter 24: Growing Virtues

B	C	V	O	E	V	F	H	O	S
S	E	I	L	I	E	O	U	B	T
F	A	N	G	B	R	R	M	O	U
I	T	P	E	D	A	T	I	E	D
D	F	H	I	F	X	I	L	D	I
E	A	O	U	E	I	S	I	I	O
L	X	E	T	M	N	C	S	E	S
I	V	I	R	T	U	S	U	N	U
S	D	I	L	I	G	E	N	S	S

Translate the English words below into Latin (just provide the masculine form) and then find the Latin words in the word search!

a. brave, strong **fortis**

b. faithful **fidelis**

c. careful, attentive **diligens**

d. wise **sapiens**

e. humble **humilis**

f. truthful, honest **verax**

g. kind, generous **beneficus**

h. eager to learn **studiosus**

i. obedient **oboediens**

j. virtue, courage, excellence **virtus**

182

Chapter 25: Review

1. Translate the English words into Latin and fill in the crossword puzzle. Try translating the words directly into the crossword puzzle!

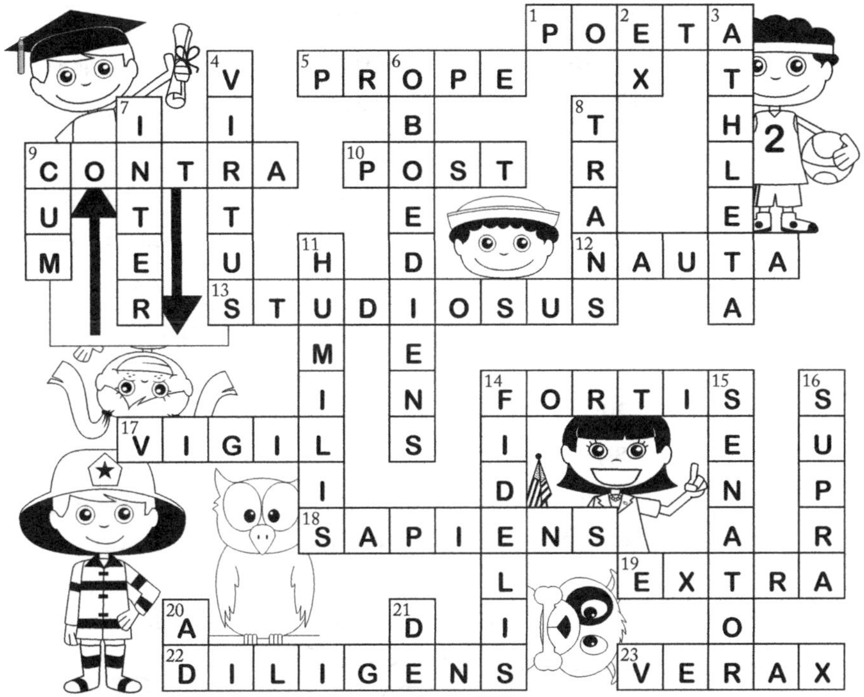

Across
1. poet
5. near
9. against
10. after
12. sailor
13. eager to learn (m)
14. brave, strong (m)
17. guard, policeman, fireman
18. wise (m)
19. outside of
22. careful, attentive (m)
23. truthful, honest (m)

Down
2. out of
3. athlete
4. virtue, courage, excellence
6. obedient (m)
7. between, among
8. across
9. with
11. humble (m)
14. faithful (m)
15. senator, politician
16. above
20. to, toward
21. down from

Note: The (m) indicates that you only need to supply the masculine form of the word.

183

2. Do you know your Latin roots and English derivatives? Draw lines to match the English words to the correct Latin root words.

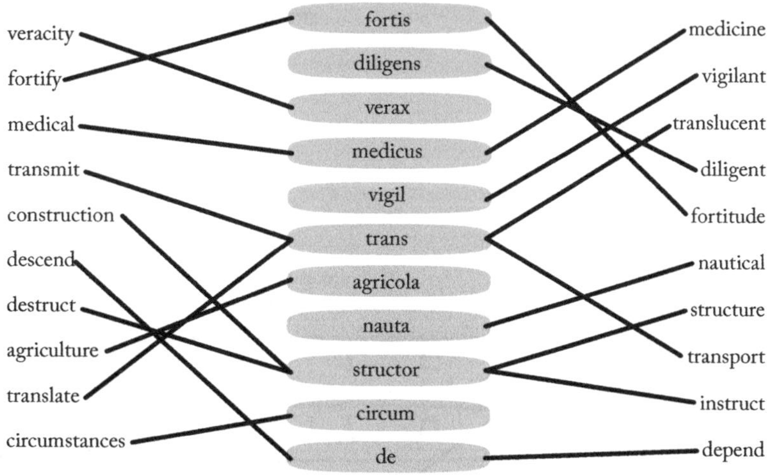

3. Can you put together the phrases from the past few chapters? Using the word bank below, translate each English phrase into Latin.

brevis spero Ars per Fortes astra longa aspera fortuna diem Ad vita Dum Carpe iuvat spiro

Fortune favors the brave: Fortes fortuna iuvat

While I breathe, I hope: Dum spiro, spero

Art is long, life is brief: Ars longa, vita brevis

Seize the day: Carpe diem

To the stars through difficulties: Ad astra per aspera

4. Do you remember the being verbs in the present, imperfect, and future tenses? Below, circle the present verbs, underline the past verbs, and color the future verbs green.

sumus eratis erunt sum eritis eris eramus ero eras es est erant estis erit erat sunt eram erimus

The future verbs are shaded for you.

5. Fill in the three charts below with the correct endings.

Present Tense	Singular	Plural
First Person	-o	-mus
Second Person	-s	-tis
Third Person	-t	-nt

Imperfect Tense	Singular	Plural
First Person	-bam	-bamus
Second Person	-bas	-batis
Third Person	-bat	-bant

Future Tense	Singular	Plural
First Person	-bo	-bimus
Second Person	-bis	-bitis
Third Person	-bit	-bunt

Chapter 26: Time for Bed!

1. Label each image with the correct Latin word. Then color the images!

dormio
(I sleep)

nox
(night)

lectus
(bed)

balneum
(bath)

2. Answer the question or complete the sentence by drawing a line to the correct word.

a. At night the *luna* gives ______. — lux

b. If a *puer* yawns, how do you think he feels? — fessus

c. Before bed, your mom might read you a ______. — fabula

d. When you close your eyes and bow your head, you say a ______. — prex

e. Let's all sing a ______. — carmen

f. What do you use to keep warm? — stratum

Word bank: fessus, fabula, lux, stratum, prex, carmen

Chapter 27: A Time for Everything

C	S	E	P	T	I	M	A	N	A
H	E	B	R	I	S	H	O	R	A
A	N	N	U	S	J	R	K	E	N
M	I	D	E	T	E	M	P	U	S
E	S	I	U	P	N	T	A	R	E
N	D	W	S	H	M	Y	B	O	O
S	M	E	R	I	D	I	E	S	Z
I	V	A	U	R	O	R	A	F	P
S	U	X	G	V	R	N	L	Q	I

Translate the English words below into Latin and then find the Latin words in the word search!

a. time tempus

b. hour hora

c. dawn, morning aurora

d. evening vesper

e. day dies

f. noon meridies

g. week septimana

h. month mensis

i. year annus

Chapter 28: Colors

Write the English translation of each Latin word in the color the Latin word describes. Then color the image using that same color!

Chapter 29: Around the Palace

Using the picture and instructions below, draw a palace scene! Check off the boxes after you do each step.

- ☐ 1. Draw a **solium** at the top of the stairs.
- ☐ 2. Draw a **gemma** on both sides of the door frame.
- ☐ 3. Draw a **tyrannus** on the **solium**.
- ☐ 4. Behind the **solium**, color the curtain the color of **aurum**.
- ☐ 5. Draw a **servus** bringing the **tyrannus** a glass of water.
- ☐ 6. Draw **populus** from the **regnum** outside the door.
- ☐ 7. Draw a speech bubble from the **tyrannus** that says, "**Regno**!"

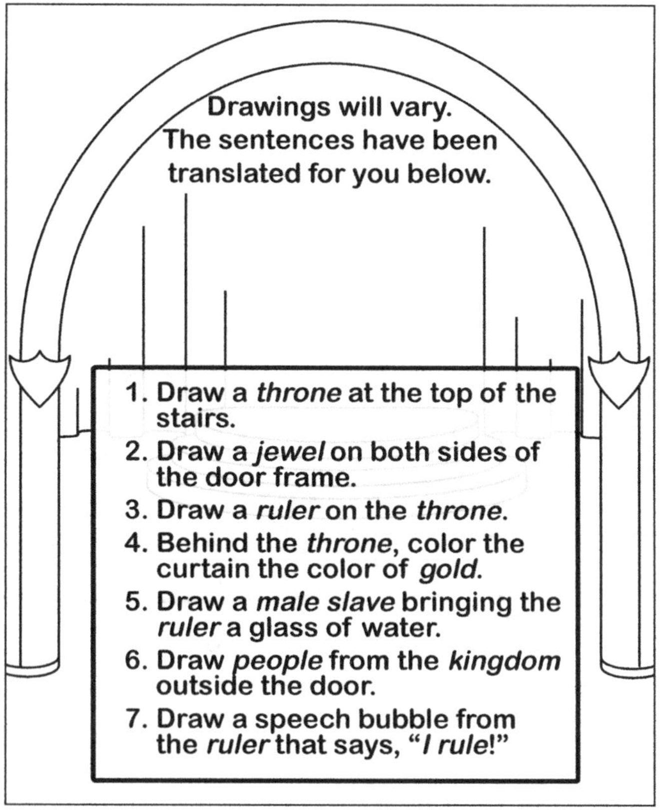

Chapter 30: Adjectives

1. Complete each sentence by drawing a line to the correct Latin word.

a. Compared to a mouse, an elephant is a ______ animal.

b. A tall cliff is very ______.

c. An A on a test is a ______ grade.

d. A ball is ______.

e. Compared to ten minutes, one second is a very ______ time.

f. Compared to an elephant, a mouse is very ______.

g. A flower could be called very ______.

h. To rob someone is a ______ action.

i. A box, or a four-sided figure, is ______.

j. When you're waiting, ten minutes seems like a ______ time.

k. A triangle, or any three-sided figure, is ______.

bonus
magnus
altus
rotundus
pulcher
brevis
quadratus
parvus
malus
triangulus
longus

2. Draw a *parva rotunda avis*,* a *longus flavus canis*, and an *aurantia feles that is *brevis* and *triangula*.**

Drawings will vary.
Every drawing should have a *small round bird*, a *long yellow dog*, and an *orange cat* that is *short* and *triangular*.

*Avis and feles are feminine nouns and so the adjectives that describe them have feminine endings, in this case *a*.

Chapter 31: Review

1. Translate the English words into Latin and fill in the crossword puzzle. Try translating the words directly into the crossword puzzle!

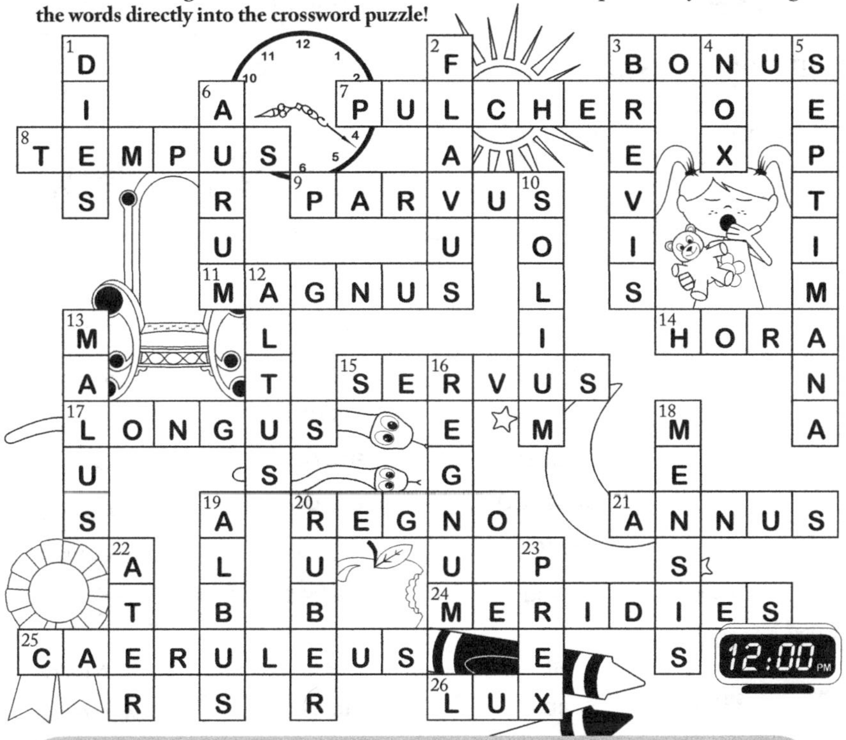

Across
3. good (m)
7. pretty, handsome (m)
8. time
9. small, young (m)
11. great, big (m)
14. hour
15. male slave
17. long (m)
20. I reign
21. year
24. noon
25. blue (m)
26. light

Down
1. day
2. yellow (m)
3. short (m)
4. night
5. week
6. gold
10. throne
12. high (m)
13. bad (m)
16. kingdom
18. month
19. white (m)
20. red (m)
22. black (m)
23. prayer

Note: The (m) indicates that you only need to supply the masculine form of the word.

Chapter 31: Review

2. Do you know your Latin roots and English derivatives? Draw lines to match the English words to the correct Latin root words.

nocturnal — nox	fabula	lucid — lux
fable — fabula	dormio	dormitory — dormio
translucent — lux	lux	fabulous — fabula
dormant — dormio	nox	tempo — tempus
diurnal — dies	tempus	annual — annus
temporary — tempus	dies	albino — albus
brief — brevis	annus	diary — dies
gem — gemma	albus	malignant — malus
malicious — malus	gemma	altitude — altus
	malus	
	altus	
	brevis	

3. Can you put together the phrases from the past few chapters? Using the word bank below, translate each English phrase into Latin.

Tempus liberabit fugit Fiat opus Regnat Magnum vos lux populus Veritas

Let there be light: **Fiat** **lux**

Time flees (flies): **Tempus** **fugit**

The truth will make you free: **Veritas** **vos** **liberabit**

The people rule: **Regnat** **populus**

A great work: **Magnum** **opus**

Chapter 31: Review

4. Chant your charts as you use the words and endings on the right to fill in the charts below.

First Declension Noun Endings	Singular	Plural
Nominative	-a	-ae
Genitive	-ae	-arum
Dative	-ae	-is
Accusative	-am	-as
Ablative	-a	-is

Hora Chant (First Declension)	Singular	Plural
Nominative	hora	horae
Genitive	horae	horarum
Dative	horae	horis
Accusative	horam	horas
Ablative	hora	horis

-a hora horis -am -arum -a horas -ae -is horae horarum -ae -ae horae horam -is hora horae horis -as

5. Adjectives are words that describe or modify what?

verbs **nouns** actions nothing

6. Color verbs *caeruleus*, nouns *ruber*, prepositions *viridis*, and adjectives *flavus*.

C regno I reign; F rotundus round; R vesper evening; R lectus bed; V supra above; V circum around; V pone behind; R gemma jewel; F bonus good; V ex out of; F brevis short; R mensis month; R dies day; C dormio I sleep; C coqueo I cook; R solium throne; C laboro I work; F parvus small

The words are labeled: C=caeruleus (blue), R=ruber (red), V=viridis (green), F=flavus (yellow).
The words are also translated for your convenience.

1. Verb Chart Chant Challenge! Chant your charts as you use the words and endings on the right to fill in the charts below.

Present Tense	Singular	Plural
First Person	-o	-mus
Second Person	-s	-tis
Third Person	-t	-nt

Laudo Present Tense	Singular	Plural
First Person	laudo	laudamus
Second Person	laudas	laudatis
Third Person	laudat	laudant

Imperfect Tense	Singular	Plural
First Person	-bam	-bamus
Second Person	-bas	-batis
Third Person	-bat	-bant

Future Tense	Singular	Plural
First Person	-bo	-bimus
Second Person	-bis	-bitis
Third Person	-bit	-bunt

laudant -o -bam -bo -bas -nt -bat laudo -bis -bunt -t -bamus laudas -s -batis -tis -bant -bimus laudat -mus -bit laudamus -bitis laudatis

2. What is the ending for a verb in the future tense, first-person singular? -bo

3. Fill in the boxes below with the stem and ending of the present tense, third-person plural form of *laboro* (one letter is done for you).

L	A	B	O	R	A	N	T

4. How do you say "they work" in Latin? laborant

5. Noun Chart Chant Challenge! Chant your charts as you use the words and endings on the right to fill in the charts below.

First Declension Noun Endings	Singular	Plural
Nominative	-a	-ae
Genitive	-ae	-arum
Dative	-ae	-is
Accusative	-am	-as
Ablative	-a	-is

Hora Chant (First Declension)	Singular	Plural
Nominative	hora	horae
Genitive	horae	horarum
Dative	horae	horis
Accusative	horam	horas
Ablative	hora	horis

-a -ae hora -arum -ae horae hora -ae -am horae horae -a horam horis -as -is horarum horas -is horis

6. What is the ending for a first declension noun in the genitive singular form?

-ae

7. What is the ending for a first declension noun in the ablative plural form?

-is

8. What is the genitive singular form of *regina*? reginae

9. What is the ablative plural form of *aqua*? aquis

10. What is the accusative singular form of *patria*? patriam

11. What is the dative plural form of *fabula*? fabulis

Chapter 32: End-of-Book Review

12. Noun Chart Chant Challenge Two! Chant your charts as you use the words and endings on the right to fill in the charts below.

-um hortus horti horto -o -orum -i -is -os hortum -us horti horto hortis -o -i hortis hortos -is hortorum

Second Declension Masculine Endings	Singular	Plural
Nominative	-us	-i
Genitive	-i	-orum
Dative	-o	-is
Accusative	-um	-os
Ablative	-o	-is

Hortus Chant (Second Declension Masculine Endings)	Singular	Plural
Nominative	hortus	horti
Genitive	horti	hortorum
Dative	horto	hortis
Accusative	hortum	hortos
Ablative	horto	hortis

13. What is the ending for a second declension masculine noun in the dative singular form?
-o

14. What is the ending for a second declension masculine noun in the ablative plural form?
-is

15. What is the genitive plural form of *gladius*? gladiorum

16. What is the nominative plural form of *ludus*? ludi

17. What is the accusative singular form of *lectus*? lectum

18. What is the dative plural form of *populus*? populis

Chapter 32: End-of-Book Review

19. Noun Chart Chant Challenge Three! Chant your charts as you use the words and endings on the right to fill in the charts below.

bonum bona -um -is boni -um -o bona bonis -orum bonum -a -i bonis bono -a -o bono -is bonorum

Second Declension Neuter Endings	Singular	Plural
Nominative	-um	-a
Genitive	-i	-orum
Dative	-o	-is
Accusative	-um	-a
Ablative	-o	-is

Bonum Chant (Second Declension Neuter Endings)	Singular	Plural
Nominative	bonum	bona
Genitive	boni	bonorum
Dative	bono	bonis
Accusative	bonum	bona
Ablative	bono	bonis

20. What is the ending for a second declension neuter noun in the accusative singular form?
-um

21. What is the ending for a second declension neuter noun in the nominative plural form?
-a

22. What is the accusative singular form of *bellum*? bellum

23. What is the nominative plural form of *balneum*? balnea

24. What is the genitive singular form of *regnum*? regni

25. What is the ablative singular form of *stratum*? strato

26. **Color the pictures according to the instructions below. Check off each box after you do each step.**

- ☐ Color the **rex ruber**.
- ☐ Color the **solium flavum**.
- ☐ Color the **epulae virides**.
- ☐ Color the **venator viridis**.
- ☐ Color the **ludus ruber**.
- ☐ Color the **gladius ater**.
- ☐ Color the **regina aurantia**.
- ☐ Color the **musica aurantia** and her **carmen atrum**.
- ☐ Color **duo coronae flavae**.
- ☐ Color the **artifex purpureus**.
- ☐ Color the **magnus albus canis** and the **parva caerulea avis**.
- ☐ Color the **quattuor gemmae purpureus**.
- ☐ Color the **nauta alba** and **caerulea**.

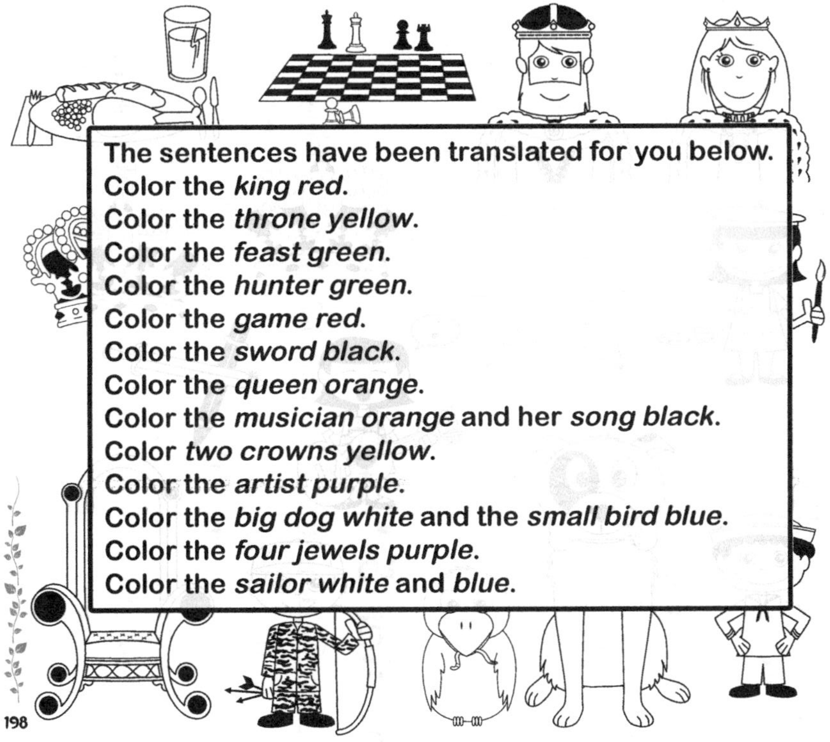

The sentences have been translated for you below.
Color the *king red*.
Color the *throne yellow*.
Color the *feast green*.
Color the *hunter green*.
Color the *game red*.
Color the *sword black*.
Color the *queen orange*.
Color the *musician orange* and her *song black*.
Color *two crowns yellow*.
Color the *artist purple*.
Color the *big dog white* and the *small bird blue*.
Color the *four jewels purple*.
Color the *sailor white* and *blue*.

27. **Read the sentences out loud. Then follow the instructions below and check off each box after you do each step.**

- ☐ Translate each italicized word on the line below it.
- ☐ Circle all the nouns.
- ☐ Underline all the verbs.
- ☐ Draw triangles around all the adjectives.
- ☐ Draw small stars on either side of all the prepositions.
- ☐ Draw small hearts on either side of all the adverbs.

a. The *vigil* *clamat.*
guard, policeman, fireman — he shouts

b. The *amicus* is ★*cum*★ the *familia.*
male friend — with — family

c. The *puer* is not *fortis* ★at★ *nox.*
boy — brave, strong — night

d. *Porto* the *gemmam* ★*inter*★ the *rotundus* bushes
I carry — jewel — between/among — round

e. *Cano* my *carmen* ♥*cito.*♥
I sing — song — fast, quickly

f. *Scribo* a *fabula.*
I write — story

g. The *optime* *mensis* *est* *Iulius.*
best — month — is — July

h. The *senator* *dicabo* ♥*diligenter.*♥
senator, politician — he will speak — carefully

Song Lyrics

Chapter 1 Song

When You Wake Up in the Mornin'
[Track 1(C)/31(E)]

When you wake up in the mornin'
and you don't know the day,
Qui dies est? is the way to say:
What's the day?
What's the day?

When you wake up in the mornin'
and you're in the know,
Hodie est is the way to show:
It's today,
It's today,
It's today!

Chapter 2 Song

Days of the Week Song [Track 2(C)/32(E)]

Sunday **Solis**
Monday **Lunae**
Tuesday **Martis**
Wednesday **Mercurii**
Thursday **Iovis**
Friday **Veneris**
Saturday **Saturni**

Chapter 3 Song

Months of the Year, Part I
[Track 3(C)/33(E)]
Ianuarius comes first in the year,
Februarius brings us coats to wear.
Martius marches into town,
Aprilis brings the showers down. *(x2)**
The first four months of the year!

Chapter 4 Song

Months of the Year, Parts I & II
[Track 4(C)/34(E)]

Ianuarius comes first in the year,
Februarius brings us coats to wear.
Martius marches into town,
Aprilis brings the showers down.
The first four months of the year!

Maius blooms in flowers and berries,
Iunius loves the bright red cherries,
Iulius starts with a bang and a flash,
Augustus—off to the beach we dash.
The next four months of the year.

September—lots of cookies to bake,
October scatters leaves to rake,
November—off to Grandma's we go,
December shovels white, white snow.
The last four months of the year.

Chapter 5 Song

Numbers Chant, Part I [Track 6(C)/36(E)]

One, two, three, four!
Unus, duo, tres, quattuor! *(x2)*

Give me one and give me two
Unus! Duo! One and two! *(x2)*

Three and four I adore
Tres and then comes **quattuor**! *(x2)*

And now **quinque** does arrive
That very special number five. *(x2)*

Unus–quinque, one to five
Chant again and look alive! *(x2)*

*That number at the end of the verse is there to tell you how many times you should sing the verse.

Chapter 6 Songs

Numbers Chant, Parts I & II
[Track 7(C)/37(E)]

One, two, three, four!
Unus, duo, tres, quattuor! *(x2)*

Give me one and give me two
Unus! Duo! One and two! *(x2)*

Three and four I adore
Tres and then comes **quattuor**! *(x2)*

And now **quinque** does arrive,
That very special number five. *(x2)*

Six, seven! Eight, nine, ten!
Five more numbers up to ten. *(x4)*

Sex, septem! Six and seven,
Two more numbers we've been given. *(x2)*

Octo, novem, eight and nine,
Right up to the borderline. *(x2)*

Now there's **decem**, number ten,
The first ten numbers in Latin. *(x2)*

Unus–decem, one to ten,
Take a breath and count again! *(x2)*

Decem Little Romans [Track 8(C)/38(E)]

Unus, duo, tres little Romans
Quattuor, quinque, sex little Romans
Septem, octo, novem Romans
Decem Roman boys!

Decem, novem, octo Romans
Septem, sex, and **quinque** Romans
Quattuor, tres, and **duo** Romans
Unus Roman boy! *(x2)*

Chapter 8 Song

The Working Song [Track 9(C)/39(E)]

Laboro, laboro, I work with my family,
Work with my family, work with my family.
Purgo, purgo, I clean up the dirty things,
Clean them happily.

I work with my family,
Work with my family,
Laboro, laboro, I work with my family,
Work with them happily.

Coquo, coquo, I help cook the food we eat,
Help cook the food we eat, help cook the
food we eat.
Pasco, pasco, I feed the cat and parakeet,
Feed them happily.

I work with my family,
Work with my family,
Laboro, laboro, I work with my family,
Work with them happily.

Lavo, lavo, I wash dishes while I sing,
Wash dishes while I sing, wash dishes
while I sing.
Purgo, purgo, I clean up everything,
Clean up happily.

I work with my family,
Work with my family,
Laboro, laboro, I work with my family,
Work with them happily.

Chapter 9 Song

Speaking and Writing Song
[Track 10(C)/40(E)]

I **dico, dico, dico**,
I love to speak, speak, speak!
I **clamo, clamo, clamo**,
I shout from mountain peak!

And when my mom is sleeping, I whisper,
oh, so soft!
Susurro, yes, I whisper,
Susurro, oh, so soft!

I **scribo, scribo, scribo**,
I write to friends away;
And **oro** when I talk to God,
I **oro** all the day.

Dico, clamo,
Susurro, oh, so soft.
Scribo, oro
Oro all the day.

Chapter 10 Song

Walk and Ride Song [Track 11(C)/41(E)]

I walk, I **ambulo**, I walk far up the hill.
Then I run, I **curro, curro, curro** down the hill.
I run to the ship at bay, I **navigo** the seas.
Navigo, yes, off I go, and sail with the breeze.

I ride, I **equito** on my horse named Captain Pie.
When I have far to go, I **volo** in the sky.
Still, I am happiest when I **navigo** the seas.
Navigo, yes, off I go, and sail with the breeze.

I walk, I **ambulo**, I walk far up the hill.
Then I run, I **curro, curro, curro** down the hill.
I run to the ship at bay, I **navigo** the seas.
Navigo, yes, off I go, and sail with the breeze.

I ride, I **equito** on my horse named Captain Pie.
But when I have far to go, I **volo** in the sky.
Still, I am happiest when I **navigo** the seas.
Navigo, yes, off I go, and sail with the breeze.

Chapter 11 Song

The Subjects Song [Track 12(C)/42(E)]

We need to learn our numbers, **mathematica**!
To add, subtract, and multiply, **mathematica**!
And to write our words and letters and sounds,
Scriptio helps us write them down.
So, let's learn **scriptio** and **mathematica**!

Historia tells me what has happened a hundred years ago,
Famous men in battles and war—tales of weal and woe!

Physica speaks of planets and snakes,
Rocks and trees and big earthquakes.
Historia and **physica** are wonderful things to know.

To learn these things we need to read, and read aloud and clear,
And **lectio**, our favorite friend, brings stories very near.
Grammatica is the way we know
The rules of words and sentence flow.
Grammatica and **lectio** are subjects we revere.

Chapter 12 Song

Celebratio Song [Track 13(C)/43(E)]

Time to **cel-e-bra-ti-o**!
Fa-mi-li-a will gather.
Invite your favorite **a-mi-cae**
To a tasty **e-pu-lae**.

Celebratio, celebratio, amici, musica, familia.
Rejoice, sing **musica**!

Birthdays, holidays, and fun,
The season has begun.
Bring another dear **amica**.
The girls will play **musica**!

Celebratio, celebratio, amici, musica, familia.
Rejoice, sing **musica**!

Prepare a tasty **epulae**.
Familia will drop by!
Gear up for a rowdy **ludus**,
Don't forget your **amicus**!

Celebratio, celebratio, amici, musica, familia.
Rejoice, sing **musica**!

Chapter 14 Song

Rex and Regina Song [Track 14(C)/44(E)]

We are the **populus** here in the land,
This is our **patria**, the fatherland.
Our king is just and has sworn to us all,
"I **rego** the land and I'm servant of all."

The **rex** and **regina**, they sit on gold thrones,
They wear gold **coronas** with beautiful stones.
The **populus** love them and frequently say,
"They've brought the land peace and a new dawning day."

Chapter 15 Song

The Mighty Miles Song
[Track 15(C)/45(E)]

I'm a mighty **miles**, I can swing a sword.
My **gladius** is my best friend when
I go off to war.
I fight to save my **patria**, **pugno**
to keep it free,
Pugno for liberty!

Video many enemies, and **vinco** all I see,
To see and conquer enemies, courageous
I must be.
A **bellum** is a tragedy, but a **miles** still must go
Pugno in rain or snow!

Chapter 16 Song

Porto-Amo Song [Track 16(C)/46(E)]

Porto—carry,
Porto—carry,
Porto books!
Porto rocks!
Specto at the horses,
Specto at the blue sky,**
Look around,
Look up high.

Amo pater,
Amo amicus,
I love you,
Yes, you, too!
Vivo in the city,
Vivo in the country,
I live high,
I live free.

Narro stories,
Narro stories,
I tell tales!
Tall, tall tales!
Voco all my best friends,
I call all my neighbors,
"Come see me,
Come to tea."

Chapter 17 Song

Cito-Lente Song [Track 18(C)/48(E)]

Put out the fire! **Cito**!
How should I do it? **Cito**!
Put out the fire, not slow.
Put out the fire, **cito**!

Walk very slowly, **lente**!
Creep up the stairs, **lente**!
Sneak around the corner, all day.
Take your time, **lente**!

Semper, always! I always do!
Saepe, often, and you, too!
Always or often, tie your shoe.
Semper, **saepe**, tie your shoe!

Nunc or **numquam**, now or never!
Nunc or **numquam**, don't wait forever!
Let's play **nunc** and play forever.
Let's play **nunc** and forever!

Chapter 18 Song

Forte Song [Track 19(C)/49(E)]

When you're scared, just face it bravely!
Like a soldier—**forte**!
And work **diligenter**—carefully!
Forte, diligenter!

Bene, do well, give your best,
Or you'll do **pessime** on your test!

Pessime—badly, **optime**—best!
Now let's give it your best!

Optime is **non pessime**,
and **pessime** is **non optime**.
Mice live in fear, **non forte**.
The word **non** means "not"!

The word **specto means "I look at," so including the English word "at" in these two lines of the song repeats the idea that's already included in the Latin word.

Chapter 20 Song

<u>The Negotium Song, Part I</u>
[Track 20(C)/50(E)]

There's lots of things that you could do
When you grow tall and strong.
The **negotium** that's right for you,
That you'll love all day long!

When Jack fell down and broke his crown
His mother called the doctor
And the **medicus** made Jack lay down
And soon Jack felt much better.

When you see a **vigil** who guards your town,
A **vigil** strong and brave,
Make sure you thank him for his work,
Give him a smile and wave.

An **architectus** draws designs
For buildings tall and bold.
An **artifex** is glad, I'm told
When his artwork is all sold.

When you walk into the general store,
Say, "Hello, **Tabernarius**!"
And buy a book of **poeta*****
And read the poems to us!

Chapter 21 Song

<u>The Negotium Song, Part II</u>
[Track 21(C)/51(E)]

An **agricola** on a summer day
Went out to plant some hay.
A **venator** shot down a deer
While the **nauta** sailed away!

The **musicus** played a pretty song,
And a **scriptor** wrote a book,
The **senators** passed a brand-new law,
And locked up every crook.

An **athleta** and a mouse did race.
The mouse, he took first place.
A **structor** built a fancy house
With lots of rooms and space.

Chapter 22 Song

<u>The Shoe Song</u> [Track 22(C)/52(E)]

"It's time to go," Dad says.
I look under and near the bed.
I look for my shoes, which I always lose,
Sub and **prope** the bed!

"Please hurry, or we'll be late.
We must drive across the state.
Trans the whole state, **ad** grandma's house,
To grandmother's house by eight!"

I look behind the chairs.
I look above the stairs.
Pone the chairs, **supra** the stairs,
Can't find them anywhere.

Our dog strolls into the house
With one of my shoes in his mouth
We circled him—**circum**—and saw
My shoe locked tight in his jaw.

Chapter 23 Song

<u>Visiting Song</u> [Track 23(C)/53(E)]

I ran up the hill with my friend,
Cum amicus, my best friend.
Sursum the hill, then **de** the hill,
Up and down the hill we went.

We went to visit the goat,
He lives **extra**, outside of a moat.
Between the trees, among the bees,
He paddles around in his boat!

After dinner, **post** eating, we went
To visit the cow in a tent.
He was building a stall, **contra** the wall,
And hoping to charge us rent.

***The phrase "of **poeta**" can mean "of a poet" or "of the poet." Remember that in Latin there is no word for "a" or "the," so **poeta** by itself could be translated "the poet" or "a poet."

While walking home in the dark,
Dum walking, we went through the park.
Ante we got home, we heard a big boom!
Ran all the way home in the dark.

Chapter 24 Song

Grow My Virtus [Track 24(C)/54(E)]

I'm gonna grow my **virtus** every day, uh-huh,
Grow **virtus** as I work and play, uh-huh.
Verax, truthful words I'll say, truthful words will win the day,
Be **fortis**, brave and strong, along the way.

Fidelis, faithful, that's what I should be,
Diligens, working carefully!
Oboediens, doing what's asked of me, obedient to my family,
And **humilis**, with humility, uh-huh.

Beneficus, helping family and friends,
Studiosus, learning my numbers, chants, and blends!
I'm going to work to be wise or **sapiens**, I'll thank my parents, teachers, and friends.
I'm gonna grow my **virtus** every day, uh-huh.

Chapter 26 Song

Bedtime Song [Track 26(C)/56(E)]

First a bath, **balneum**,
Then I tidy my bedroom,
Then my **pater** tucks me in,
In my fuzzy blue **stratum**.

A **fabula**,
A bedtime tale,
Makes me sleepy, without fail.*(x2)*

I say a **prex**, say a prayer,
Sing a **carmen** with my **mater**,
But she tells me that time flies
So I close my **fessus** eyes.

Nox brings rest
For a new day,
Strength for work and for play. *(x2)*

Dormio, I sleep tight
In my **lectus**, through the **nox**, night
With my **nox lux**, shining bright light,
Keeping company tonight.

Dormio, sweetly sleep
In my **lectus**, counting sheep. *(x2)*

Chapter 27 Song

Grand Old Father Time [Track 27(C)/57(E)]

The grand old Father Time,
He marches every day.
The **Pater Tempus** chimes
Every **hora**, while we play.

Each **dies**, day, he calls,
As **aurora** breaks the sky,
And then as evening, **vesper**, falls
He bids **dies** good-bye.

Each **septimana** is a week,
Five days for work and school,
Then two days for rest and play
But remember your lunch at **meridies**
Each day when you're at school.

Each **mensis** a new moon comes
For **nox** to light the night.
Every **annus**, every night,
Pater Tempus brings us light.

The grand old Father Time,
He marches every day.
The **Pater Tempus** chimes
Every **hora**, while we play.

Chapter 28 Song

The Colores Song [Track 28(C)/58(E)]

I love to paint when it's time for art,
I make each color play a part.
Ruber is the color of my go-cart.
Aurantius is the color of morning sky, morning sky, morning sky.

It's also the color of a fruit I like
And **flavus** is the color of banana pie!

My favorite animal is black and white.
It loves to kick and it just might bite,
The stripes are a style that's quite the sight.
The black stripes we'll call **atra, atra, atra.**
The snowy white stripes are **alba**, white,
But the black stripes we'll call **atra**.

Viridis, green, are the leaves in spring.
Caeruleus, blue, are the birds on wing.
Purpureus, the royal robes of a king.
Flavus, the glow of candlelight, candlelight, candlelight.
Purpureus, the royal robes of a king,
And **flavus** is color of his golden ring.

Well, I love to paint and I love art,
Yes, and every color has a part
And I think the colors all look smart.
Atra, **alba**, and **ruber** bright, **ruber** bright, **ruber** bright.
Atra and **alba** sure look nice,
But I'm in love with **ruber** bright.

Chapter 29 Song

Mr. King Folium [Track 29(C)/59(E)]

There was an old **rex**
Named Mr. King **Folium**.
He sat on a throne
Named Mr. **Solium**
And told his **servus**
To bring him a nummy-num.
Hungry old Mr. King **Folium, Folium**.

There was a little queen
Named Mrs. Queen **Regina**.
She loved to dress up
In her gold, gold **corona**.
That **aurum** crown
Had a great big **gemma**
Always on Queen **Regina, Regina**.

A frog one day said,
"I'll take over.
I'll make a fine **tyrannus, tyrannus**, ruler.
I'll steal the crown **gemma**
from the royal jeweler.
Regno, I rule, I'm the ruler, ruler!"

Queen **Regina** and Mr. King **Folium**
Had a powwow
And took back the **regnum**.
"Mr. Mean Frog, your time has finally come.
Leave our **solium** and our **regnum, regnum**!"

Chapter 30 Song

Adjectives Chant [Track 30(C)/60(E)]

My puppy is small, he's cute and kind of **parvus**,
And most of the time he's really very **bonus**.
His tail is long; it's a tail **longus**,
His tummy is round and just a bit **rotundus**.

Is your puppy **brevis**, short and small?
Or is your puppy **altus**, high and tall?
Magnus, parvus, big or small?
Is it round and **rotundus**, shaped like a ball?

Maybe it's **quadratus**, shaped like a square?
Malus, bad and hairy, and mean like a bear?
Or **triangulus**, like an arrow in the air?
Or **pulchra, pulcher**, beautiful, and fair?

Your Latin Journey

Lower Grammar

You Can Start Here

Grades 1–2

Grades 2–3

Upper Grammar

Start or Continue Here

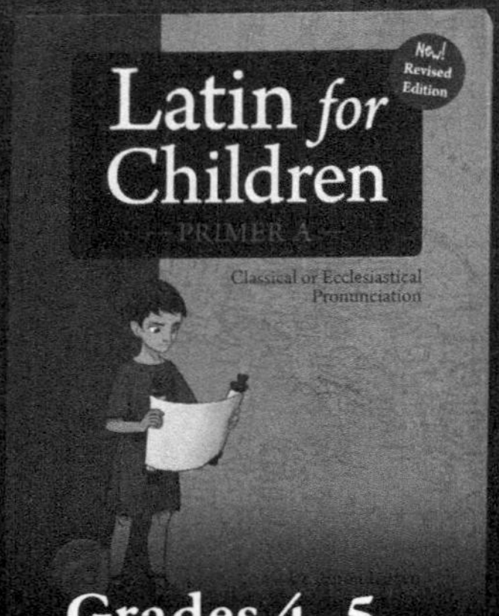

Grades 4–5

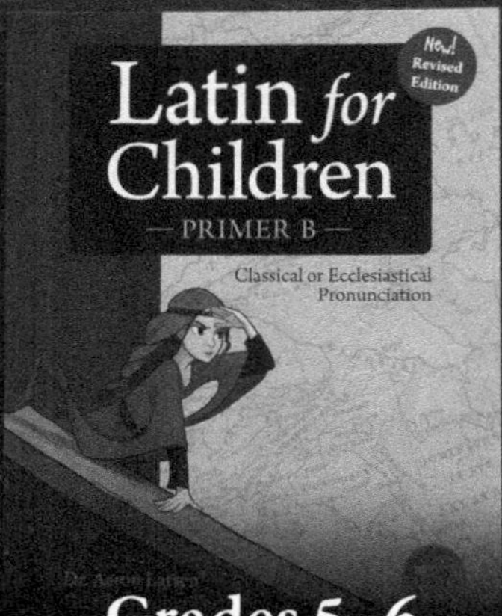

Grades 5–6

Grades 6–7

Ready for National Latin Exam Prep

Middle & High School

or Here

Grades 7–8+

Grades 8–9+

Grades 9–10+

Grades 10–Adult

Ready for

Grades 7–8+	Grades 8–9+	Grades 9–10+	Grades 10–Adult
National Latin Exam Level I	National Latin Exam Level II	National Latin Exam Level III or IV Prose	National Latin Exam Level III or IV Prose